AF884736

The American Constitutional Tradition

The Fairleigh Dickinson University Press Law, Culture, and the Humanities Series

Series editor: Caroline Joan "Kay" S. Picart, MPhil (Cantab), PhD, JD, Esquire Attorney at Law; former associate professor of English and Humanities, Florida State University

The Fairleigh Dickinson University Press Series in Law, Culture, and the Humanities publishes scholarly works in which the field of Law intersects with, among others, Film, Criminology, Sociology, Communication, Critical/Cultural Studies, Literature, History, Philosophy, and the Humanities.

Publications

H. Lowell Brown, *The American Constitutional Tradition: Colonial Charters, Covenants, and Revolutionary State Constitutions, 1578–1780* (2017)
Arua Oko Omaka, *The Biafran Humanitarian Crisis, 1967–1970: International Human Rights and Joint Church Aid* (2016)
Marouf A. Hasian, Jr., *Representing Ebola: Culture, Law, and Public Discourse about the 2013–2015 West Africa Ebola Outbreak* (2016)
Jacqueline O'Connor, *Law and Sexuality in Tennessee Williams's America* (2016)
Caroline Joan "Kay" S. Picart, Michael Hviid Jacobsen, and Cecil E. Greek, *Framing Law and Crime: An Interdisciplinary Anthology* (2016)
Caroline Joan "Kay" S. Picart, *Law In and As Culture: Intellectual Property, Minority Rights, and the Rights of Indigenous Peoples* (2016)

On the Web at http://www.fdu.edu/fdupress

The American Constitutional Tradition

Colonial Charters, Covenants, and Revolutionary State Constitutions, 1578–1780

H. Lowell Brown

FAIRLEIGH DICKINSON UNIVERSITY PRESS
Madison • Teaneck

Published by Fairleigh Dickinson University Press
Copublished by The Rowman & Littlefield Publishing Group, Inc.
4501 Forbes Boulevard, Suite 200, Lanham, Maryland 20706
www.rowman.com

Unit A, Whitacre Mews, 26-34 Stannary Street, London SE11 4AB

British Library Cataloguing in Publication Information Available

Library of Congress Cataloging-in-Publication Data

The hardback edition of this book was previously cataloged by the Library of Congress as follows:

Names: Brown, H. Lowell, author.
Title: The American constitutional tradition : colonial charters, covenants, and revolutionary state constitutions, 1578-1780 / H. Lowell Brown.
Description: Lanham, Maryland : The Fairleigh Dickinson University Press, 2017. | Series: Series in law, culture, and the humanities | Includes bibliographical references and index.
Identifiers: LCCN 2017004980 (print) | LCCN 2017008741 (ebook)
Subjects: LCSH: Constitutional law--United States--History. | Constitutional law--United States--States.
Classification: LCC KF4550 .B743 2017 (print) | LCC KF4550 (ebook) | DDC 342.7302/90903--dc23
LC record available at https://lccn.loc.gov/2017004980

ISBN 9781683930495 (pbk. : alk. paper)
ISBN 9781683930471 (cloth : alk. paper)
ISBN 9781683930488 (Electronic)

∞™ The paper used in this publication meets the minimum requirements of American National Standard for Information Sciences Permanence of Paper for Printed Library Materials, ANSI/NISO Z39.48-1992.

Printed in the United States of America

On the cover: The chair from which President George Washington presided over at the 1787 Constitutional Convention in Philadelphia. James Madison noted that on the last day of the convention,

The members then proceeded to sign the instrument. Whilst the last members were signing it, Doctor Franklin looking towards the President's Chair, at the back of which a rising sun happened to be painted, observed to a few members near him, that Painters had found it difficult to distinguish in their art a rising from a setting sun. I have, said he, often in the course of the Session, and the vicissitudes of my hopes and fears as to its issue, looked at that behind the President without being able to tell whether it was rising or setting: But now at length I have the happiness to know that it is a rising and not a setting sun.

James Madison, *Notes on the Constitutional Convention of 1787* (New York: Oxford University Press, 1918), 96–97.

Dedication

For my wife, Ella

Contents

Acknowledgments

I am indebted to friends and colleagues who have given me aid and comfort along the way, but particularly to Charles W. Blau, Esq., who graciously reviewed an earlier version of this book. I am also deeply indebted to Professor Robert Allison whose thoughtful comments and critique resulted in this book. Without their consideration and encouragement, and that of my wife, Ella, this work would not have been possible.

Foreword

When the Constitutional Convention adjourned in September 1787, the Framers proffered to the states a constitution of government that was a radical departure from the accepted constitutionalism of the time, as exemplified by the British constitution. This new conception of a federal constitution was not simply the invention of the assembled delegates over the preceding several months, but was instead the culmination of an American tradition of constitutionalism rooted in the royal charters and covenants upon which their colonies' governments had been founded. This book is a study of that constitutional tradition.

In September 1786, representatives from the states of Delaware, Maryland, New Jersey, New York, Pennsylvania, and Virginia met at Annapolis, Maryland, to discuss measures that could be taken to redress the "important defects in the federal government" that by then were generally regarded as being "of a nature so serious . . . as to render the situation of the United States delicate and critical," and that called for "an execution of the united virtue and wisdom of all members of the confederacy." To that end, the delegates expressed "their earnest and unanimous wish, that speedy measures be taken, to effect a general meeting, one of the States, in a future Convention, for the same and such other purposes, as the situation of public affairs, may be found to require." The delegates proposed that a meeting of commissioners appointed by their states be convened in Philadelphia the following May, "to take into consideration the situation of the United States, to devise such other provisions as shall appear to them necessary to render the constitution of the Federal Government adequate to the exigencies of the union."[1]

After consideration of the report of the Annapolis proceedings by the convention's chairman, John Dickenson, Congress resolved that such a convention should be called for the second Monday in May 1787. Congress directed, however, that this convention should be held

> for the sole and express purpose of revising the Articles of Confederation and reporting to Congress and the several legislatures such alterations and provisions therein as shall when agreed to in Congress confirmed by the States render the federal constitution adequate to the exigencies of government and the preservation of the union.[2]

Notwithstanding the limitations of this charter, however, what emerged from the convention that met in Philadelphia on Friday, May 25, 1787, was nothing less than a revolutionary and transformative reconception of social authority in the American polity—what Akhil Amar described as "America's legal city on a hill."[3]

The origins of the American Constitution have been the source of broad scholarship, including landmark works by Bernard Bailyn,[4] Jack N. Rakove,[5] and Gordon S. Wood.[6] The primary focus of this constitutional scholarship has been the political ideologies of the revolutionary period.[7] Although, to be sure, the Framers' conception of government was strongly influenced by the European enlightenment and the influence of the writings of John Locke, Montesquieu, and Jean-Jacques Rousseau on their thinking on the nature of governmental authority and the proper relationship of the people to their government cannot be denied. To the extent that any attention has been paid to American constitutionalism before 1787, it has been in the context of the constitutions adopted by the revolutionary states, particularly in Virginia (1776) and in Massachusetts (1780). Willi Paul Adams[8] and Marc W. Kruman[9] have admirably examined these inchoate constitutions, tracing their salient features to later enshrinement in the federal Constitution.

Largely overlooked, however, has been the legacy of the colonial charters and enactments of the nascent colonial legislatures in shaping the conception of the national Constitution of 1787 as the seminal source of the federal government's legitimacy and authority, as well as the fundamental document establishing the relationship of the national republican government with the states and ultimately with the people. It is to that legacy that this book is addressed.

Well more than a century ago, Sydney George Fisher wrote that "histories of the Constitution usually describe the labors of its Framers in the Convention of 1787 and the contests of political parties" over adoption by the states. These histories, Fisher wrote, have treated the Constitution "as invented by the convention that framed it, or have sought in England or other European countries for forms of government that were like it or might have suggested its various provisions." Instead, in his *Evolution of the Constitution of the United States*, Fisher viewed the colonial charters, the state constitutions, and the plans of government as being the social experiments that resulted in the federalism of the Constitution.[10]

Thirty-six years later, in his Anson G. Phelps Lectures at New York University, Andrew C. McLaughlin put forward an evolutionary analysis of "the fundamental and elementary principles of the American constitutional system," that included the plantation covenants and charters of the New England colonies because they shaped the colonists' theories of representative government.[11]

In his *Origins of American Constitutionalism*, Donald S. Lutz expressed his appreciation for McLaughlin's "excellent work, all but forgotten by historians and political scientists alike." Although Lutz said that he had employed "entirely different historical methods" than McLaughlin had, Lutz nevertheless "ended up supporting many of McLaughlin's general conclusions" concerning the influence of these original documents on the later constitutional thinking of the Framers.[12]

This work differs in methodology and focus from that of both McLaughlin and Lutz and concludes that the constitutionalism of the late eighteenth century that produced the federal Constitution was informed fundamentally by a constitutional tradition having its genesis in the earliest formation of the American colonies. Although the works of Lutz and McLaughlin were firmly grounded in historical research, their analysis of the evolution of the Constitution was more jurisprudential than historical. In contrast, the study underlying this book concentrates on the documentary record, read in the larger historical context. Although this focus differs from that of Lutz and McLaughlin, like them, this study seeks to illuminate the striving of the colonists from the earliest days to structure societies that sought to harmonize their aspirations for just institutions and individual rights with the imperatives of order and security in an often hostile and alien environment. From these shared, though disparate, experiences emerged a tradition of constitutionalism that was uniquely American.

In the United States, the federal Constitution is the foundational law of the nation. It is the Constitution that "defines and contains the way government operates and politics is conducted."[13] Lutz observed with regard to the political and legal centrality of the Constitution that "by setting forth procedures and publicly recognized political institutions," the Constitution "not only defines a regime but also establishes the regime's authority."[14]

The constitution that resulted from the Philadelphia Convention represented a radical departure from the constitution of eighteenth-century England. Before the Convention of 1787, the British constitution was considered to be comprised of the accumulated customary practices, legal principles, and individual rights that evolved over centuries in the courts and parliament and in administrative institutions.[15] As Viscount Bolingbroke famously wrote in 1734, "By constitution, we mean . . . the assembly of laws, institutions and customs derived from certain fixed principles of reason directed to certain fixed objects of public good, that compose the general system, according to which the community hath agreed to be governed."[16]

By crafting the constitution of the federal government in a unified document, the Framers dramatically transformed national constitutionalism. Under this new American conception of a constitution, the fundamental law of the institutions of government was made available to everyone, without the necessity of recourse to legal specialists. This egalitarianism resonated with the enlightenment principles expressed in the Declaration of Independence and other revolutionary writings. Lutz saw the setting forth of the foundational law in a single written document as "a strong commitment to broad citizen participation then and in the future."[17] In sum, the Constitution was said to be "society in its political aspect."[18]

As such, the British constitution was not conceived of as the single source of governmental authority and legitimacy or of the fundamental liberties of citizens. Instead, these first principles were thought to be "embedded in the institutions of a nation," that could be ascertained only by reference to those institutions.[19]

Also under the British conception of a constitution, there was no "constitutional law that was superior or that had greater authority than other laws." Instead, "laws of the constitution do not differ from any other laws either in form or in source of origin," as parliament was considered to be both a legislative body and "constituent assembly." Therefore, there was "less facility in distinguishing between what . . . would be called basic law, and other law."[20]

The Convention of 1787 created a new constitutional paradigm. The Framers fashioned a charter of enumerated powers and first principles upon which the federal government was to be founded that would not be subject to legislative modification except by a specific process of amendment requiring the assent of the majority of states. Through this unitary written constitution, the fundamental law of government was available to everyone without the necessity of recourse to legal specialists, an egalitarianism that resonated with the Enlightenment principles embraced by the Revolutionaries.[21]

This conception of the written constitution as being antecedent to government differentiated the American political system from that of Britain and has been haled as the great innovation of American constitutionalism.[22]

The central question remains, however, why it was when the time came for the Constitution's framers to fashion the first federal constitution of the newly independent nation, they did not hew to the familiar, but abandoned centuries of British constitutional history and practice? It is the thesis of this study that this new constitutional form was the continuation of an American tradition of constitutionalism that had its origins in the royal charters for the exploration and exploitation of the new world.

Thus, from the original charter granted to Sir Humphrey Gilbert by Queen Elizabeth in 1578 and continuing through the adoption of the revolutionary constitutions for the newly independent states, this uniquely American constitutional tradition emerged as the settlers labored to structure stable societies grounded on fundamental and immutable principles enshrined in written plans of government and statements of fundamental rights. The evolution of this American constitutional tradition set forth in this book is the story of that struggle.

THE ROYAL CHARTERS AND COLONIAL COVENANTS

The charters first granted to Gilbert and to his half-brother, Sir Walter Raleigh, and later to the Virginia Company, established their colonial enterprise as a "body politic" apart from, though related to, British political society. These enterprises were invested with broad authority to adopt laws for the colonies and to put them into execution. The charters also granted these enterprises the authority to erect governmental structures of governors, councils, and other executive offices necessary to administer those laws.

Even in the absence of a royal charter or patent, the settlers of what would become the New England colonies of Connecticut, New Hampshire, New Haven, Plymouth, and Rhode Island solemnly covenanted among themselves and declared themselves to be bodies politic with authority to enact laws and to form governments for their general welfare. Like the charters, their agreements of self-government were set forth in mutually assented-to writings.

First under the reign of Charles I and following the Restoration, under his two sons Charles II and James, palatine colonies were established in Maryland, New York, New Jersey, Pennsylvania (which spawned the Delaware colony), and the Carolinas. The Georgia colony was later chartered by William and Mary to serve both strategic and colonial purposes.

These royal charters informed the expectations of the various merchant adventurers, palatines, and religious dissidents that the source of governmental legitimacy and the structure of the government, as well as individual and civic rights that were secure from governmental interference, could be ascertained by reference to a central, recognized, and authoritative written document. Over time, those charters gave rise to representative assemblies that, while sharing power with the colonial authority in the person of appointed governors, enacted laws for the governance of the colony and the preservation of individual liberties.

ACTS OF THE COLONIAL LEGISLATURES

Beginning with the assembly of the burgesses in Virginia on June 30, 1619, legislative bodies comprised of elected representatives became a common feature of colonial governments, even those such as Maryland and Pennsylvania that were in effect proprietary provinces. Through landmark acts of legislation, such as the Fundamental Orders of Connecticut (1639), the Fundamental Articles of New Haven (1639, 1643), the Massachusetts Body of Liberties (1641, 1647), the Acts and Orders of Rhode Island (1647), and the New York Charter of Liberties and Privileges (1647), colonial assemblies defined the foundational architecture and principles for the governance of the colonies and the revolutionary states that succeeded them following independence. In addition to enacting codes of civil and criminal law regulating conduct in their respective colonies, these statutes apportioned the authority of the executive and legislative branches of government and established the judiciary. Statutes provided for the imposition of taxes for raising revenue for public purposes, including education. These enactments also introduced bicameralism into the legislative structure with an upper chamber comprised of the governor and privy council and a lower chamber of elected representatives. In several instances, term limits for remaining in public office were imposed. In Rhode Island, legislation separated the church from the civil affairs of the colony.

Colonial legislation secured a variety of civil liberties as well. Individuals were to have access to the courts in both civil and criminal matters. Persons accused of crimes were guaranteed due process, including the right of indictment by a grand jury, bail pending conviction and sentencing, the assistance of counsel at trial, adjudication of guilt by a jury, and the prohibition of being twice put in jeopardy for the same offense. The use of torture to obtain a confession and "inhumane and barbarous" punishments were likewise prohibited. The imposition of martial law was restricted, as was the mandatory quartering of military personnel in private homes.

The colonial legislatures apportioned governing authority between the colonial governments and local governments (usually towns). These local governments were often the product of covenants and agreements between the inhabitants of a settlement, as they were in Massachusetts under the agreements in Cambridge (1632, 1634, 1652), Dedham (1636), Dorchester (1633), and Watertown (1634), in Maine by the Combination of Piscataqua (1641), and in Rhode Island through the Newport and Portsmouth Agreements (1639), the Providence Agreements (1637, 1640), and the Warwick Agreement (1647).

Although diminished in authority after the crown reasserted control over the colonial governments, these colonial legislatures continued to function. As a consequence, when the exigencies of the revolution demanded that the newly independent states form governments, they did so through the adoption by their elected assemblies of written plans of government and declarations of rights, which gave form to the fundamental tenets of representative government, the influence of which on the formation and ratification of the federal Constitution cannot be ignored or underestimated.

THE REVOLUTIONARY STATE CONSTITUTIONS

This American tradition of constitutionalism was carried on during what has been described as the "most eventful constitution-making epoch in America,"[23] which followed the declaration of independence from Great Britain and the dissolution of the crown governments in the colonies. The rebellious states erected governments of limited and enumerated powers founded on republican principles of elected representation, and the separation of legislative, executive, and judicial functions. Informed by their experiences under the colonial governments, the revolutionary constitution writers erected their plans of government in written constitutions. Indeed, all of these state constitutions provided for an elected legislature, predominantly comprised of two chambers.[24] Qualifications for election to the two chambers often differed,[25] as did the constituencies that each represented.[26]

To one degree or another, each of the revolutionary constitutions incorporated principles of the separation of powers. In the majority of constitutions, there was an explicit recognition of the separation of powers as an organizing principle.[27] However, implementation of that principle of constitutionalism varied widely. With the exception of Massachusetts, New York, and Vermont, the governor and other executive officers were chosen by the legislature.[28] Virginia was the first state to establish the judiciary as the third branch of government. Virginia's example was followed subsequently in Georgia, Maryland, Massachusetts, New Hampshire (in the second constitution of 1784), New York, North Carolina, Pennsylvania, and Vermont. In other states (Delaware, New Jersey, and South Carolina), either the executive or the legislature carried out at least some of the judicial functions. In a majority of the states, the independence of the judiciary was preserved by providing that judicial offices were to be held "during good behavior."[29]

In addition to the separation of governmental functions, the revolutionary constitutions included mechanisms for limiting the powers of the executive and legislature. A common feature of the constitutional schemes of government was a prohibition on holding more than one public office simultaneously.[30] Limitations were also imposed on the length of time in which some offices could be held.[31] As a further check on the authority of the legislature, Massachusetts, New York, and South Carolina empowered the governor to veto legislation.[32]

The authority of the governor to act unilaterally was restricted by a requirement of the advice and consent of a privy council, usually appointed by the legislature.[33] The authority to make appointments to public offices was also divided frequently between the executive and the legislature.[34] Civil officers of state governments including, the governor, were subject to impeachment and removal by the legislatures in several states for malfeasance or misfeasance in office.[35]

As a further limitation on the authority of the governor and the legislature, the constitutions of eight states (Delaware, Pennsylvania, Maryland, Massachusetts, North Carolina, Vermont, Virginia, and the second constitution of New Hampshire) included or were accompanied by a specific declaration securing enumerated civic and individual rights and liberties of citizens. The constitutions of four states (Georgia, New Jersey, New York, and the second constitution of South Carolina) embedded these rights in the body of the constitutions themselves.[36]

Of perhaps even greater significance, however, the constitutionalism of the revolutionary states gave rise to the recognition of constitutional law as having greater dignity and authority than other legislative enactments and therefore, that constitutional provisions were not as transitory or as subject to legislative modification as other statutory laws. Indeed, the elevation of constitutional law to a paramount position over other laws has been considered "*the* great innovation and achievement of American eighteenth century constitutionalism."[37]

In their earliest experiments in constitution-making in the heat of rebellion, the revolutionary states of New Hampshire, South Carolina, and Virginia enacted constitutions of government in the same manner in which they enacted other legislation. However, first in Pennsylvania and then in Delaware, special conventions were called for the express purpose of adopting a constitution.[38] In Maryland, a provincial congress was elected for the stated purpose of adopting a constitution as well as enacting other necessary legislation. A similar approach was followed in North Carolina, Georgia, and New York. In 1777, the breakaway state of Vermont held a convention specifically to adopt a constitution and a declaration of rights.

The necessity of calling a special constitutional convention had been the subject of communications from several of the town meetings in Massachusetts that objected to the writing of the constitution by the legislature. Although an attempt was made to authorize the legislature to adopt a constitution that would then be submitted to the voters for approval, a variety of objections were made to the proposed constitution and the constitution was rejected. Finally, on June 21, 1779, elections were announced for a constitutional convention and on September 1, the constitutional convention came together in Cambridge. The draft that emerged from the convention was then submitted to the towns for ratification.[39]

In fashioning its procedure, Massachusetts established the precedent both for the calling of a special constitutional convention in 1787 and for the process by which the Constitution was ratified by the states.[40] The Massachusetts approach also gave concrete recognition to constitution-writing as being in all respects distinct from ordinary legislation and to constitutional law as being the immutable principles upon which the government was founded and individual rights and liberties were secured against encroachment by that government.

The revolutionary state constitutions created centralized representative governments that were discrete from town or county governments, whose authority was supreme within their own spheres. The state constitution writers drew upon the learning and experience that had grown out of the colonial charters and covenants, spanning more than two centuries. The delegates later carried with them this colonial experience when the federal constitutional convention met in Philadelphia during the summer of 1787. Their experiences coalesced in their deliberations at the Philadelphia convention and in the ratification proceedings in the states. Thus, it was that this American constitutional tradition found its most lasting expression in the new federal Constitution.

NOTES

1. Proceedings of the Commissioners to Remedy Defects of the Federal Government (September 11, 1786), reprinted in Arthur Taylor Prescott, *Drafting the Federal Constitution* (Baton Rouge: Louisiana State University Press, 1941), 3–8.
2. Prescott, *Drafting the Constitution*, 11.
3. Akhil Reed Amar, *America's Constitution: A Biography* (New York: Random House, 2005), xi.
4. Bernard Bailyn, *The Ideological Origins of the American Revolution* (Cambridge, MA: Harvard University Press, 1992).
5. Jack N. Rakove, *Original Meanings: Politics and Ideas in the Making of the Constitution* (New York, Knopf, 1997).
6. Gordon S. Wood, *The Creation of the American Republic: 1776–1787* (Chapel Hill: University of North Carolina Press, 1998).
7. Additional examples of note are Henry Steele Commager, *The Empire of Reason: How Europe Imagined and How America Realized the Enlightenment* (Garden City, NY: Anchor Press, 1977); Jack P. Greene, *Peripheries and the Center: Constitutional Development in the Extended Polities of the British Empire and the United States 1607–1788* (Athens: Georgia University Press, 1986); and Forrest McDonald, *Novus Ordo Seclorum: The Intellectual Origins of the Constitution* (Lawrence: University of Kansas Press, 1985).
8. Willi Paul Adams, *The First American Constitutions: Republican Ideology and the Making of State Constitutions in the Revolutionary Era* (Lanham, MD: Rowman & Littlefield, 2001).
9. Marc W. Kruman, *Between Authority and Liberty: State Constitution-Making in Revolutionary America* (Chapel Hill: University of North Carolina Press, 1997).
10. Sydney George Fisher, *The Evolution of the Constitution of the United States* (Philadelphia: Lippincott, 1897).
11. Andrew C. McLaughlin, *Foundations of American Constitutionalism* (Greenwich: Fawcett Publications, 1961), 13. McLaughlin's emphasis on the New England colonies reflected the

purpose of the author to provide lectures "upon the early history of America, particularly with reference to New England, with the purpose of inculcating a knowledge of the principles which animated the Puritan Fathers and early colonists; and the influence they have exerted upon modern civilization."

12. Donald S. Lutz, *The Origins of American Constitutionalism* (Baton Rouge: Louisiana State University Press, 1988), 14.

13. Keith E. Whittington, *Constitutional Construction* (Cambridge, MA: Harvard University Press, 1991), 1.

14. Lutz, *The Origins of American Constitutionalism*, 14.

15. Jack P. Greene, "The Origins of American Constitutionalism," in A. E. Dick Howard, ed., *The United States Constitution: Roots, Rights, and Responsibilities* (Washington, DC: Smithsonian Press, 1992), 23–24.

16. Henry, Viscount Bolingbroke, "Letter X" (January 26, 1734), in David Armitage, ed., *Political Writings* (Cambridge: Cambridge University Press, 1999).

17. Lutz, *The Origins of American Constitutionalism*, 9.

18. H. R. G. Greaves, *The British Constitution* (London: Allen & Union, 1965), 11.

19. Charles Howard McIlwain, *Constitutionalism: Ancient and Modern* (Ithaca, NY: Cornell University Press, 1940), 14.

20. Greaves, *The British Constitution*, 20. Nevertheless, Greaves cited a variety of laws that he considered to be of "major constitutional importance," including: Magna Carta; the Bill of Rights; the Settlement Act; the Abdication Act; the Royal Marriages Act; the Civil List Acts; the Parliament and the Representation of the Peoples Acts; the Judicature Act; the acts establishing particular ministries; public boards and dominion constitutions; the Statute of Westminster; the Ballot Act; the Corrupt Practices Act; and the Redistributions Acts. *The British Constitution*, 15.

21. Lutz, *The Origins of American Constitutionalism*, 9.

22. See Jack N. Rakove, *Revolutionaries: A New History of the Invention of America* (Boston: Houghton Mifflin Harcourt, 2010); Merrill D. Peterson, "The Idea of a Written Constitution in the Thought of the Founders," in Howard, ed., *The United States Constitution*, 43. Referring to the revolutionary constitution of Virginia discussed in chapter 5, Rakove wrote that this new American constitutionalism "treated a constitution not as a working description of government but as a single authoritative document, written at a known moment of historical time, under rules that made it legally superior to all other acts that the government it created would subsequently adopt." Rakove further observed that "No longer would Americans appeal to custom or tradition or the myth of an 'ancient constitution' lost in the dim mists of history as the sources of their political values and institutions. The Americans had instead become a people who defined themselves by the constitutions they framed and who saw their opportunity to 'alter or abolish' constitutions as the great achievement their own struggle for independence should bequeath to the wider world." To Wood, the "most obvious difference" between the British and American constitutionalists of the late eighteenth century "was the American Revolutionaries' conception of a constitution as a written document, as a fundamental law circumscribing the government." In this connection, Wood cites Thomas Payne's observation in 1791 that a constitution was "a thing *antecedent* to a government," such that "a government is only a creature of a constitution." Gordon S. Wood, *The Idea of America: Reflections on the Birth of the United States* (New York: Penguin Press, 2011), 174–75 (emphasis original). Ronal Peters also remarked that among the most significant differences between the American political system and the British system out of which it grew was "the fact that the American system is based on written constitutions while the English system is not." Ronald M. Peters, "The Written Constitution," in George J. Graham and Scarlett G. Graham, eds., *Founding Principles of American Government: Two Hundred Years of Democracy on Trial* (Bloomington: Indiana University Press, 1977), 168.

23. Adams, "The State Constitutions as Analogy and Precedent," in Howard, ed., *The United States Constitution*, 3.

24. Bicameral legislatures were established under the provisional constitutions of New Hampshire and South Carolina and under the more permanent constitutions of Virginia, New Jersey, Delaware, Maryland, North Carolina, New York, and Massachusetts.

25. Different qualifications for election to the two chambers of the legislature were specified in the constitutions of Massachusetts, New Jersey, New York, North Carolina, South Carolina, and Virginia.

26. Members of the senate represented different geographic divisions of the state from those represented by the members of the house in Massachusetts, Maryland, New Hampshire, New York, North Carolina, South Carolina, and Virginia.

27. Explicit reference to the separation of powers was made in the constitutions of Georgia, Maryland, Massachusetts, North Carolina, Vermont, and Virginia.

28. Provision for the direct election was later made in the 1784 New Hampshire constitution.

29. Tenure during "good behavior" was secured in the constitutions of Delaware, Maryland, Massachusetts, New Hampshire, New York, North Carolina, South Carolina, and Virginia. Fixed terms for judicial offices were established by the constitutions of New Jersey and Pennsylvania.

30. The holding of multiple offices was prohibited in Delaware, Georgia, Maryland, Massachusetts, New Hampshire, New York, North Carolina, Pennsylvania, and South Carolina.

31. Limitations on time in office were established in the constitutions of Delaware, Georgia, Maryland, North Carolina, Pennsylvania, Vermont, Virginia, and South Carolina.

32. The gubernatorial veto in the first South Carolina constitution was not carried over in the second constitution. In New York and New Hampshire, the veto could be overridden by the legislature. In Georgia and Vermont, legislation was required to be submitted to the governor and council for their "perusal and advice," after which they could propose amendments. Additionally, in Vermont, if the governor and council were not satisfied with the legislature's response to their proposed amendments, they could suspend passage of the legislation until the next legislative session.

33. The advice and consent of the privy council was required by the constitutions of Delaware, Georgia, Maryland, Massachusetts, New Hampshire, North Carolina, Virginia, and South Carolina.

34. The appointment power was shared by the executive and the legislature in Delaware, Massachusetts, New York, South Carolina, Vermont, and Virginia.

35. Authority to impeach and remove the governor and other civil officers was conferred on the legislature in Delaware, Massachusetts, New Hampshire, New York, North Carolina, Pennsylvania, South Carolina, Virginia, and Vermont.

36. These constitutional guarantees of rights and liberties were the predicate to the Bill of Rights amending the Constitution after ratification. Although beyond the scope of this study, it is noteworthy that only Delaware and Vermont (which was at the time an independent nation) confronted the illegality of slavery in their constitutions, which would not be addressed in the federal Constitution until after a civil war eighty years later.

37. Gerald Stourzh, "Constitution: Changing Meanings of the Term from the Early Seventeenth to the Eighteenth Century," in Terence Ball and J. G. A., eds., *Conceptual Change and the Constitution* (Lawrence: University of Kansas Press, 1988), 47 (emphasis in the original).

38. To Willi Adams, the decision by Pennsylvania and Delaware was "a great step forward in the practical development of modern constitutionalism." Adams, *The First American Constitutions*, 73.

39. Despite some legerdemain on the part of the reconvened convention in tabulating the town's responses, the constitution was declared to have been accepted by at least two-thirds of the voters.

40. As Peterson observed, "No theory or model of a constitutional convention existed in 1776. It came about gradually through trial and error. As finally realized, the new institution involved three main elements: first, the popular election of delegates to a convention specifically authorized to frame a constitution; second, the convention's deliberate choice of a frame of government reduced to written form; and third, the consent (or dissent) of the people to the proposed constitution through a process of ratification. . . . The institution rested on a distinction, unknown to English theory and practice, between the constitution-making authority and the law-making authority." Peterson, "The Idea of a Written Constitution in the Thought of the Founders," in Howard, ed., *The United States Constitution*, 45.

Part I

Constitutionalism in Colonial America

Chapter One

The Enterprise Colonies of Virginia

Settlers were drawn to the American colonies from a variety of backgrounds for different reasons. The earliest settlements in Virginia and Maine were primarily mercantile adventures motivated by the prospect of plunder and the exploitation of fishing and fur trading. The New England colonies had their genesis in the repression of religious dissenters. The colonies established in Maryland, New York, New Jersey, Pennsylvania, Delaware, and the Carolinas were in essence feudal provinces under the control of a proprietary palatine, given as a reward for service and loyalty to the crown. Georgia, the last of the colonies, was intended to serve geopolitical strategic and social welfare ends.

The colonization of America was effected primarily through grants of royal authority either made to commercial enterprises, usually joint stock companies, or to individual nobles. Nevertheless, when the colonialists established their New World settlements, each in their own way sought to establish a social order where there was none. In each of the colonies, the settlers structured their societies by reference to a commonly acknowledged written document manifesting the delegation of authority to govern, either from the crown or from the settlers themselves.

In Virginia and New England, joint stock companies were formed by investors and merchant adventurers,[1] who pooled their capital and subscribed for stock in the corporation to finance a common commercial enterprise. Like modern corporations, these joint stock companies enjoyed an existence independent of their individual owners and could engage in commerce—such as the ownership of land and the erecting of settlements—in the same way as a natural person. Their existence, however, was dependent on a charter from the crown. As Herbert Osgood has noted, the charter was "a document used for the transmission of rights and powers," that "Since its introduction by the

Roman priesthood into England," had been "used by the Crown for the conveyance of powers in great number and variety."[2]

These charters established the framework under which the corporations would be governed. Executive officers (typically a "treasurer" and a council) were designated and legislative authority was conferred on the stockholders, who were to meet in general assembly (referred to as "general courts") at times specified in the charter. These charters also made provision for general assemblies of representatives of the settlers that were to enact legislation for their own governance.

The charters granted to individuals for the establishment of proprietary colonies similarly specified the governing authority of the palatine. Although the authority of the palatine was virtually feudal, these charters provided for some degree of local participation and consent to the ordinances of the proprietor.

The royal charters granted rights to land in specified territories and the authority to establish and construct settlements. Even in their most rudimentary form, the charters served as the foundational documents for the societies they were to form. The charters authorized the adoption of laws and ordinances for the government of the colonies. Pursuant to the charters, civil and criminal violations of those laws were adjudicated by judicial authorities created under the charters. The charters also authorized the raising of land and naval forces to defend the colonies from external threats and to subdue insurrections among the settlers themselves.

Significantly, the charters provided for the sharing of executive and legislative powers between the grantees in England and the colonial governments in America. Over time, the colonists enjoyed greater autonomy in part as a means of attracting settlers who would remain in the colonies forming a stable population and in part as a consequence of political developments in England. Throughout these changes in the political order, the charters secured the rights of English citizens for the colonists.

The royal charters have been rightly viewed as a distant source of principles later enshrined in the Constitution.[3] Derived from the early English guilds, the colonial charters established the legitimacy of the executive, legislative, and judicial bodies in the colonies and provided a framework within which their authority was to be exercised.[4] Importantly, these charters formed the basis on which the colonists themselves fashioned their own covenants and agreements and ultimately their state constitutions for their own self-governance after the withdrawal of the crown governors.

THE COLONIAL EXPEDITIONS OF GILBERT AND RALEIGH: 1578–1590

In the papal bull *Inter Caetera* of 1493, Pope Alexander divided the territory of the New World between the Catholic kings of Spain and Portugal, both of whom laid claims to the territory by virtue of the expedition of Christopher Columbus. The pope drew a line of demarcation running north to south from a point west of the Azores and Cape Verde Islands. The lands to the east of the line were to be the domain of Portugal and the lands to the west were to be under the dominion of Spain.[5] Although Spain and Portugal assented to the pope's plan by executing the Treaty of Tordesillas on June 7, 1494, the authority of the pope and the legitimacy of the exclusive claims of Spain and Portugal were not recognized by the English crown. Thus, although among Catholic Europe, the pope was regarded as "an inspired administrator," who "distributed the newly discovered regions according to his inclination and infallible discretion," as head of the church in England, Henry VIII "claimed authority to empower his subjects to discover remote, heathen and barbarous lands . . . with no reference to the supremacy of the Roman pontiff."[6]

To that end, King Henry VII had sent the adventurer, John Cabot, on a voyage of discovery in 1496. However, it was Elizabeth I who launched the "first serious gestures toward colonization." George Louis Beer observed that England's bitter conflict with Spain had directed royal attention to the colonization of America. Proponents of colonization, like Sir George Peckham and Richard Hakluyt, argued that Spain's monopoly on the resources of America posed a significant risk to Britain's national security. Hakluyt advocated a colonial enterprise in the territory north of Florida that was still "unplanted by Christians." Also, adventurers like Francis Drake had plundered Spanish treasure while searching for the Northwest Passage between Asia and America, known as the Strait of Anian. Thus, there were strong geopolitical and economic motives underlying Britain's colonial aspirations.[7]

Elizabeth's colonial initiative was carried out by Humphrey Gilbert, and later by his half-brother, Walter Raleigh.[8] Gilbert had had a distinguished military career as captain of the English forces sent to aid the Huguenots in 1652 and later to confront the Munster Revolt in Ireland. It was during his service in Ireland that Gilbert published his *Discourse* in which he endorsed the establishment of colonies in North America to support trade and to secure the riches of China, an interest he may have acquired from the Huguenots who had colonial aspirations in Florida.[9] Gilbert was knighted for his service in aid of the Dutch in their revolt against the Spanish, and on June 11, 1578, Elizabeth granted Gilbert letters patent to found a colony on the North American coast between Labrador and Florida.[10]

Pursuant to the letters patent, like those issued to Cabot before him, Gilbert was to "discover, find, search out, and view such remote, heathen and barbarous lands, countrys and territories not actually possessed by any Christian prince or people." The lands discovered and possessed by Gilbert under authority of the letters patent were granted to him as a proprietary "in fee simple or otherwise, according to the order of laws of England."[11]

The letters patent imposed certain obligations on Gilbert and delegated governmental authorities to fulfill those obligations. Gilbert was to provide for the defense of his colony and to that end, Gilbert was authorized to "encounter, expulse, repel and resist" anyone who attempted to settle in his territory "without specific license and liking" of Gilbert. He was further authorized to take "As of good and lawful prize," the "vessels, and other goods and fortunes" of anyone found to be "trafficking into any harbor or . . . creek," except those "driven by force or tempest and shipwreck."[12]

Gilbert was also granted broad legislative, executive, and judicial authority to govern the colony, as much as "Necessary for safety of all men that shall adventure themselves in those journeys or voyages, to determine to live together in Christian peace and civil quietness each with the other." The laws adopted under this grant of authority were to be "As near as conveniently may, agreeable to the form of the laws and policy of England," as well as "not against the true Christian faith or religion," nor that would "withdraw any of the subjects or peoples of those lands or places from allegiance to us . . . as their immediate Sovereigns under God."[13]

The authority of the crown was to extend to the territory acquired by Gilbert, which "from henceforth shall be of the allegiance to us, our heirs and successors." So too, those who accompanied Gilbert who had been born in England, Ireland, or "any other place within our allegiance," were to enjoy "all the privileges of free denizens and persons native of England."[14]

In contrast to the colonial endeavors of France, Portugal, and Spain, which received public funds, English colonialism was to be funded through private investment and Elizabeth I refused to provide any capital for the venture.[15] However, emboldened by the royal patent, Gilbert was able to marshal sufficient support to outfit a fleet of eleven ships at Dartmouth, with five hundred men provisioned for one year. There is general agreement, however, the primary mission of the expedition was plunder rather than colonization, although Gilbert's intentions included establishing a base in the New World.[16]

To pursue their desire for Spanish treasure, the expedition chose a southern route rather than following Cabot's course northward across the Atlantic.[17] That decision proved to be a fateful one.

As a result of disagreements among the backers in the face of royal opposition to provoking Spain, four ships carrying 160 men withdrew before the expedition could get underway. Eventually seven ships, with 389 men, embarked on a southwesterly course intending to raid the West Indies before continuing on to America. However, while still off the coast of Ireland, one of the ships was lost in a storm and the others returned to England. It would be five years before Gilbert was again able to secure the resources for a second expedition to the New World.[18]

By June 1583, Gilbert had secured sufficient investment to outfit five ships and 250 men for a second expedition to North America. The agreement with the investors, among whom was an association of merchant adventurers in Southampton, established a governance structure for the company that served as a model for later royal charters, although no rights of government of the colonies were included as they would be later. The agreement provided that the affairs of the company would be overseen by a governor, a group of eight assistants, and several other officers including a treasurer and a secretary. The agreement further provided that there were to be meetings at least twice a year of all the investors, called a "general court," and in addition to a return on their investment, the investors were to receive land in the North American colony.[19]

Gilbert led the expedition personally. Raleigh had set out with the expedition, but he and his ship soon turned back. By the end of June 1583, the fleet entered Saint John's Bay, Newfoundland, which Gilbert claimed in the name of the English crown.[20]

As Gilbert continued his explorations, other ships and men abandoned the venture and returned to England. Eventually, storms forced the remaining ships to return. En route, Gilbert and his ship were lost.[21]

Gilbert's colonial aspirations were carried on by his younger half-brother Raleigh, who like Gilbert had seen military service in France and Ireland. Upon his return to court in 1582, Raleigh soon became a favorite of Elizabeth who conferred lucrative privileges on him.[22] On March 25, 1584, Raleigh was granted a royal charter for the exploration of North America, which had been modeled after the letters patent previously awarded to Gilbert.[23]

A party under the leadership of Arthur Barlowe and Philip Amadas was sent out a short time later. Their ships reached the outer banks of the Carolinas before returning to England with glowing reports of fertile soil and hospitable native peoples. Barlowe and Amadas brought with them to England two inhabitants of Roanoke Island, Montaco and Wanchese. Raleigh named this territory Virginia in honor of Elizabeth, the "Virgin Queen."[24]

Encouraged by the reports of Amadas and Barlowe, in 1585, Raleigh dispatched Richard Greenville with 108 men to establish a colony in Virginia. The party landed south of the Chesapeake Bay on Roanoke Island with the intention of establishing a base for trading and for privateering against the Spanish in the Caribbean, rather than a self-sustaining settlement.

This was consistent with the prevailing view in England that the value of establishing posts in the New World lay in the exploitation of natural resources and the facilitation of trade and not in the establishment of new, semi-autonomous societies, which had been the view expressed in Gilbert's writing and that of Richard Hakluyt, another influential proponent of New World colonization.[25] As D. W. Meinig has pointed out, however, Hakluyt's vision of New World colonization was fundamentally flawed in that "Hakluyt had not yet grasped the first principal of colonization, that colonies must first be able to feed themselves."[26] This flawed conception of the colony as being first and foremost a profit-making economic enterprise, rather than a social organization capable of sustaining itself before generating a return on the investment, affected the entire course of the Virginia colony thereafter and ultimately resulted in the failure of the Virginia Company.

Because the Roanoke settlement had not been intended to be self-sustaining, Grenville returned to England two months later to procure supplies for the colony. Grenville's return was delayed, however, by a privateering excursion in the Caribbean. In the meantime, when Admiral Drake's fleet stopped at Roanoke on its return from the West Indies in 1586, the settlers returned with the fleet to England. Thus, upon arriving in Roanoke, Grenville found the settlement deserted.

Grenville left a party of fifteen men to garrison the settlement when he returned to England. This party was killed by the native peoples in retaliation for an attack on their village by the earlier settlers and the killing of one of their chiefs.[27]

Raleigh organized a second colonial enterprise in Virginia, this time comprised of eighty-nine men, seventeen women, and eleven children. Despite Raleigh's instructions that a new site was to be found for the settlement, the ship's captain put the settlers ashore at Roanoke to pursue the hunt for Spanish treasure ships.[28]

Dissension erupted among the leadership of the colony and the governor, John White, returned to England. The ships carrying supplies and reinforcements for the colony were diverted by their captains to capture Spanish prize ships and after being crippled, did not continue on to Roanoke. Later in 1588, the war with Spain delayed sending supply ships, and when supplies finally arrived at Roanoke in 1590, no trace of the settlers was found.[29]

Thereafter, Raleigh abandoned his colonial ambitions in America.[30] The failure of Raleigh's colonial effort has been attributed to several causes including the choice of an inhospitable and disease-ridden site for the colony, inadequate organization as a result of lack of funding, and a lack of motivation and practical skills on the part of the colonists. In essence, the colony was regarded as little more than an adjunct to the privateering activities in the Caribbean, which were directed at plundering the Spanish treasure fleets.[31] Raleigh transferred his remaining rights under his royal charter to a group of London merchant adventurers.[32] Inspired by reports of valuable fisheries and opportunities for trade, the London adventurers joined by investors in Plymouth petitioned James I for their own charter to engage in commerce in America.[33] The charters granted to these merchant adventurers closely resembled that of the East India Company of 1601.[34]

THE FIRST VIRGINIA COMPANY: 1606–1609

On April 10, 1606, King James I granted the London and Plymouth adventurers a license "to deduce a colony of sundry of our people into that part of America commonly called Virginia."[35] Such a charter has been said to have been "by far the most formal and authoritative instrument by which the king can express his will or grant powers and privileges."[36] The charter was perpetual in duration but could be terminated either by voluntary surrender of the charter holder or by judicial process through the issuance of the writ *quo warranto* or *scire facias*, as would later be the case with the Virginia Company.

Two companies were formed. The first, centered in the City of London, came to be known as the Virginia Company. The other, which was comprised of investors from Bristol, Exeter, and Plymouth, became the Plymouth Company.[37] The territory conferred under the charter extended from the St. Croix River in the north to Cape Fear in the south.[38] The Virginia Company was given control over the southern tract running from Cape Fear to modern-day New York City, whereas the Plymouth Company was to control the northern tract from the Potomac River to what is now Bangor, Maine.[39] Each company was given a 100-mile square tract on which to locate their own settlements and the middle region was to be available for joint settlement.[40]

The royal charter established a governance structure that differed substantially from the structure under the Gilbert and Raleigh patents. Under the 1606 charter, there was to be a thirteen-member "Council for Virginia" appointed by the crown and situated in London. There was to be an element of local control through thirteen-member colonial councils located in the colonies, whose members were to be appointed by the Council of Virginia.[41] This charter has aptly been described as a constitution for the Virginia colony, "for it prescribed the form of government and made regulations that none could disregard."[42]

The colonial councils were invested with broad powers to effectuate the laws and instructions issued by the Council of Virginia in England. The colonial councils were empowered to "govern and order all matters and causes, which shall arise, grow, or happen to or within the same or several colonies, according to such laws, ordinances, and instructions, as shall be, in that behalf, given and signed" by the crown. The councils were also authorized to "take and surprise" persons who attempted "to inhabit" the colonies "without the especial license of the said several Colonies and Plantations."

Additionally, the councils were given the authority to impose duties on goods "trafficked, bought and sold" in the colonies and to seize the "ships, vessels, goods and other furniture" of those who do did not pay the duties.[43]

Lastly, the Charter of Virginia contained a guaranty of personal liberties and rights. Inhabitants of the colonies, as well as any children born there, were to "have and enjoy all Liberties, Franchises, and Immunities . . . to all Intents and Purposes, as if they had been abiding and born, within this our Realm of England." This signal feature of English colonialism in America would largely inform the evolution of constitutionalism that followed.

The significance of this grant of authorities and rights cannot be overstated. To H. D. Hazeltine, the 1606 charter marked "the real beginning of English settlement in America and an opening of a new era in the history of colonization in general." The charter, which Hazeltine noted was the work of Lord Coke, not only asserted the crown's right to colonize the New World but also "asserted the principle that English colonists in this territory were to enjoy the same constitutional rights possessed by Englishmen in the homeland."[44] Warren Billings viewed the grant to the colonists of full English rights to be significant in that "colonial Englishmen carried to America a centuries-old legal tradition founded upon the belief that the conduct of civilized society was governed by rules, and that every man irrespective of his station, was obliged to obey the laws of the realm."[45]

As Billings pointed out, however, the charter did not provide further illumination of what those rights were that the colonists would enjoy, and accordingly, it was left to the Virginia Company to fill in the interstices.[46] To that end, the company issued "Instructions for Government" on November 20, 1606, that obliged the colonial councils to

> constitute, make, and ordain such constitutions, ordinances and officers for the better order, government and peace of the people of their several colonies, so always as the same ordinances and constitutions do not touch any party in life or member; which constitutions shall stand and continue in full force until the same shall be otherwise altered or made void by us . . . so always as the same alterations be such as may stand with and be in substance consonant unto the laws of England or the equity thereof.

The councils were instructed to exercise judicial powers including the punishment of criminals, and in that connection, council presidents were authorized to reprieve but not pardon criminal offenders.[47]

On December 20, 1606, the Virginia Company dispatched three ships, the *Sarah Constant*, the *Godspeed*, and the *Discovery*, to establish a colony in Virginia. The ships carried 105 prospective settlers, all of whom were men. Roughly one-third were described as "gentlemen," including a physician, an Anglican minister, and several privateers. Forty of the settlers were former soldiers and the remainder were artisans and laborers.[48]

Unfortunately, many of the errors that had doomed the Roanoke settlement were repeated. The ships followed the southern route to the West Indies, finally reaching the Chesapeake Bay on April 26, 1607. The settlers landed at what would become the Jamestown settlement on May 24. Thirty-nine of the settlers had been lost en route.[49]

Although something other than a base for privateers had been envisioned—dwellings, a fort, and a church were erected, and some effort was made to plant grain—the colony was still conceived of as a mercantile enterprise rather than a self-sustaining colony, and the settlers were expected to search out valuable commodities such as precious metals, medicinal plants, dyes, and spices that could be sold in England.[50] As Charles Andrews noted,

> the contemporary idea of colonization had advanced no further than to conceive of settlements in terms of ships, reasonably well equipped and captained, of hardy men sufficient in number but of any class or quality, drawn together in part by the prospect of gold and plunder, and in part by the need of employment, and of supplies adequate for the purpose at hand.

Andrews observed that like the Roanoke adventurers, the Jamestown settlers "were not above gold and plunder and were interested in barter with the Indians." However, "neither they nor the company in England had yet learned in the hard school of experience the fundamental lesson that a colony to be successful and permanent must be self-supporting."[51] As a consequence, the Jamestown settlers, like those of the previously failed Roanoke colony, were wholly dependent on supplies from England.[52]

The settlers of Jamestown faced sickness and starvation. Jamestown was located on the edge of a swamp, which provided a rich environment for the malaria, typhoid, and dysentery that the settlers had unwittingly brought with them. Additionally, in the summer months, the drinking water was contaminated with seawater, which led to salt poisoning.[53] Four out of five of the settlers succumbed to starvation, disease, and attacks from the native peoples. Andrews described the first year of the colony, at the end of which only thirty-eight men survived, as a "ghastly epic of misfortune," and Sarson likened life in the colony "to that in a Hobbesian State of Nature: hard, nasty, brutish and short."[54]

THE SECOND VIRGINIA COMPANY: 1609–1611

Conditions at Jamestown began to improve after John Smith assumed the leadership of the colony in September 1608 and imposed strict martial discipline on the settlers (e.g., Smith threatened to expel anyone unwilling to tend the crops and livestock and leave them to starve in the wilderness).[55] The continuing hardships in the colony led the Virginia Company to seek, "such ample and large privileges and powers" to reform the company's governance structure and to eliminate the dissension that had paralyzed the colonial council.[56] It was also felt that a fatal weakness of the 1606 charter was that the crown had retained decisional authority but left it to the investors to bear the cost of implementing the crown's decisions. As the prospect of immediate profit became unlikely, the crown willingly eschewed its involvement.[57]

A new joint stock company, "The Treasurer and Company of Adventurers and Planters of the City of London and the First Colony of Virginia," was formed by a charter granted by James I on May 23, 1609. This company was to enjoy perpetual existence and was empowered to acquire and dispose of property in its own name and to sue and be sued in the courts of England. The territorial grant was enlarged to comprehend the territory 200 miles north and 200 miles south of Point Comfort, the place where the James River enters the Chesapeake Bay.[58]

The second charter also effected significant changes in the company's governance structure. Although authority was centralized in the London Council, as it had been under the previous charter, both the general court of the investors and the colonial councils were eliminated.[59]

Executive authority was conferred on the treasurer who was to be assisted by a council. Initially, the treasurer and council were appointed by the crown, but thereafter, they were to be elected by the shareholders. A deputy treasurer was to be designated by the treasurer with the concurrence of the council.[60]

The authority of the treasurer and council over the government of the Virginia colony was also enlarged. The treasurer and council were given the authority to appoint such officers for the colony "as to them seem good." The laws adopted under the previous charter were nullified, and in their place, the council was to "make, ordain, and establish all Manner of Orders, Laws, Directions, Instructions, Forms and ceremonies of Government and Magistracy" that the council deemed "fit and necessary for and concerning the Government of Said Colony and Plantation."

Laws adopted by the council were to be in effect not only in the colony "but also upon the seas, in going to and from said colony," and were to be "as near as conveniently may be . . . agreeable to the Laws, Statutes, Government and Policy of this our Realm of England." The charter also reiterated the provision of the 1606 charter conferring on the colonists the rights of English subjects.[61]

The charter authorized the colonial officers appointed by the treasurer and council to enforce the laws and ordinances adopted by the council. The governor of the colony was given "full and absolute power and authority to correct, punish, pardon, govern and rule" the inhabitants of the colony and that authority extended equally to "cases capital and criminal, as civil, both marine and other."[62]

Additionally, in light of the perceived breakdown of discipline under the 1606 charter, the second charter authorized the imposition of martial law "in cases of rebellion or mutiny." As Billings observed, resort to martial law reflected "the Londoners' awareness that traditional modes of legal administration were ill-suited to a virtually all-male frontier settlement that lacked even the rudiments of English society" and "was prompted by a belief that an insufficiency of discipline among the settlers was a key reason for the lack of the colony's success." It was the hope therefore, that reorganization along military lines would produce order. To accomplish that reorganization, the company selected two experienced military officers, Lord De La Warr and Sir Thomas Gates, to serve as the leaders of the colony.[63]

Under its new treasurer, Sir Thomas Smith, who had been a governor of the highly lucrative East India Company for twenty years, nine ships were dispatched from London and Plymouth on May 15, 1609, carrying eight hundred settlers. The leaders of the expedition were detained in Bermuda by weather and did not reach Virginia until May 23, 1610.

In the meantime, the colony had gone through another "starving time" due to the lack of supplies and the settlers' inability to sustain themselves in the wilderness. Many of the settlers resorted to cannibalism, and it was decided to move the settlement to Newfoundland in the hope of obtaining supplies and transport back to England. However, as the colonists were making way, they encountered Lord De La Warr, the new colonial governor, who ordered them to return to Jamestown.[64]

De La Warr was able to make some improvements but illness forced his return to England, and Thomas Gates assumed the leadership of the colony. In May 1609, instructions for the governance of the colony were issued to Gates. Under those instructions, cases of rebellion, mutiny, and "all such cases of provident necessity" were to be subject to martial law, "as of most dispatch and terror and fittest for this government." In all other matters, Gates and his government were to proceed "rather as chancellor than as judge" on the basis of "natural right and equity" rather than "the niceness and letter of the law which perplexes in this tender body." Gates was further instructed that "to beget reverence for your authority" and to "refresh" in the minds of the colonists "the gravity of those laws under which they were borne," Gates was given "power to make, add, or distinguish any laws or ordinances at your discretion according to the authority limited in your commission."[65]

Under this authority, Gates issued the first comprehensive codification of the laws of the colony. Gates was of the view that the past failures of the colony were the direct result of the colonists' proclivity to savagery and lawlessness, and therefore, strong external controls and discipline were required.[66] The result was the draconian "Articles, Laws, and Orders, Divine,

Politic and Martial for the Colony of Virginia," published on June 12, 1610.[67]

The code proposed to establish military discipline in the colony. Colonial officers were obliged to ensure "that the Almighty God be duly and daily served," and it was made a capital offense to "speak impiously or maliciously" against the Holy Trinity or to "blaspheme God's holy name." Settlers were required to attend church services twice a day and to keep the Sabbath.

It was also a capital offense to "use any traitorous words against the Majesty's Person or royal authority." The code contained the common law crimes of murder, rape, sodomy, adultery, false witness, and slander. It was a criminal offense, as well, to engage in unauthorized trade with or theft from the native peoples.[68]

The Gates code contained penal provisions relating directly to the colony's welfare. It was a crime to embezzle from the stores of supplies or to steal from someone who had died or who was absent from the settlement. It was also a crime for a settler to sell a tool or other "instruments necessary and useful for the business of the colony" or for a settler to kill livestock or to discharge laundry water within twenty feet of a well. Settlers were further required to store their tools, clean their houses and to clean the streets in front of their houses, and to attend work. Seamen who were considered "greedy and ill disposed" and who sold supplies to settlers "at unreasonable rates and prices unconscionable" faced death.[69] Actions adversely affecting the colony's good order were also criminalized. Flight from the colony (or assisting another to flee), conspiracy against the governor or other officers, and the failure to report such acts of treason within one hour were all punishable by death. The unauthorized transport of goods away from the colony for private gain or the removal of a ship without the governor's authorization were capital offenses, as well. Offenders were hung and then burned to death, broken on the wheel, or staked out and starved to death. Loss of ears was the punishment for thefts or frauds by bakers, cooks, and fishermen. But as harsh as these punishments were, it has been noted that the large number of capital crimes in the Gates code was typical of the English common law at the time, although the punishments were not.[70]

THE THIRD VIRGINIA COMPANY: 1611–1624

Despite the Jamestown colony having assumed an aura of greater stability, there continued to be dissatisfaction among the shareholders. It was thought that the Virginia Company's authority over the colony was not sufficient to address the problems of mutiny and unauthorized flight by the settlers. The shareholders also objected to their loss of direct control under the second charter.

As new capital became more difficult to attract, the shareholders sought to enhance the economic base of the enterprise. To do so, the shareholders sought an enlargement of the territory available for colonization, to include the Bermuda Islands, as well as other sources of revenue.[71]

On March 12, 1611, James I granted a third charter for the Virginia Company. This charter significantly expanded the territory and permitted additional adventurers, including the Archbishop of Canterbury.[72] Of much greater import, however, were the reorganization of the corporation's governance structure and the restoration of the shareholder's control over the affairs of the corporation. As Homer Hockett observed, under the third charter, "the Virginia Company became a self-governing corporation similar to the East India Company, with the privilege not only of managing its own business affairs but of governing the inhabitants of the plantation."[73] Of equal significance, as Osgood noted, the evidence in the records of the Virginia Company "abundantly proves not only that the corporation directly exercised governmental power, but that it was the source whence that power was immediately derived."[74]

The third charter invested the general court of the shareholders with the authority for "Handling, Ordering and Disposing of Matters and Affairs of general Weight and Importance" having to do with the "Weal Public and general good of the said company and the Plantation," including "the Manner of Government," the disposition of land, and the establishment of trade. The general court was to elect the members of the council and "such officials as they shall think fit and requisite." The charter also conferred on the general court broad legislative power "to ordain and make such Laws and Ordinances, for the "good and welfare of the said Plantation."[75]

This investiture of governing authority in the members of the corporation would have a broader significance for American constitutional development. As Hockett noted, "The democratic charter of the Virginia Company . . . tended to familiarize stockholders with the idea that officials derive their powers from the consent of the members of the corporate body, of which they are not the masters but the responsible agents. When members of the company were transformed by events into residents of a de facto political community, the concept of derivative power was readily carried over from things economic to affairs political." In this, Hockett saw the inchoate conception of a written constitution as the fundamental document of government.[76]

Thereafter, conditions improved both in the company and in the Jamestown colony. The third charter had granted the corporation a license to conduct lotteries that substantially increased revenue. The introduction of tobacco cultivation in 1612, together with the seventeen-year exemption from English customs duties provided in the charter and the subsequent prohibition against planting tobacco in England and Wales imposed on December

30, 1619, greatly contributed to the stability of the colony. Also by 1619, the investors had come to recognize that the success of the colony required that the colonists themselves have a stake in the enterprise. As a consequence, provision was made for the settlers to be allocated three acres of land that they could farm for their own use. Such private land ownership, and the income there from, as well as the improvement in the system of supply, through an enterprise known as the "magazine," made life in the colony more hospitable.[77]

The meeting of the shareholders' general court in November 1618 was a momentous one for American constitutional history. It was at this meeting that the Charter of Grants and Liberties was ratified. Although lost to history, the charter is believed to have been written at the instance of Sir Edwin Sandys, Treasurer of the Virginia Company, and to have been carried to Jamestown by the colonial governor, George Yardley. It is believed that the charter was an extensive statement of orders, laws, and privileges that were to govern life in the colony, including the creation of four boroughs: Charles City, Henrico, Jamestown, and Kiccowtan. The charter is most memorable, however, because it is believed to have contained an instruction to convene a general assembly of the representatives of the residents of Jamestown. Representatives were elected in accordance with the charter and on June 30, 1619, the first legislative body in America was convened.[78]

In all likelihood, Sandys and the corporation were responding to the imperatives of the Jamestown settlers themselves. As Joseph Story wrote in his *Commentaries on the Constitution of the United States*, "As the colony increased, the spirit of its members assumed more and more the tone of independence; and they grew restless and impatient for the privileges enjoyed under the government of their native country."[79]

This transformation of the colonial government under the Charter of Grants and Liberties marked a fundamental shift in the colonial paradigm. It has been observed that "The alteration of government that occurred in Virginia in 1619 was constitutionally significant as the first instance in which the corporation principle provided the basis for a self-governing policy," and "signified the transformation of the business into a political society."[80] This shift in the colonial paradigm also reflected the recognition that some element of self-government would be necessary to attract "those kinds of settlers who could turn land to profitable uses" but who would not venture to Virginia "unless it took on the attributes of home," including "a legal system that resembled English rather than martial law."[81] Thus, Sarson has written that "Gradually, settlers and company men alike realized that if Virginia were to be a colony at all it would have to be a colony of settlement and as such would require a good measure of self-government."[82]

In any event, the establishment of a representative assembly marked a turning point both in the history of Virginia and in American constitutional history. To Billings, "It was the first positive step towards the creation of permanent legal institutions in the colony, and it stands out as one of the London Company's most enduring contributions towards the transformation of English culture to the New World."[83]

Between August 2 and August 4, 1619, the first general assembly enacted a series of laws regulating the temporal and spiritual life of the colony. Laws were enacted against "idleness, gaming, drunkenness, and excess in apparel;" as well as laws requiring the planting of certain crops, including mulberry trees, flax, anis, and grapes. Stores of corn were required to be maintained for every household servant, and an additional "one spare barrel" was to be "delivered out yearly" for sale or trade. The killing of cattle and oxen was prohibited without the permission of the governor. The theft of boats, oars, or canoes, either from other colonists or from the native peoples was declared a felony.

Laws were enacted regulating commercial relations as well as the operation of the magazine. Tradesmen were to be paid "according to the quality of his trade and work." Contracts made in England between landowners and tenants were to be adhered to and violations were subject to punishment by the governor. Enticement of tenants and servants from one place of employment to another was prohibited and "both the seducer and the seduced" were to be "severely punished" by the governor. A registry of servants and the terms and conditions of their service was to be maintained by the Secretary of State.

In like fashion, a variety of laws were enacted to regulate relations with the native peoples that reflected the brittle nature of the relationship. Thus, it was decreed that "no injury or oppression be wrought by the English against the Indians whereby the present peace might be disturbed and ancient quarrels might be revived." With regard to the integration of native peoples into the English communities, the burgesses "counseled those of the colony neither utterly to reject them nor yet to draw them to come in," but instead, "five or six may be admitted" to assist in "killing deer, fishing, beating corn and other works," with the consent of the governor, so long as "good guard in the night be kept over them." Nevertheless, settlements were to provide for the education of the native peoples "in the true religion and civil course of life" and boys "of wit and graces of nature" were to receive instruction in literature "so as to be fitted for the college intended for them." Freemen were permitted to trade with the native peoples, except that the sale of weapons would be considered "traitorous" and be punishable by death. Sale of "any of the greater hoes" or of any "English dog of quality" was also prohibited. Travel to "any Indian towns, habitations, or places of resort" also required the governor's permission.

Restrictions were placed on other travel as well. The governor was to be notified of any travel more than twenty miles from the traveler's home or of any absence of more than seven days. Travelers to and from Kiccowtan were obliged to stop at James City "to know whether the governor will command him any service." Entry by ship into Chesapeake Bay required the permission of the governor and the posting of security that "neither himself nor his company shall force or wrong the Indians."

The Church of England was established as the recognized church and ministers and church wardens were enjoined to "seek to prevent all ungodly disorders" and to "not forebear" such "scandalous offenses" as "suspicions of whoredoms, dishonest company keeping with women, and such like." Persons who did not "amend his or her life in point of evident suspicion on incontinency or the commission of any other enormous sins," were subject to excommunication, apprehension, and the seizure of goods. Swearing was also specifically prohibited.

The authority of the colonial legislature was confirmed and made permanent by the London council in the Ordinances and Constitution that was carried to Jamestown by Governor Francis Watt in August 1621.[84] The Ordinances and Constitution established two "supreme councils." The first, denominated the Council of State, was comprised of the governor and other named councilors, whose charge it was to "bend their care and endeavors to assist the said governor first and principally in advancement of the honor and service of Almighty God and the enlargement of His kingdom amongst those heathen people, and in erecting the said colony in one obedience to his Majesty and all lawful authority from his Majesty's derived, and lastly in maintaining the said people in justice and Christian conversion among themselves and in strength and ability to withstand their enemies."

The second council, the general assembly, was to be comprised of the governor and the Council of State and two representatives, called "burgesses," from each political division of the colony, "respectively chosen by the inhabitants." The general assembly was given "free power to treat, consort, and conclude as well of all emergent occasions concerning the public weal of the said colony and every part thereof as also to make, ordain, and enact such general laws and orders for the behalf of the said colony and the good government thereof as shall from time to time appear necessary or requisite.

All matters were to be decided by majority vote, "reserving always to the governor a negative vote," and were "to imitate and follow the policy of the form of government, laws, custom, manners of loyal and other administration of justice used in the realm of England." The laws enacted by the burgesses were subject to approval by the general court in London.[85]

Once the colonial government had been "well framed and settled," the orders of the general court in London would not "bind the said colony unless they be ratified in like manner in their general assembly." Although originally conceived of as fulfilling administrative and judicial roles as well, the burgesses over time became a purely legislative body.[86]

Despite this remarkable constitutional transformation, both the Virginia Company and the Jamestown colony suffered significant economic reverses that substantially undermined the company's ability to carry on. In 1621, the company lost the lucrative lottery franchise. By 1622, barely 25 percent of the four thousand settlers who had come to the colony since 1618 still survived. Also in 1622, there was a devastating attack on the colony by the native peoples that left approximately four hundred of the settlers dead. As a consequence, expansion of the colony effectively ended and the attitude of the English toward the native population changed from what has been described as "pragmatic accommodation," to one of "total intolerance."[87]

These reverses exacerbated the rift that had grown among the shareholders that began with the displacement of Sir Thomas Smith as treasurer in 1619 and the attack on Smith and his son-in-law over the management of the Jamestown magazine. The attacks were seen as the work of Sandys and the Earl of Warwick, and when Sandys and Warwick eventually split in 1622, the company's management was left incapable of meeting the company's worsening financial and political situation.[88]

By July 1623, the Virginia Company had effectively been placed under the management of the privy council and on July 31, the Attorney General and the Solicitor General recommended that the government of the Jamestown colony be returned to the control of the crown. When the company refused to surrender its charter voluntarily, the Attorney General instituted *quo warranto* proceedings and on May 24, 1624, the charter was vacated and the Virginia Company ceased its corporate existence.[89]

In the end, however, the Virginia Company failed because of its flawed conception of the colonial enterprise as a source of immediate revenue. Unlike the East India Company and other joint stock companies that the Virginia Company's investors hoped to replicate, "which found their markets and sources in the eastern world already prepared and immediately available for profit," as Andrews noted,

> the Virginia Company had first to create its colony in America before any adequate profit from it could be expected. It failed in the effort to accomplish this result and lost its charter before it could bring into existence a working agricultural and industrial community such as it needed in order to return to its subscribers any earnings on their investment.[90]

By royal proclamation on May 13, 1625, the Virginia colony was remanded to the care of the king, becoming the first royal colony in English history. Two governing bodies were constituted. The first was to be located in London and was to be comprised of "a few persons of understanding and quality" appointed by the king. The second was to be seated in the colony and was inferior in authority to the council in London. Governing officials were to be appointed by the crown, which also pledged "Men, Munitions and Fortification," for the defense of the colony. The proclamation assured the preservation of the "Rights and Interests of every Planter and Adventurer" in the colony.[91]

Virginia remained a royal colony thereafter.[92] The standing of the assembly, which came to be known as the House of Burgesses, was uncertain after the reassertion of royal control over the colony, and for the first several years after the crown reasserted its authority, the burgesses were primarily an advisory body.[93] However, in 1638, the king directed the royal governor to convene a formal meeting of the House of Burgesses, and thereafter, the burgesses again served as the lower chamber of the bicameral legislature. Over time, the authority of the burgesses increased, first over the laying of taxes and later, over all legislation, which required the assent of the burgesses to become law. In this way, the House of Burgesses remained at the center of the Virginia colonial government until the colonial governor abdicated his office in 1776.[94]

Among the legislative actions taken by the burgesses was the establishment of qualifications for voting in the election of representatives and the procedures under which elections would be held. The compensation of the burgesses was fixed by law, and the giving of gifts and entertainment to elected members of the House of Burgesses was prohibited. Public officials were also prohibited from attempting to influence the election of burgesses, and individuals were barred from holding multiple public offices. Other acts such as those establishing procedures whereby petitions for the redress of grievances and conferring immunity from arrest for burgesses attending legislative sessions were incorporated into the constitution of the newly independent Commonwealth of Virginia and eventually into the federal Constitution.[95]

NOTES

1. The term *merchant adventurer* refers to groups of traders, usually in the English port cities, who formed organizations to pursue commercial ventures. The oldest of these organizations was the Merchant Adventurers of York that was formed in 1357 and was incorporated in 1518. Charles M. Andrews, *The Colonial Period of American History* (New Haven: Yale University Press, 1934) vol. 1: 28–29.

2. Herbert L. Osgood, "The Corporation as a Form of Colonial Government, Part I," *Political Science Quarterly*, (June 1896) vol. II: 260.

3. See for example, Fisher, *The Evolution of the Constitution of the United States*, 26.

4. Burleigh Cushing Rodick, *American Constitutional Custom: A Forgotten Factor in the Founding* (New York: Philosophical Library, 1953), 20.

5. Frances G. Davenport, ed., *European Treaties Bearing on the History of the United States and its Dependencies of 1648* (Washington, DC: Carnegie Institution of Washington, 1917), vol. 1: 71–78.

6. Samuel F. Haven, *History of Grants Under the Great Council for New England* (Boston: John Wilson, 1869), 4.

7. Susan Brigden, *New Worlds, Lost Worlds: The Rule of the Tudors 1485–1603* (New York: Penguin Group, 2000), 274–80; George Louis Beer, "The Early English Colonial Movement, Part I," *Political Science Quarterly* (March 1908), vol. 23: 76–80.

8. Anthony Pagden, "The Struggle for Legitimacy and the Image of Empire in the Atlantic to C. 1700," in Nicholas Canny, ed., *The Oxford History of the British Empire: The Origins of Empire* (Oxford: Oxford University Press, 1998), 34.

9. Anthony McFarlane, *The British in the Americas 1480–1815* (New York: Longman, 1992), 21–22.

10. D. W. Meinig, *The Shaping of America: A Geographical Perspective of 500 Years of History* (New Haven: Yale University Press, 1986), 30; Kenneth R. Andrews, *Trade, Plunder and Settlement: Maritime Enterprise and the Genesis of the British Empire, 1480–1630* (London: Cambridge University Press, 1984), 183–87.

11. Thorpe, Frances N., ed., *The Federal and State Constitutions, Colonial Charters, and Other Organic Laws of the States, Territories, and Colonies Now or Heretofore Forming the United States of America* (Washington, DC: U.S. Government Printing Office, 1909), vol. 1: 49–50. The reference to "lands not actually possessed by any Christian prince or people," parallels the language of the *Inter Caetera* and is consistent with Elizabeth's statement to the Spanish ambassador in response to Spain's protest of Sir Francis Drake's earlier expedition in 1577, that Spain had no exclusive claim to the Americas "except they have established a few settlements and named rivers and capes," and that "Perscription without possession is not valid." Melvin I. Urofsky, *A March of Liberty: A Constitutional History of the United States* (New York: Knopf, 1988), 7.

12. Thorpe, *The Federal and State Constitutions*, vol. 1: 50.

13. Thorpe, *The Federal and State Constitutions*, vol. 1: 51.

14. Thorpe, *The Federal and State Constitutions*, vol. 1: 51.

15. Richard Middleton and Anne Lombard, *Colonial America: A History to 1763*, 4th ed. (Chichester: Wiley-Blackwell, 2011),42.

16. Andrews, *Trade, Plunder and Settlement*, 187–88; Herbert I. Osgood, *The American Colonies in the Seventeenth Century* (New York: Macmillan, 1904), vol. 1: 8; Steven Sarson, *British America 1500–1800* (New York: Oxford University Press, 2005), 31.

17. Osgood, *The American Colonies in the Seventeenth Century*, vol. 1: 7–8.

18. Osgood, *The American Colonies in the Seventeenth Century*, vol. 1: 8; Andrews, *Trade, Plunder and Settlement*, 189–90; John C. Appleby, "War, Politics, and Colonization, 1558–1625," in Canny, ed., *The Oxford History of the British Empire*, 63.

19. Osgood, *The American Colonies in the Seventeenth Century*, vol. 1: 9–10.

20. Andrews, *Trade, Plunder and Settlement*, 194–95.

21. Osgood, *The American Colonies in the Seventeenth Century*, vol. 1: 12–14; Andrews, *Trade, Plunder and Settlement*, 195–96; M. Edward Haies, *Sir Humphrey Gilbert's Voyage to Newfoundland: A Report of the Voyage and Success Thereof, Attempted in the Year of Our Lord 1583 by Sir Humphrey Gilbert, Knight* (Boston: Directors of Old Southwork, 1902).

22. Andrews, *Trade, Plunder and Settlement*, 200–1; Raleigh Trevelyn, *Sir Walter Raleigh* (New York: Holt, 2002), 1–77; Robert Lacey, *Sir Walter Raleigh* (New York: Athenaeum, 1974), 20–63.

23. Thorpe, *The Federal and State Constitutions*, vol. 1: 53–57.

24. MacFarlane, *The British in the Americas*, 23; Appleby, "War, Politics, and Colonization, 1558–1625," in Canny, ed., *The Oxford History of the British Empire*, 64; Middleton and Lombard, *Colonial America*, 42–43.

25. Carl Brent Swisher, *American Constitutional Development* (Boston: Houghton, 1943), 8.

26. Meinig, *The Shaping of America*, 31.

27. Osgood, *The American Colonies in the Seventeenth Century*, vol. 1: 15–20; Andrews, *Trade, Plunder and Settlement*, 211; Appleby, "War, Politics, and Colonization, 1558–1625," 64–65; McFarlane, *The British in the Americas*, 23; Meinig, *The Shaping of America*, 30.

28. Meinig, *The Shaping of America*, 30; David Beers Quinn, *England and the Discovery of America:1481–1620* (New York: Knopf, 1974), 437.

29. Osgood, *The American Colonies in the Seventeenth Century*, vol. 1: 21–22; Appleby, "War, Politics, and Colonization, 1558–1625," in Canny, ed., *The Oxford History of the British Empire*, 64–65; Meinig, *The Shaping of America*, 30; Middleton and Lombard, *Colonial America*, 44–45.

30. McFarlane, *The British in the Americas*, 24; Quinn, *England and the Discovery of America*, 282–306.

31. Middleton and Lombard, *Colonial America*, 45.

32. Sarson, *British America 1500–1800*, 49.

33. Osgood, *The American Colonies in the Seventeenth Century*, vol. 1: 24–26; William R. Polk, *The Birth of America: From Before Columbus to the Revolution* (New York: Harper Collins, 2006), 105; Middleton and Lombard, *Colonial America*, 47–48.

34. Osgood, "The Corporation as a Form of Colonial Government, Part I," *Political Science Quarterly* (1896), vol. ii: 263–64.

35. Thorpe, *The Federal and State Constitutions*, vol. 7: 3784.

36. Leonard Woods Labaree, *Royal Government in America: A Study of the British Colonial System Before 1783* (New Haven: Yale University Press, 1930), 7.

37. Joseph Story, *Commentaries on the Constitution of the United States* (Boston: Hilliard Gray, 1833), vol.1: 22–23.

38. Meinig, *The Shaping of America*, 37.

39. Sarson, *British America*, 37.

40. Thorpe, *The Federal and State Constitutions*, vol. 7: 3784–85; Osgood, *The American Colonies in the Seventeenth Century*, vol. 1: 26.

41. Thorpe, *The Federal and State Constitutions*, vol. 7: 3785–86. At the request of the investors, the Council of Virginia was increased in size to forty members in March 1607. Osgood, *The American Colonies in the Seventeenth Century*, vol. 1: 28.

42. Thomas J. Wertenbaker, *Virginia under the Stuarts, 1607–1688* (New York: Russell and Russell, 1959), 2.

43. Thorpe, *The Federal and State Constitutions*, vol. 7: 3785–87.

44. H. D. Hazeltine, "The Influence of Magna Carta on American Constitutional Development," *Columbia Law Review* (1917) vol. 17: 6. Although Quinn did not consider the charter to be "a first-rate instrument of colonization," he wrote that "What it was excellent for was committing the English at last to a sustained program of settlement." Quinn, *England and the Discovery of America*, 483.

45. . Warren M. Billings, "The Transfer of English Law to Virginia: 1606–1650," in Kenneth R. Andrews, Nicholas P. Canny, and P. E. Haires, eds., *The Westward Enterprise: English Activities in Ireland, The Atlantic, and America* (Liverpool: Liverpool University Press, 1978), 215.

46. Billings, "The Transfer of English Law to Virginia," in Andrews, Canny, and Haires, eds., *The Westward Enterprise*, 216.

47. Osgood, *The American Colonies in the Seventeenth Century*, vol. 1: 28–29; Kavenagh, *Foundations of Colonial America: A Documentary History* (New York: Chelsea House, 1973), 1856–61.

48. Middleton and Lombard, *Colonial America*, 55–56.

49. Andrews, *The Colonial Period of American History*, vol. 1: 98.

50. Middleton and Lombard, *Colonial America*, 56.

51. Andrews, *The Colonial Period of American History*, vol. 1: 99–100.

52. Osgood, *The American Colonies in the Seventeenth Century*, vol. 1: 35. As Osgood further observed, "At Jamestown, under the first charter, they measured time by the intervals between supplies; later the periods in the history of the colony were measured by governorships."

53. Middleton and Lombard, *Colonial America*, 56–57.

54. Andrews, *The Colonial Period of American History*, vol. 1: 100; Sarson, *British America 1500–1800*, 51.
55. Andrews, *The Colonial Period of American History*, vol. 1: 100–1.
56. Osgood, *The American Colonies in the Seventeenth Century*, vol. 1: 44–45; Billings, "The Transfer of English Law to Virginia, 1606–1650," 216.
57. Middleton and Lombard, "Colonial America," in Andrews, Canny, and Haires, eds., *The Westward Enterprise*, 59–60.
58. Thorpe, *The Federal and State Constitutions*, vol. 7: 3795–96.
59. Thorpe, *The Federal and State Constitutions*, vol. 7: 3796–97.
60. Thorpe, *The Federal and State Constitutions*, vol. 7: 3797.
61. Thorpe, *The Federal and State Constitutions*, vol. 7: 3800–1.
62. Thorpe, *The Federal and State Constitutions*, vol. 7: 3801.
63. Billings, "The Transfer of English Law to Virginia," in Andrews, Canny, and Haires, eds., *The Westward Enterprise*, 217.
64. Middleton and Lombard, *Colonial America*, 61.
65. Kavenagh, *Foundations of Colonial America*, 1861–69.
66. Middleton and Lombard, *Colonial America*, 61–62.
67. Andrews, *The Colonial Period of American History*, vol. 1: 111–14; Osgood, *The American Colonies in the Seventeenth Century*, vol. 1: 67–71; Billings, "The Transfer of English Law to Virginia, 1606–1650," 217–18; Sarson, *British America 1500–1800*, 54–55; Charles E. Hatch, *The First Seventeen Years, Virginia 1607–1624* (Charlottesville: University of Virginia Press, 1957), 10–12.
68. Donald S. Lutz ed., *Colonial Origins of the American Constitution: A Documentary History* (Indianapolis: Liberty Fund, 1998), 314–19; Kavenagh, *Foundations of Colonial America*, 1869–76.
69. Lutz, *Colonial Origins of the American Constitution*, 319–23.
70. Lutz, *Colonial Origins of the American Constitution*, 314; Middleton and Lombard, *Colonial America*, 62.
71. Andrews, *The Colonial Period of American History*, vol. 1: 116; Osgood, *The American Colonies in the Seventeenth Century*, vol. 1: 60.
72. Thorpe, *The Federal and State Constitutions*, vol. 7: 3802–4.
73. Homer Carey Hockett, *The Constitutional History of the United States, 1776–1826, The Blessings of Liberty* (New York: Macmillan, 1939), 22.
74. Osgood, "The Corporation as a Form of Colonial Government, Part I," *Political Science Quarterly*, vol. 11: 272.
75. Thorpe, *The Federal and State Constitutions*, vol. 7: 3802–8.
76. Hockett, *The Constitutional History of the United States*, 24–25.
77. Andrews, *The Colonial Period of American History*, vol. 1: 118–40, 150–64; Hatch, *The First Seventeen Years*, 16–18; Middleton and Lombard, *Colonial America*, 66.
78. Osgood, *The American Colonies in the Seventeenth Century*, vol. 1: 92–95; Hatch, *The First Seventeen Years*, 23–24.
79. Story, *Commentaries on the Constitution of the United States*, vol. 1: 25–26.
80. Alred H. Kelly, Winfred A. Harbison, and Herman Belz, *The American Constitution: Its Origins and Development*, 7th ed. (New York: W.W. Norton & Co., 1991), vol. 1: 5.
81. Billings, "The Transfer of English Law to Virginia, 1606–1650," in Andrews, Canny, and Haires, eds., *The Westward Enterprise*, 218.
82. Sarson, *British America 1500–1800*, 55.
83. Billings, "The Transfer of English Law to Virginia 1606–1650," 218.
84. Andrews, *The Colonial Period of American History*, vol. 1: 182–87; Story, *Commentaries on the Constitution of the United States*, vol. 1: 26.
85. Thorpe, *The Federal and State Constitutions*, vol. 7: 3811–12; Lutz, *Colonial Origins of the American Constitution*, 336–38; Kavenagh, *Foundations of Colonial America*, 1889–90.
86. Billings, "The Transfer of English Law to Virginia, 1606–1650," 224–25.
87. Sarson, *British America 1500–1800*, 53; Middleton and Lombard, *Colonial America*, 70–71. See Hatch, *The First Seventeen Years*, 28–29. Thus, it has been said that—to the English—the Jamestown attacks "revealed that the two cultures were incompatible," and that

ultimately, "one culture would have to give way." Middleton, *Colonial America*, 68. To the English it was clear which culture that would be.

88. Andrews, *The Colonial Period of American History*, vol. 1: 137–40, 165–73; Appleby, "War, Politics, and Colonization, 1558–1625," in Canny, ed., *The Oxford History of the British Empire*, 74.

89. Story, *Commentaries on the Constitution of the United States*, vol. 1: 27.

90. Andrews, *The Colonial Period of American History*, vol. 1: 178.

91. Kavenagh, *Foundations of Colonial America,* 1722–24; Jack P. Greene, *Great Britain and the American Colonies 1606–1763* (Columbia: South Carolina University Press, 1970), 36–37; G. E. Alymer, "Navy, State, Trade, and Empire," in Canny, ed., *The Oxford History of the British Empire*, 476.

92. Andrews, *The Colonial Period of American History*, vol. 1: 174–79; Hatch, *The First Seventeen Years*, 29–30.

93. Andrews, *The Colonial Period of American History*, vol. 1: 204; Sarson, *British America 1500–1800*, 57–58.

94. Lutz, *Colonial Foundations of the American Constitution*, 327.

95. Kavenagh, *Foundations of Colonial America*, 1900–8.

Chapter Two

The Covenant Colonies of New England

At the time the Virginia Company made its first colonial foray to Roanoke, the Plymouth Company, which was the second company formed under the charter from James I, established its own settlement on the Sagadahoc River in what is now Phippsburg, Maine. In May 1607, 120 men were sent to establish an outpost for fishing and trade with the native peoples, and like the Virginia Company's Roanoke settlement, the Plymouth adventurers were almost wholly dependent on supplies from England to survive. The Sagadahoc settlement failed after two years and was abandoned.[1]

Despite the failure of the Sagadahoc expedition, the territory remained of interest to the Plymouth Company's investors who, in 1614, engaged Captain John Smith, the former governor of the Jamestown colony, to explore their grant. It was Smith who named the region "New England."[2]

However, the failure of the Sagadahoc settlement "paralyzed the energies of the Northern Company of Virginia."[3] Nevertheless, exploitation of fishing and opportunities for trade continued and led to conflicts between the two companies over territory and fishing rights.[4] To resolve these conflicts, in 1620, James I granted a new charter to the Council established at Plymouth "for the planting, ruling, ordering and governing of New England in America." Reflective of the evolutionary change in the royal charter, the Plymouth Council was established as "one body politic and corporate" with the requisite power to create a government for New England.[5]

Under the charter, the council was to choose its own president and was given power to admit members. The council was also authorized to choose the governor and other officers of the colony and to "make, ordain, and establish" those laws and ordinances "fit and necessary for and concerning the Government of the said Colony and Plantation."[6]

The colonial governor was given power to "correct, punish, pardon, govern and rule the colony." In the event of a rebellion, as had occurred in Jamestown ten years previously, the governor could impose martial law.[7] Deserters from the colony were to be returned, "there to be proceeded against and punished as the Governor's deputy or council . . . shall think meet."[8]

Like the Virginia Company, the Council for New England, as it came to be known, was authorized to defend the colony by force of arms. The colonial government was also empowered to seize ships and their cargo coming into the colony without the permission of the governor and council.[9]

The charter of 1620 marked a significant departure from the previous charters of the Virginia Company in several respects. As noted, the council was created as a body politic and corporate, which meant that unlike the Virginia Company under the 1609 charter, the governing council was not simply part of the corporation with no separate existence, but rather as Osgood observed, "the council was the corporation, and thus was the grantee of all powers."[10] As a result, the relations between the council and the king were direct, and therefore, the Council for New England enjoyed plenary authority over its own governance. In 1621, the Council for New England succeeded to the interests of the Plymouth Company, which was dissolved in bankruptcy in 1626.[11]

The independence granted to the Council for New England, and to later colonial enterprises in New England, coupled with the historical accident (or misdirection) of a group of religious separatists from Leyden, Holland, now known in the American lexicon as the "Pilgrims," set into motion forces and events that profoundly shaped the American constitutional tradition that emerged from the seventeenth-century colonial experience.

THE PLYMOUTH COLONY

The Pilgrims, like the Puritans who settled the Massachusetts Bay Colony, were part of a broad reform movement within the Church of England that objected to the influence of the Church of Rome on the doctrines and ceremonies of the Anglican Church. Their objections compelled the Pilgrims to separate from the Church of England, and as a consequence, they found England to be inhospitable.[12] The Pilgrims are believed to have learned of the American wilderness from Smith's accounts of his exploration of New England and from reports of fishermen who plied the waters there.[13] Having decided on a plan to establish a community in the New World, the Pilgrims proceeded with stealth so as not to make their intentions known.

Petition was made to the Virginia Company for a patent to establish a colony in Virginia. The petition was made to the Virginia Company because the reorganization of the Plymouth Company that resulted in the formation of the Council for New England had not yet been completed. The petition was also made in the name of an English clergyman, John Wyncop, rather than by the Leyden Church in its own name, "for that would have made public a purpose they desired to conceal."[14]

Negotiations for the patent had begun as early as 1617 but had come to naught. Instead, "The most . . . that James could be induced to do was to connive at their removal, and refrain from molesting them, provided they kept the peace."[15] The patent was eventually granted in 1619 but was never used in part because William and Thomas Brewster, leaders of the Pilgrim colonial efforts, published a pamphlet in 1619 denouncing James's attempt to impose an episcopacy on the Scottish church, and as a consequence, the Brewsters were forced into hiding.[16]

A second patent was procured by a London ironmonger and adventurer named Thomas Weston, who, together with several co-venturers, agreed to fund the Pilgrims' settlement under the Weston patent in exchange for their labor once they were settled in the New World.[17] The Pilgrims agreed to forgo any profits from their labor for the first seven years, and it has been observed, "Under these terms, the Pilgrims knew they were unlikely to grow rich in America,"[18] thus distinguishing the Pilgrims from their predecessors.

The Pilgrims availed themselves of Weston's offer and on September 16, 1620, they set off for America in two ships: the *Mayflower* and the *Speedwell*, both of which had been provided by Weston and his investors. The *Speedwell* showed itself to be unseaworthy shortly after leaving lands' end and returned to England, leaving the 101 passengers and the crew of the *Mayflower* to make the crossing alone.[19]

After what the *Mayflower*'s captain, Christopher Jones, described as a "long beating at sea," the Cape Cod coast was sighted. Although the Pilgrims may have intended to make landfall along the Hudson River, Weston apparently favored New England for its abundant fishing opportunities. In any event, the *Mayflower* became entangled in shoals and lost wind in Cape Cod Bay, and after exploring parties found Plymouth Bay, it was decided that the Pilgrims would go ashore there.[20]

Before going ashore, however, the Pilgrims established the basis on which they would order their new society. There had been conflicts between the Pilgrims and others on board the *Mayflower* who were not part of their congregation, whom the Pilgrims referred to as "Strangers." The decision to remain in Cape Cod Bay provoked a near mutiny by the Strangers, and it has been suggested that the agreement reached on board the *Mayflower* was intended as much to dampen dissension as to establish the basis for their government.[21] Forty-one of the male passengers entered into a solemn compact among themselves that they would govern themselves in the management of their own affairs.

Their agreement was known initially as the "Plymouth Combination," and later as the "Mayflower Compact." There, the men of the settlement stated that they would

> solemnly and mutually, in the presence of God and one another, covenant and combine ourselves together into a civil body politic, for our better ordering and preservation, and in furtherance of the ends aforesaid: and by virtue hereof so enact, constitute, and frame, such just and equal Laws, Ordinances, Acts, Constitutions and Officers . . . as shall be thought meet and convenient for the general good of the colony; unto which we promise all due submission and obedience.[22]

Covenants were common, particularly in the church life of the Pilgrims, and as such, the compact has been seen as "a perfectly simple extension of the ordinary form of church covenant with which they were familiar, to cover the crisis which they now faced."[23] But the Mayflower Compact has been accorded even greater import to the structuring of the community the Pilgrims were about to construct. As Sarson observed, the Mayflower Compact "acted as the basis of Plymouth's politics and set a precedent for representative government under a written constitution."[24] Although Lutz did not consider the compact to be a true constitution, he found the compact to possess certain constitutional attributes, such as creating a basis of government and laying out the community's fundamental values and commitments.[25] To Story, the compact represented "in its very essence a pure democracy," on the basis of which the colonists selected their leaders and enacted their laws.[26]

This declaration of the Pilgrim's independence reflected the reality of their circumstances in America. Under their agreement with Watson and the other merchant adventurers, the Pilgrims were equal co-venturers, and as such, they were at liberty to ignore the advice transmitted from England. Although the Pilgrims were not dependent on the king or a council to authorize their actions, they were certainly aware of their ambiguous legal standing to occupy the land they were settling because their patent rights derived from the Virginia Company but the territory was in the dominion of the Plymouth Company, with which they enjoyed no privity. In essence, the Pilgrims were "squatters, destitute of legal rights of settlement."[27]

Although the Pilgrims acknowledged the king's temporal authority, they recognized their tenuous legal status, and faced with the possibility of revolt, the Pilgrims, "solemnly agreed to assume such power as was necessary for the framing of just and convenient ordinances, and the creating and filling of offices; and to such ordinances and officials they promised obedience."[28] To accomplish this, the Pilgrims drew on religious custom in which church government was ordained by the congregations with all authority vested in the assembly of church members.[29]

The composition of the Pilgrims and their motivation for coming to America distinguished them from their Virginia counterparts and contributed significantly to their self-conception as one body politic. Except for those persons who had been hired to accompany the expedition such as artisans and crew members (i.e., the Strangers), the Pilgrims shared a deep and abiding common bond of faith. Many of the *Mayflower*'s passengers were families (of the 101 passengers, 36 were married and 31 were children, 2 of whom had been born during passage), and a number of the men had left their wives behind with the expectation that they would be reunited when the settlement was established.[30]

Despite the deaths of approximately half of the original settlers because of the hardships of life and of sickness during the "general visitation," there was nether the threat to abandon the enterprise, nor the sloth among the settlers that had characterized the early years of the Virginia colony.[31] Instead, spurred by the increase in demand for their livestock and grain from the new population in the larger and more prosperous Massachusetts Bay Colony to the north, the population of the colony grew as a result of the immigration of new settlers from 124 in 1624 to nearly 300 in 1630.[32] As a consequence of this dramatic growth, after 1626, the government of the Plymouth Colony took on greater formality.

A settlement was reached with Watson and the English investors under which their claims would be relinquished for a payment of £1800. To settle this and other debts, it was resolved to conduct the affairs of the colony for a period of six years as a joint stock company, comprised of the Pilgrims, in the form of a chartered government.[33]

Nevertheless, despite the greater stability and increased population, the legal status of the colony remained highly uncertain. As Story noted, "the Weston patent had never been confirmed by the crown," and "the colonists were never, by act of the crown, created a body politic and corporate with any legislative powers." Instead, Story observed, the colony's legal existence and the framework of government were grounded on a principle of mutual assent that may have been grounded on the English custom of "social contract" or in maritime law, which recognized the passengers' ability to govern themselves by mutual assent during a sea voyage.[34]

To resolve the uncertainty of the colony's legal standing, petition was made to the Council for New England, which in 1629 granted a patent for the Colony of New Plymouth to William Bradford and others in recognition of their having "nine years lived in New England" and their having "inhabited and planted a town called by the name of New Plymouth at their own proper cost and charges."[35] Story remarked, "The charter of 1629 furnished them . . . with the colour of delegated sovereignty, of which they did not fail to avail themselves."[36]

Bradford held the patent in trust for the colony. After 1632, meetings of the governing council and the general court were held regularly, and over time, towns were formed and delegates from those towns joined the general court.[37]

As a consequence of this growth, the general court enacted the Plymouth Agreement on November 15, 1636. Also referred to as the Great Fundamentals, the agreement proclaimed that

> We, the associates of New Plymouth coming hither as free born subjects of the State of England endowed with all and singular privileges belonging to such being assembled," ordained that no law or ordinance could be "made or imposed upon us . . . but shall be imposed by the Consent of the body of associates or their representatives legally assembled; which is according to free liberties of England.[38]

The Plymouth Agreement was in its essentials a constitution for the Plymouth colony. The agreement established an overarching government structure, which provided for the annual election of the governor and seven assistants and the appointment by them of the other colonial officers, including the treasurer and the coroner.[39]

The agreement enumerated the powers of these elected officials. The governor was to see to "the execution of such laws and ordinances as are or shall be made and established for the good of this corporation." The assistants were to give their "best advice both in public court and private council with the governor," and they were charged to "keep secret, such things as concern the public good and shall be thought meet to be concealed by the governor and council of assistants."[40]

In furtherance of his responsibility to see to the execution of the laws, the governor was authorized "to arrest and commit to ward any offenders provided that with all convenient speed he shall bring the case to hearing either of the assistants or general court, according to the nature of the offense." In doing so, the governor was to "examine any suspicious person for evil against the colony" and to "intercept or oppose such as he conceives may tend to overthrow the state."[41]

The judicial function of government was to be carried out by the governor and assistants as well. In cases involving minor offenses, the assistants were to have "a voice in the censuring of such offenders as shall be brought to public court." In more serious cases when the assistants judged the case to be "too great to be decided by them," the governor was to call a general court at which the governor was to "propound cases, and go before the assistants in the examination of particulars," and to impose "such sentences as shall be determined."[42]

Under the Plymouth Agreement, the colony was socially and politically stable, such that by 1641, Bradford gave over the patent to the freemen, thereby formally vesting in them the authority to govern the colony.[43] Because of the culture of its separatist origins and the lack of substantial financial backing, the colony grew slowly, however.

By the end of its first decade, the population had risen to just three hundred persons. By 1657, the population had grown to only thirteen hundred, resulting in Plymouth being completely overshadowed by the more sophisticated and entrepreneurial Puritan colony of Massachusetts Bay to the north. By 1691, without a royal charter of its own and dependent on the port of Boston for trade, Plymouth succumbed to its symbiotic relationship with Massachusetts Bay, into which it was absorbed in 1691.

THE MASSACHUSETTS BAY COLONY

The Puritans who settled in America were not separatists like the Pilgrims but considered themselves reformers. Also in contrast to the Pilgrims, the Puritans were not a small insular group but rather were part of a significant movement within the English church that had a number of powerful adherents. Thus, although similarly grounded in ex patriot Puritanism, the rise of the Massachusetts Bay colony was a stark contrast to the retiring settlement of Plymouth.

The first of the Puritan settlers arrived three years after the *Mayflower*'s voyage. Under the leadership of the Reverend John White, a band of adventurers attempted the establishment of a settlement and fishing station at Cape Ann. Although shelters were constructed and corn planted to sustain the settlers, the effort failed and the settlement was abandoned in 1626. Although some of the settlers returned to England, others led by Roger Conant relocated to what is now Salem, Massachusetts.

Meanwhile in England, White and others sought a means of establishing a Puritan colony in Massachusetts. The Plymouth colony was not considered to be hospitable to the Puritans because of the Pilgrims' complete renunciation of the Anglican Church, with which the Puritans were not in accord. Meetings were held in London with a view toward establishing a separate colonial venture for the Puritans, and in 1628, the nearly moribund Council for New England granted the Puritans a patent for the territory of Massachusetts, which included the fledgling Salem community. In June of that year, a party of settlers was dispatched to join the others already in Salem.

Other colonial interests also laid claim to the Massachusetts territory by virtue of patents from the Council for New England, however. In view of those competing claims, the Puritans petitioned Charles I for a charter modeled after the charter granted to the Virginia Company twenty years earlier by Charles's father, James I. Charles granted the charter in 1629. Included within the charter was a substantial part of the territory previously conferred on the Council for New England, in effect, merging the Council for New England into the newly formed Massachusetts Bay Company.[44]

The charter created the Massachusetts Bay Colony as a body politic and corporate under the direction of a governor, deputy governor, and eighteen assistants, who were to be elected by the freemen of the colony. There were also to be general courts held four times a year and at one of them (the Easter term), the governor and other officers were to be elected for the following year.[45] In a significant departure from the previous royal charter of the Council for New England, the Massachusetts Bay charter conferred "the right to rule and administer the territory it owned," without recourse to the crown government.[46] This was a grant, in Story's view, of "the most ample powers of government."[47]

Under the charter, the governor and the council were given "Full and Absolute Power and authority to correct, punish, pardon, govern and rule," the colony's inhabitants. Laws were to be enforced by the governor and the council through the imposition of fines, imprisonment "or other correction." The colonial government was also empowered to defend the colony by force of arms or all "fitting ways and means whatsoever."[48]

The most significant departure from the preceding charters was that the Massachusetts Bay charter did not require the corporation to be resident in England. On that basis, when John Winthrop, the leader of a group of East Anglian Puritans, announced that his group would settle in Salem if the patent and the seat of government went with them, the court of the corporation complied, and on August 29, 1629, the charter was transferred to Salem, and on October 20, Winthrop was elected governor of both the company and the colony.[49]

Opinions differ whether the omission of a residence requirement was inadvertent[50] or had been a purposeful gambit on the part of Winthrop to secure control of the colony in the hands of the Puritans.[51] In either event, as Story remarked, "this transaction stands alone in the history of English colonization," and "the boldness of the step is not more striking than the silent acquiescence of the king in permitting it to take place."[52] Removal of the charter from London to Salem was also significant because, as Virginia DeJohn Anderson noted, "New Englanders valued the colonial charters that granted them extraordinarily broad powers of self-government precisely because these documents offered the king and parliament little role in their affairs."[53]

There followed what has been described as "the largest single expedition in the history of the seventeenth century English colonization," when Winthrop led a fleet of eleven ships carrying one thousand Puritans to join the settlement in Salem.[54] This mass migration demonstrated that in contrast to both Virginia and Plymouth, the Massachusetts Bay Puritans had "considerable financial resources" and "realistic expectations."[55]

The general court of the company convened in Salem on October 19, 1630, and with that event, the transfer of the governance of the company and the colony was complete. The establishment of the charter government in Salem has been seen as "a fact of greatest importance, not only for the history of New England, but also in the development of modern social and governmental forms."[56]

The prevalence of disease eventually forced the government to relocate first to Charleston and then to Boston, which became the permanent seat of government.[57] Also at this time, the number of freemen was increased first by inviting people to submit their names for consideration, and second by changing the definition of freeman from a stockholder in the company to a person who was eligible to hold office and to vote as a citizen of the colony.[58]

However, to respond to the concern that this enlargement of the freemen would jeopardize the religious character of the colony, the general court decreed on May 18, 1631, that to be admitted into "the freedom of this body politic," it was necessary to be a member "of some of the churches within the limits of the same."[59] This imposition of a religious qualification for full citizenship, "seriously strained, if it did not violate the terms of the charter."[60]

The general court also took several actions to enlarge its authority. At its meeting on May 9, 1632, the general court reserved to itself the sole authority to select the governor, deputy governor, and the assistants (from whom one would be selected governor).[61] A year later, on May 14, 1634, the general court enacted the Massachusetts Agreement on Legislation, under which the general court had sole authority to "make and establish laws," as well as to levy taxes and dispose of property. The general court also asserted the authority to remove the governor and the colonial officers "upon misdemeanor."[62]

The Agreement on Legislation also established the judicial authority of the general court. The agreement declared that

> The General Court . . . is the Chief Civil Power in this Commonwealth . . . and may act in all affairs of this Commonwealth according to such power, both in matters of counsel, making laws and matters of judicature, by impeaching and sentencing any person or persons according to law and by receiving and hearing any complaints orderly presented against any person or court.[63]

Lastly, the agreement established the general court as a representative body. Under the agreement's scheme, the freemen in each town were to elect two representatives "with the full power and voices of all the said freemen."[64] Thus, the general court of the Massachusetts Bay colony became the second elected, representative legislature in America. Described as the "crowning order" of the general court,[65] the agreement has been seen as involving such elements of a constitution as the formal establishment of legislative power, the manner of electing members of the legislature, and the frequency of meeting.[66]

After what Massachusetts governor James Sullivan described as a "chain of blunders,"[67] the Council for New England was forced to surrender its charter to the crown in 1635.[68] Among those blunders was the manner in which the patent for Massachusetts Bay had been granted to Winthrop, which eventually led to an inquiry by the privy council in London.[69]

Despite these events, the Massachusetts general court continued to govern the colony and to enact landmark legislation. Massachusetts had no comprehensive body of laws. Instead, justice had been administered along the lines of Mosaic law, grounded on scripture. In 1636, John Cotton had fashioned a code, which Governor Winthrop described as a "model of Moses." This code was modified by the Reverend Nathaniel Ward in 1639, but Cotton's code retained its Mosaic character.[70] To remedy the perceived arbitrariness of decisions under the code, in 1641, the general court enacted the Massachusetts Body of Liberties, considered the seminal source document for the civil liberties secured in the federal Bill of Rights a century and a half later.[71] This exhaustive compendium of individual rights was considered necessary by the Massachusetts colonists because they feared "their liberties were not safe from arbitrary power because these liberties were not embodied in positive law,"[72] a view shared by the later proponents of the Bill of Rights.

In another significant legislative act, on May 7, 1644, the general court created a bicameral legislature by dividing itself into two chambers: the Chamber of Magistrates and the Chamber of Deputies. The Chamber of Deputies was comprised of the elected representative of the towns, and they, in turn, elected the members of the Chamber of Magistrates.

Legislation was to be drafted by the magistrates for consideration by the deputies. Once the deputies had consented, the legislation was returned to the magistrates who could then either consent to or disallow the legislation.[73]

On January 14, 1647, this bicameral general court enacted a second comprehensive codification of the laws of the colony. Known as the Book of General Laws and Liberties Concerning the Inhabitants of Massachusetts, the code has been said to contain "everything we might today expect in a constitution" and indeed the General Laws functioned as the constitution of the colony until being supplanted by the royal charter in 1691.[74]

The foundational principal was set forth in the preamble that that no one in the colony was to be deprived of life, liberty, or property except "by virtue or equity of some express law of the country warranting the same, enacted by the general court or otherwise by the Word of God."[75]

The representatives elected from "every plantation," were to have full authority "for the making and establishing of laws, granting of lands, and to deal in all other affairs of the common-wealth." Elections for colonial officers were to be held annually. For choosing the assistants, the freemen were to cast "Indian corn" in favor of a candidate and beans in opposition. The governor and other officials were to be elected by paper ballot, "open or once folded."[76]

The bicameral legislature was maintained under the General Laws. Bills and orders were to be drawn up by the magistrates for presentation to the deputies, who after consideration of "how good and wholesome such orders are for the Country," either assented to or dissented from them. Likewise, the deputies were authorized to propose legislation to the magistrates, "as they in their discretion and experience find meet for the common good." Once both houses of the legislature had agreed, the legislation was to be engrossed and read again on the last day of the session, after which they became law.

The General Laws established the basis of a judicial system for the colony. Four "quarter courts" of the assistants were to be held annually comprised of the governor and the magistrates and of the county courts comprised of the magistrates "as shall reside in, or near the same." The courts were to sit in Boston and "hear and determine all civil cases & criminal, not extending to life, member or banishment." Those cases were to be decided by the court of assistants. Quarter courts with the same jurisdiction were to be held in the various towns by the magistrates. Cases involving "strangers" to the colony were to be decided by the governor and two of the magistrates. Appeals from decisions of the county courts were to be heard by the court of assistants.[77]

The General Laws also codified the rights of litigants. A party to litigation had the right to choose a trial by jury or by a judge sitting without a jury.[78] Jurors were to be chosen from among the freemen of the town and had jurisdiction to decide all cases but those decided by a judge in equity, such as forfeiture of an obligation or breach of a covenant. Cases in which the punishment was "life or banishment" were to be decided by a "special jury" summoned for that purpose. Grand juries were also empanelled every year to determine whether criminal charges should be filed.[79] Courts were empowered to compel the attendance of individuals to be examined under oath at a trial and to award damages in cases of vexatious litigation.[80]

Lastly, the General Laws secured a variety of individual civil rights, many of which were carried over from the 1641 Body of Liberties. Every person was to "enjoy the same justice and law that is general for this Jurisdiction," and, whether "free or not free" was to have the liberty of participating in public meetings, including moving "any lawful, reasonable, or material question," and presenting "any necessary motion, complaint, petition, bill or information," over which the meeting had cognizance. Free movement within the colony was guaranteed and impressments, such as compelled public work, the taking of property for a public purpose, or military service outside the colony were prohibited. No one could be compelled to engage in defensive warfare "unless enterprised by the council" and consented to by the general court.[81]

Persons accused of crimes were also guaranteed fundamental liberties. Torture was prohibited in all cases except capital cases when guilt was established by "clear and convincing evidence," and it was apparent that others were involved in the crime; but even then, torture that was "barbarous and inhumane" could not be employed.[82] Persons accused of crimes, other than capital offenses, were entitled to bail and were not to be imprisoned until they had been sentenced.[83] No one could be sentenced twice for the same offense, and like torture, "inhumane, barbarous, or cruel" punishments were prohibited.[84]

By 1652, the Massachusetts Bay colony had transformed itself into a commonwealth, independent of the English crown, governed by a written constitution of its own making. As Andrews observed, "By 1652, the Massachusetts Bay Company had gone a long way from the path marked out for it by the charter; it had evolved into a political organism, with all the essential features, though in a somewhat rudimentary form, of a modern state."[85]

The system for distributing land also led to a different political structure than had developed in Virginia. Land in Massachusetts was initially distributed to a group of people (usually a church congregation) to be held communally pursuant to a covenant entered into by the members.[86] Once a sufficient amount of land had been cleared, plots were allocated to families according to their initial investment. As a consequence, settlers generally lived in towns that became the central locus of civic activity in the colony.[87]

It has been said that "Restoration imperialism faced its most difficult test in Puritan Massachusetts."[88] Massachusetts had delayed recognizing the restoration of Charles II until December 1660, and in what has been described as a "major attempt by the colonists to create a political foundation based completely upon their own consent," on June 10, 1661, the general court declared that the colonial government had "full power and authority, both legislative and executive, for the government of all the people here." The general court warned that "we conceive any imposition prejudicial to the country contrary to any just laws of ours, not repugnant to the laws of England, to be an infringement of our right."[89] The Massachusetts general court rebuffed the overture of Charles II to renew the charter, which would have required royal appointment of the governor and officers of the militia, and resisted the efforts of the royal commissioners led by Colonel Richard Nichols to secure the colony's "obedience and loyalty."[90]

This backhanded attitude toward parliament and the crown, with its intimation of independence, did not go unnoticed in England. In 1676, the Committee on Plantations, a committee of the privy council that came to be known as the Lords of Trade,[91] dispatched Edward Randolph to investigate the situation in Massachusetts Bay. Randolph reported that the Navigation Acts, which had been enacted by parliament to control colonial trade, were being evaded routinely. Randolph also reported that the Puritan theocracy had prevented members of the Church of England from conducting worship services and from voting. Randolph recommended that the Massachusetts charter be rescinded. Instead, the Lords of Trade proposed a new charter that would reserve certain rights to the king that Massachusetts failed to recognize, including royal appointment of the governor and officers of the militia.

Massachusetts remained intransigent and after prolonged negotiations proved unsuccessful, the Lords directed the Attorney General to initiate *quo warranto* proceedings resulting in the revocation of the Massachusetts Bay charter in 1684.[92] James Truslow Adams attributed this royal antipathy to the colony's extraordinary ability and persistence in the "gentle art of making enemies." As Adams explained,

> the crux of the whole problem was that the theocratical party there had developed a theory—based apparently on an extension of the church-covenant idea through the plantation covenant—that the charter itself was a covenant which reserved no rights to the king and imperial government save those specifically mentioned. From this she deduced that her obligation to the empire was so tenuous as to be virtually non-existent.[93]

The revocation of the Massachusetts charter harmonized with the Stuart vision of concentrating royal authority over the colonies in centralized dominions similar to the Dominion of New France under Louis XIV.[94] When James II ascended to the thrown following his brother's death, he moved to form the first of these centralized colonies, the Dominion of New England, into which the colonies of Connecticut, Massachusetts Bay, New Hampshire, New Jersey (East and West), New York, Plymouth, and Rhode Island were subsumed.[95] The Dominion of New England proved to be short lived and did not survive the removal of James II by the Glorious Revolution in 1689.[96]

Following the dissolution of the Dominion of New England, a royal charter for the Province of Massachusetts was promulgated in 1691. This charter consolidated the colonies of Maine, Massachusetts Bay, and Plymouth under one royal government. Provision was made for a general court comprised of the governor, his council of seven assistants, and twenty-eight elected representatives, with the power to enact laws and ordinances, including taxes, fines, and penalties, that were not contrary to the laws of England, and to appoint the civil officers of the colonial government.

Otherwise, the government of the colony was in the hands of the royal governor who was charged, among his other duties, with the defense of the colonies and who had authority to declare martial law. The royal governor was empowered to veto any legislation enacted by the general court, and all laws were required to be transmitted to the crown for approval before becoming law. The colonists were guaranteed the rights of Englishmen, including liberty of worship and conscience.[97]

The 1691 charter has been said to be "the nearest approach to the creation of a constitution for a royal province by means of a single document that we have before the passage of the Quebec Act of 1774."[98] Indeed, the 1691 charter served as the constitution of the newly independent Massachusetts from 1776 until 1780.

THE RHODE ISLAND COLONY

On October 9, 1635, the Reverend Roger Williams was convicted by the general court of Massachusetts Bay of sedition and heresy for spreading "dangerous opinions" attacking the validity of royal charters and urging separation of civic affairs from those of the church. As a consequence, Williams was banished from the colony. Although the Massachusetts authorities intended that Williams be deported to England, Williams was warned of his imminent apprehension and escaped from the colony leaving his family in Salem, where he had been the assistant minister of the church.[99]

Williams made his way to the eastern shore of Narragansett Bay, and en route, Williams was joined by other "wanderers" who like the settlers of Connecticut and New Hampshire, believed their opportunities lay elsewhere than Massachusetts. Together, they established a settlement that they named Providence, and on August 20, 1637, they entered into a compact known as the Providence Agreement.[100]

The settlers pledged their "active and passive obedience" to the laws "as shall be made for the public good of the body . . . by the major consent of the present inhabitants." In keeping with Williams' separatist views, the agreement limited the government's authority "only in civil things." In this, the Providence Agreement has been credited with being the earliest expression in America of the principle of separation of church and state.[101]

In April 1638, another group of dissidents left Boston under the leadership of William Coddington to found a settlement more amenable to their Antinomian views, which questioned whether outward signs of piety, such as church-going, obedience to Puritan leaders, and "good works" (e.g., secret prayer, reverence toward ministers, and glorification of the Sabbath) were necessary duties of a Christian. Coddington joined with the prominent Antinomian, Anne Hutchinson (who herself had been banished from Massachusetts as a blasphemer) in Providence, and with other "exiles," they made their way to the island of Aquidneck. There, with the help of Williams, land was purchased from the native peoples and the settlement of Portsmouth was founded.[102]

The Portsmouth settlers also entered into a covenant on March 7, 1638, agreeing to conduct themselves as one body politic and to "submit our persons, lives and estates unto our lord Jesus Christ, the King of Kings and Lord of Lords and to all those perfect and most absolute laws he has given us in his holy word of truth, to be guided and judged thereby." After signing the covenant, the settlers elected Coddington to govern the settlement.[103]

Within a year, however, a rift with Hutchinson caused Coddington and his followers to quit Portsmouth on April 28, 1639, and to establish their own settlement at the southern end of the island. They named the settlement Newport.[104]

Hutchinson and her followers signed their own covenant on April 30, 1639, in which they acknowledged their loyalty to Charles II and bound themselves as a body politic to the laws of England. The settlers agreed to govern themselves by the will of the majority with one person elected as "ruler and judge among us." A judicial system was fashioned under which an adjudicatory court would be held quarterly with a twelve-member jury. Minor cases were to be decided by an elected judge and "eight men chosen unto him."[105]

Despite their differences, Coddington pursued a union of the two Aquidneck settlements, and in March 1642, a written framework of government was agreed upon. The most salient feature of their plan was a common representative body in which it was declared that the government would be a popular democracy in which the "freemen orderly assembled, or the major part of them" were empowered "to make or constitute Just Laws, by which they will be regulated, and to depute from among themselves such Ministers as shall see them faithfully executed between Man and Man." The plan also mandated a degree of religious tolerance, in that no one would be "accounted delinquent for doctrine" so long as that doctrine was not repugnant to the government or the laws.[106]

In 1644, the Aquidneck colony, comprised of Newport and Portsmouth, took the name Rhode Island. Their plan of union remained the foundation of the colony's government until 1647 when Portsmouth voted to break away.[107]

As this was happening, the Plymouth and Massachusetts Bay colonies laid claims to parts of the territory of Providence and Rhode Island, neither of which enjoyed British authority but rather were founded on purchases of land from the native peoples, which Williams considered to be morally superior to a royal grant.

However, despite his personal repugnance to English charters, in March 1643, Williams sailed from New Amsterdam to England (Williams was barred from entering Massachusetts Bay) for the purpose of obtaining a patent for the Providence colony from Parliament. With the aid of the Earl of Warwick, Williams was successful, and in September 1644, Williams returned to Providence (this time through Massachusetts, having been guaranteed safe passage by Warwick) with the patent for the colony.

Although not fully a charter, the patent granted the settlers the civil authority to govern themselves. Of equal importance, the patent included the settlements of Newport, Portsmouth, and Providence and covered the territory bounded by Massachusetts Bay and Plymouth for a distance of twenty-five miles inland.[108]

The patent was not put into effect immediately because of the union of Newport and Portsmouth, which was not dissolved until 1647. In the meantime, a fourth settlement, Warwick, was organized within the boundary of the patent.

The Warwick settlement was founded by another group of Antinomians led by Samuel Gorton who had fled from Boston in 1637 and who had supported Hutchinson in the Portsmouth revolt against Coddington in 1639. Described as a "strange and much maligned man,"[109] Gorton's Antinomian views had put him in conflict with the governing authorities of Portsmouth, particularly the judiciary whose jurisdiction he denied. In 1638, Gorton was charged with misconduct in open court and with "stirring up the people to mutiny in the face of the court," and after falling out with Hutchinson, Gorton was expelled from Portsmouth. Gorton next settled in Providence but he fared no better there, and he and his followers were expelled from Providence as well. Gorton moved on to the settlement in Pawtuxet where he remained until 1642, when Pawtuxet announced its intention to join the Massachusetts Bay colony from which Gorton was barred. Fearing prosecution by Massachusetts Bay authorities, Gorton again moved to an area south of Pawtuxet where he and his followers established the Warwick settlement.[110]

The governing structure of Warwick was not formalized until August 8, 1647, after Williams had secured the patent for the Providence Plantation, which included Warwick. In the Warwick Agreement, the settlers acknowledged the sovereignty of the king and his "just and equal laws." Gorton and three others were denominated in the agreement as the "commissioners" and representatives of the Warwick inhabitants.[111]

Contemporaneously, a general assembly of the freemen of Newport, Portsmouth, Providence, and Warwick was called for the purpose of establishing a government in accordance with the Providence Plantation patent, and of enacting laws for the governance of the whole colony. This assembly adopted the Acts and Orders of 1647, which in its essentials served as the constitution of Rhode Island for the following 195 years.[112]

Considered to be a "true constitution," the Acts and Orders recognized the respective powers of the colonial government and the governments of the towns, including Warwick, which had not at that point established its government formally. The Acts and Orders also acknowledged that the authority of the colonial government was derived from the voluntary consent of the governed.[113]

The plan of government under the Acts and Orders included executive, legislative, and judicial functions. The executive function was to be carried out by a president and assistants from each of the four towns as well as by a treasurer, general recorder, and sergeant, all of whom were to be elected by paper ballots (including absentee ballots by those "necessarily detained") in elections conducted by a Court of Election (or by the towns in the case of the assistants).[114]

Legislation originated in the six-member town councils. After approval in the town meeting, proposed legislation regarding "general matters for the colony" was sent to the three other towns, where the proposal was also voted on. The votes of each of the towns were forwarded to a six-member Committee for the General Court, whose members were elected by the towns. If this committee found that the proposal had been approved by a majority of the towns, the proposal became law until the next meeting of the general assembly at which consideration was given to whether the legislation should become permanent.[115]

Legislation could also originate in the general assembly. After an act was passed by the assembly, the delegates returned to their respective towns to "declare what they have done in the case or cases premised." The towns then voted on the legislation, and their votes were transmitted to the general recorder who counted the votes in the presence of the president. If approved, the law became effective until the next session of the general assembly when the law would be "confirmed or nullified."[116]

The judicial function was the responsibility of the General Court of Trial, composed of the president and the assistants. This court had jurisdiction over criminal offenses "as may hazard life, limb, disenfranchisement or banishment," as well as civil disputes between individuals and between towns.[117]

The Acts and Orders conferred the responsibility for the defense of the colony on the Council of War, comprised of the president, the assistants, and the captains of the militias of each of the towns. Every male between the ages of sixteen and sixty was to be provided with a weapon, ammunition, and other equipment and was to receive training at least eight times a year.[118]

Lastly, the Acts and Orders set out a comprehensive code of the laws, which were to be "comfortable to the laws of England, so far as the nature and constitution of our place will admit." Individual rights of persons accused of crimes were also secured, including the right to a public trial by jury at which the accused was represented by counsel and could confront the accusers and witnesses. The procedures to be followed in both civil and criminal cases were also specified in the Acts and Orders.[119]

Two years later, however, the tension between the island settlements of Newport and Portsmouth and the mainland communities of Providence and

Warwick erupted in schism. In 1649, Providence formed its own government and for the next seven years, the general assembly was comprised of delegates from the mainland. Eventually, Williams, who had resumed the presidency in 1645, induced the dissident followers of Coddington to submit to the authority of the Acts and Orders.[120]

The restoration of Charles II to the English throne in 1660 revived the uncertainty as to the legitimacy of the Providence patent and the legal standing of the colony. To the end of finally resolving the legitimacy of the colony, John Clarke, who had accompanied Williams to petition for the original patent in 1651 and who had remained in England, was commissioned to seek "a more absolute, ample and free charter of civil incorporation" for the colony.

Decision on the Rhode Island petition was delayed first by consideration of Connecticut's petition, which was given precedence, and by the conflicting claims of Connecticut and Rhode Island to Narragansett Bay. The boundary dispute was ultimately resolved in favor of Rhode Island, and in July 1663, the new Charter of Rhode Island and Providence Plantations received the royal seal.[121]

The charter conferred on Rhode Island the same legal status as that of its neighbors and rivals. Of greater significance, the charter confirmed, with some modification, the governmental structure of the 1647 Acts and Orders.

Like the charters that preceded it, the Rhode Island charter conferred the necessary corporate attributes of perpetual existence as a body politic and legal authority to hold property and to sue and be sued. Although both the Connecticut and Rhode Island charters purported to be corporate for the purpose of trade, "they were in reality constitutions of government unlike anything seen in commercial charters before."[122]

The Rhode Island charter provided for a governor and up to ten assistants and charged them "to take care for the disposing and ordering of the general business affairs "of the colony. The charter mandated a twice-yearly meeting of the general assembly, which was to consist of the governor, the assistants, and elected representatives apportioned among the towns. The general assembly was to elect the governor and the assistants for a one-year term.[123]

In addition to the broad legislative authority to enact laws for the "good and welfare" of the colony, consistent with the laws of England, the general assembly was to construct a system of judicial courts, with defined jurisdiction over disputes. The general assembly was to exercise jurisdiction over criminal cases and matters involving the native peoples. The general assembly also had responsibility for military affairs and the charter specifically provided that other colonies could not take hostile action against the native peoples without informing the governor and assembly.[124]

In another significant departure from preceding charters, the guaranty of religious liberty was significantly enlarged. The citizens of Rhode Island were to enjoy "full liberty in religious concernments," and acknowledging that some in the colony could not "in their private opinions" conform to the liturgy of the Church of England, the charter expressly, provided that it was "Our royal will and pleasure" that no one would be "molested, punished, disquieted, or called into question" for any difference in opinion regarding religious matters. Instead, everyone in the colony was to "freely and fully have and enjoy his and their own judgments and consciences, in matters of religious concernment."[125] In this, Story remarked, "Rhode Island enjoys the honour of having been if not the first, at least one of the earliest of the colonies, and indeed of modern states, in which liberty of conscience and freedom of worship were boldly proclaimed among its fundamental laws."[126]

Three years later, the general assembly followed the example of Massachusetts and divided itself into two houses, one for the representatives of the towns and one for the governor and the assistants. Although this may have been an emulation of parliament, Lutz has suggested that colonial bicameralism reflected the desire to distinguish the representation of local interests by the elected delegates of the towns from the representation of colony-wide interests by the governor and assistants. In any event, the general assembly's order dividing the houses made clear that each was to have equal power in putting forward legislation and that neither of the houses "shall have power without the concurrence of the major part of the other House, to make any law or order to be accounted as an act of the General Assembly."[127]

As noted, the charter of 1663 (together with the Acts and Orders of 1647) remained the foundational document of the Rhode Island government until well into the nineteenth century.

THE OUTWARD MIGRATION FROM MASSACHUSETTS

The years 1635–1637 were a challenging time for the Puritan leaders of Massachusetts. Dissent from the Covenant of Deeds, which taught that salvation could be gained through good works, led to the expulsion of the English Puritan minister Roger Williams in October 1635. Proponents of Antinomianism, the belief that salvation was preordained by God and therefore could not be earned (called the "Covenant of Grace"), which directly challenged the role and necessity of the ordained clergy, also engendered the ire of the Puritan elite and resulted in the banishment of leaders of the Antinomian movement, including William Coddington, Anne Hutchinson, and Hutchinson's brother-in-law, the Reverend John Wheelock, in 1637. Williams and Hutchinson established settlements in what would become the Rhode Island colony, and Wheelock and his followers settled their community in New Hampshire.

Another charismatic minister, Thomas Hooker, although not sympathetic to the Antinomians and the separatists, objected to their arbitrary treatment by the general court and Hooker quit Massachusetts with his congregation to settle in Connecticut. Also in June 1637, the Reverend John Davenport and his congregation acquired land and founded the colony of New Haven.[128] Although each of these groups of settlers shared a common history in the Massachusetts colony, which informed their ideas of civic government, each group sought to erect their ideal society away from Massachusetts.

The New Hampshire Colony

As was the case in the Rhode Island colony, the catalyst for settlement of New Hampshire was the expulsion of a charismatic leader by the Puritan elite of Massachusetts Bay. The colonization of New Hampshire did not result from the desire of a dominant religious group to establish a haven, however. Rather, the settlement of New Hampshire represented small-scale efforts at colonization, while in the shadow of and at times under the dominion of the stable and prosperous Massachusetts Bay colony.

Settlement of New Hampshire had begun after the Council for New England granted an extensive patent to Sir Fernando Gorges and John Mason for the Province of Maine, encompassing the territory between the Kennebec and Merrimac Rivers. When plans to exploit the territory foundered in 1629, the Council for New England partitioned the territory, and Mason received the land lying between the Piscataquis and Merrimac Rivers. Mason named this territory New Hampshire.[129]

Over the next several years, the towns of Little Harbor and Dover were founded on the Piscataquis River. Strawberry Bank (what is now Portsmouth) was settled just south of the river in 1630.[130]

After being expelled from Massachusetts Bay for his Antinomian views in 1638, the Reverend John Wheelwright and his followers founded the Exeter Settlement.[131] The following year, on July 5, 1639, the Exeter settlers entered into a written covenant establishing the basis of their civil society. Their stated intention in doing so was "to erect & set up amongst us such government as shall be our best discerning, agreeable to the will of God." The settlers further professed themselves to be "subject to our sovereign Lord King Charles according to the liberties of our English colony of Massachusetts." Their covenant bound them

> solemnly by the grace and hope of Christ & in his name & fear to submit ourselves to such group & Christian laws as are established in the realm of England to our best knowledge & to all other such laws which shall upon good grounds, be made & enacted among us according to God, yet we may live quietly & peaceably together, in all godliness and honesty.[132]

Controversy surrounded the Essex Covenant, however. Despite their general agreement as to the form of government, there were sharp divisions among the settlers over the allegiance that was owed to the English monarch. Informed, as they were, by the governance of Massachusetts Bay and its restricted view of the proper role of the imperial government in the colony's affairs, two different compacts were rejected before the majority of settlers agreed in 1640 that they were subjects of Charles I, according with the liberties of Massachusetts, and that they were bound to obey the "Godly and Christian Laws" of England together with the laws "according to God" that the settlers enacted themselves.[133]

Conflicting land claims between the heirs of John Mason and others led to a petition to the general court of Massachusetts asking that Massachusetts assume jurisdiction over New Hampshire. Despite the resistance of the Strawberry Bank and Exeter settlers, by 1643, all of New Hampshire had submitted to the authority of Massachusetts, and it was during this period of Massachusetts's control that New Hampshire achieved greater stability.[134]

In what Philip Haffenden described as "a temporary expedient to improve Crown control over New England,"[135] New Hampshire was declared to be a royal province in 1680, and for the next sixty years, the governing authority over the colony shifted between New Hampshire and Massachusetts. On March 11, 1680, the general assembly of New Hampshire met in Portsmouth and enacted a comprehensive code of laws, the General Laws and Liberties of New Hampshire.

The General Laws defined a variety of criminal offenses and included a rudimentary bill of rights. The General Laws also defined the basic structure of the colony's government, and for that reason, the General Laws are considered to have been the constitution of the New Hampshire colony.[136]

Under the General Laws, legislative authority was apportioned between the governments of the towns and the general assembly of the colony, in the same way as they had been prior to the separation from Massachusetts. The freemen of the towns were to adopt "such laws and constitutions as may conduce [the] welfare of [the] town, provided they be not of a criminal but of a prudential nature" and provided that "nothing be done by them contrary to [the] laws and orders" of the province.[137]

The general assembly of the colony was to enact legislation "as may best conduce to [the] good government of this his majesty's province." Much as the general court of Massachusetts had done in 1661, the New Hampshire assembly declared its supremacy in the General Laws, stating that "no Act, Imposition, Law or Ordinance" was to be "made or imposed upon us but such as shall be made by the said assembly and approved by the President and Council from time to time."[138]

Also like the Laws and Liberties of Massachusetts, the General Laws established the basis for the judicial system in the colony. All trials were to be to a jury of twelve "good and lawful men," presided over by the president and six members of the council, who were given "full power to hear and determine all cases civil and criminal." Appeals were to be heard by the general assembly with the president and his council, and in the case of an "equivote," the president was to have the "casting vote." Members of the president's council were authorized to hear lesser criminal cases in which fines could not exceed 40 shillings or punishment be more than "ten stripes or committing to stocks."[139]

New Hampshire was returned to the control of Massachusetts from 1681 until 1691, at which time, Samuel Allen purchased the interest of the heirs of John Mason, effectively making New Hampshire a proprietary colony under Allen. Although the royal governor of Massachusetts, the Earl of Belmont, had authority over the colony, Belmont visited New Hampshire only once, briefly, in 1700. Thus, New Hampshire functioned independently of Massachusetts until 1701, when Joseph Dudley was appointed by the crown to be governor of both Massachusetts and New Hampshire. This joint administration continued until 1741, when Massachusetts and New Hampshire again became separate royal colonies.[140]

THE CONNECTICUT COLONY

Like New Hampshire, the settlement of Connecticut took place largely out of the sight of the crown government. The early settlers were "Puritans to the core," and they brought with them the political and social sensibilities of the Massachusetts Bay colony, their former home. As a consequence, the Connecticut settlers "established a system in which political independence was even more prominent than was commercial and territorial isolation."[141]

As early as 1632, adventurers from Massachusetts Bay had penetrated the dense wilderness that extended from the borders of the Massachusetts settlement, a few miles in land from the coast, to the Hudson River. During this time, trading posts were established along the Connecticut River, including one by Dutch traders from New Amsterdam.[142] Thus, from the very beginning, the Connecticut territory was subject to conflicting claims by Massachusetts, New Amsterdam, and Plymouth, as well as by a group of investors in England who had obtained a patent from the Council for New England.[143]

Interest in settling the territory along the Connecticut River intensified, and as there was no chartered trading company with dominion over the land and there was no direct oversight by the crown, the would-be colonists petitioned the general court of Massachusetts to found a colony.

On March 3, 1636, the general court authorized a "Commission for a Provisional Government," providing the basis for the settlement of Connecticut.[144] This commission delegated the powers of government to four "magistrates," including the authority to declare martial law and to make war, if necessary; to adjudicate disputes and to punish criminals; and to issue orders and decrees considered conducive to "the peaceable and quiet ordering of the affairs of said plantation." The magistrates were to convene assemblies of the towns to carry out these governmental functions, suggesting that the government was to act with the consent of the settlers. The commission was to be only for a short duration until there was agreement among the settlers on the form of government.[145]

A general court of the colony was called for May 1, 1637, for the apparent purpose of going to war with the Pequot tribe of native peoples. Representatives of the towns met with the magistrates in Hartford. Thereafter, the general court met on at least eight occasions between 1637 and 1638, to adjudicate criminal and probate matters and to carry out other financial and administrative functions.[146]

The question arose whether the Springfield settlement would be part of Connecticut or Massachusetts, and although the general court decided in favor of Massachusetts, the issue focused the settlers' attention on their need for a formal constitution of government for the Connecticut colony. Indeed, apart from the expired commission from the general court of Massachusetts, Connecticut, unlike Massachusetts Bay and Plymouth, had no formal instrument of government.[147]

The increasing interest of the settlers in structuring their government coincided with a sermon preached by the charismatic minister, Thomas Hooker, who had been one of the colony's founders. Hooker's message to the settlers was that the temporal authority to govern derived from the consent of the people, expressed through elections, and largely on the strength of Hooker's message, a general court was called in May 1638.

On January 14, 1639, the general court adopted the Fundamental Orders, which has been described as being possibly "the earliest written constitution in America." As a testament to the prescience and care that general court brought to its task, the royal charter subsequently granted to the colony in 1662 ratified the government established by the Fundamental Orders, and after independence, the charter, with references to the king redacted, served as the constitution for the state until 1816. Thus, the Fundamental Orders effectively served as the constitution of Connecticut for 177 years.[148]

The government was founded on the mutual pledge to be one commonwealth, "guided and governed" by the laws decreed pursuant to the terms of the General Orders. This pledge has been likened to the church covenant, "the outward visible sign of civil as contrasted with a religious compact."[149]

Following Hooker's previous injunction that the government's authority derived from the consent of the people, the governor and six magistrates were to be elected annually by the "admitted inhabitants" of the towns, who had taken an oath of fidelity. Voting was by paper ballot submitted to "persons deputed to receive them," and these deputies were to meet as the Court of Election. To be eligible for election as either governor or magistrate, a candidate had to be a member "of some approved church." Term limits were also imposed for the first time, such that no one was permitted to hold office "above once in two years."[150]

The governor and magistrates were to "administer justice according to the laws here established, and . . . according to the rule of the Word of God." However, the "supreme power of the Commonwealth" resided in the general assembly of the colony, established by the Fundamental Orders. This assembly was invested with broad authority to make and repeal laws, to impose levies and to dispose of lands, to exercise the judicial authority of the commonwealth, and otherwise to "deal in any other matter that concerns the good of the commonwealth," except for the election of the governor and magistrates, which was reserved for "the whole body of the freemen." Although the Fundamental Orders specified the number of representatives to be elected from the principal towns of Hartford, Wethersfield, and Windsor, the assembly was authorized to determine the number of representatives from the other towns.[151]

The government of the Fundamental Orders is interesting in a number of respects. The government was founded on the principle of popular sovereignty.[152] In contrast to Massachusetts Bay, "an indispensible qualification" for voting in elections was not membership in an approved church congregation. Perhaps the most significant innovation of the Fundamental Orders was the distinction between the representatives elected by a majority in the towns (i.e., the deputies), who were more responsive to matters of local interest, and the representatives who were elected by colony-wide majorities (i.e., the magistrates), a distinction later incorporated in the 1787 federal constitution.

It is also worthy of note that the Fundamental Orders made no mention of English crown. It is thought that this omission was not inadvertent, but that it reflected the settlers' attitude of independence from Britain that they shared with their fellows in the Massachusetts Bay colony.[153]

Like Massachusetts, communities in Connecticut were organized in towns founded on covenants. On October 10, 1636, the general court enacted legislation establishing the structure of town governments and clarifying the respective jurisdictions of the town government and the government of the colony. Each town was to elect a council of three to five members, one of whom would serve as "moderator." The council was to appoint other officers, including the secretary and the town registrar or clerk. The council was to have judicial authority over cases arising in the town and over the estates of residents who died. The towns were to have authority over the disposition of land and were empowered to enact ordinances for the "well ordering" of the town's affairs, "not being repugnant to any law" enacted by the general court.[154]

Later, in 1650, the general court enacted a comprehensive code of laws for the colony, which was in effect an extension of the 1639 Fundamental Orders. As an initial matter, the code set forth the principle that no one was to be deprived of life, honor, liberty, family, or property except in accordance with an express law of the general court. The general court also reiterated its authority to ensure that "the peace, ordinances and rules of Christ" were observed in every church.

The code set forth a variety of criminal offenses and extensive rules concerning relations with the native peoples. The grand jury was to be empanelled at least annually for the presentment of criminal cases, and the code called for a Court of Magistrates who were to adjudicate claims of up to forty shillings and to oversee trials by jury, the right to which the code guaranteed. Additionally, any one criticizing either a verdict, a sentence or a magistrate would be subject to punishment. Anyone found to have committed "any scandalous offense" would be denied the right to vote or to serve on a jury.

The code also required the towns to provide public education. Every township of fifty or more households was required to engage a teacher at public expense to teach the children of the town to read and to write. Towns with one hundred or more households were required to establish a grammar school to see that the youth were "fitted for university." [155]

THE NEW HAVEN COLONY

A second colony was established in what is now Connecticut when, after the end of the Pequot War of 1637, the Reverend John Davenport sailed with a party from Boston on March 30, 1638, and landed in the harbor where the Quinnipiac River empties into Long Island Sound. There they joined an advance party who had spent the winter and who had begun construction of a rudimentary settlement.[156] Soon after landing, the expeditionary party confirmed their intention to form a social community by adopting the New Haven Plantation Covenant (also known as the Quinnipiac Plantation Covenant), in which they mutually agreed to be governed in all secular matters "by those Rules which scripture holds forth for us." The covenant contemplated that these scriptural rules would govern the choice of representatives, the making and repealing of laws, and the disposition of property.[157]

Like the colonists in Plymouth and their brethren to the north in Connecticut, the New Haven colonists had no royal charter on which to found their colony or base their government. As a consequence, they too were left to their own devices to acquire land from the native peoples and to form a government. With regard to the latter, as the settlers and their leaders, John Davenport and Theophilus Eaton, had come from Massachusetts Bay, their conception of government was largely informed by that of Massachusetts.[158]

In June 1639, approximately a year after signing the covenant, seventy colonists met in the barn of Frances Newman's farm for ten days, "to consult about settling civil government according to God, and about nominations of persons that might be found by consent of all fittest in all respects for the foundation work of a church which was intended to be gathered at Quinnipiac." From this gathering emerged a constitution for the New Haven colony, the Fundamental Articles of New Haven, which are both a record of the colonists' deliberations and a statement of their agreed upon six fundamental principles of government.[159]

The Fundamental Articles are infused with the colony's theological underpinnings. The first principle was that scripture provided the "perfect rule for the direction and government of all men." The second principle reaffirmed the earlier covenant. The third principle established the rule that all those who came to the colony with the "desire that they be admitted into church fellowship according to Christ," would be received as "free planters," able to participate in the functions of government. The fourth principle bound the colonists to establish "such civil order as might best conduce to the securing of the purity and peace of the ordinances to themselves and their posterity according to God."

The fifth and sixth principles dealt with the formation of the government. The fifth principle established the qualifications and the method of selection of the burgesses to be elected, and their authority, which occasioned debate among the colonists. In the end, however, it was unanimously agreed that the burgesses would be chosen from the church members and would be authorized to select the magistrates and other officers, to enact and repeal laws, and to adjudicate disputes including matters of inheritance.

The sixth and final principle concerned the selection of the "seven pillars," those men who would form the nucleus of the governing structure. To accomplish this, Davenport proposed that twelve freemen be chosen by the settlers and that the twelve would elect the seven from among themselves. Davenport's proposal was unanimously adopted.[160]

In due course, the Seven Pillars were chosen and included Davenport and Eaton. A general court was formed on October 25, 1639. The Court was comprised of members of the First Church of Christ in New Haven (established by the Seven Pillars) and members of other "approved churches." Eaton was elected to serve as magistrate for a one-year term with four deputies. This structure remained in place until the growth of the colony necessitated revision in 1643.

In that period between 1639 and 1643, the colony experienced dramatic growth with the establishment of Stamford (1641); Southold (1642); Guilford (1643); Milford (1643); and Branford (1643). Thus, in the space of just four years, the New Haven colony grew from a single settlement to a far-flung collection of towns on both shores of Long Island Sound.[161]

The demands created by this expansion of territory and growth in population led to the alteration of the government structure erected by the Fundamental Articles. On October 27, 1643, the general court, which was now comprised of the governor, deputy governor, the magistrates, and two representatives from each of the towns, adopted a new constitution for the colony, known as the New Haven Fundamentals.

Under the New Haven Fundamentals, the primary political power of the colony was invested in the "free burgesses "of the towns, which had authority to elect local officials, adjudicate "inferior" cases, and to elect the officers of the colony, including the governor, deputy governor, secretary, treasurer, and the marshal. To serve as a burgess and to vote in elections, a freeman had to be a member of "some or other of the approved churches of New England."[162]

There was also to be a general court of the colony, consisting of the governor, deputy governor, and all of the magistrates and representatives that met twice yearly. The members of the general court were to "sit together till the affairs of the jurisdiction be dispatched or may be safely respited."[163]

Certain legislative and judicial powers were specified in the Fundamentals to be exercised by the general court. Thus, the general court was to:

1. See to the purity of religion and to "suppress the contrary;"
2. Impose oaths on magistrates for the faithful performance of their duties and hold the magistrates accountable "for the breach of any laws . . . or for other misdemeanors;"
3. Impose on the colony's inhabitants oaths of fidelity and "subjection to the laws;"
4. Impose levies and " contributions" to support public services; and
5. Adjudicate cases referred by other courts, which were to be decided "according to the scriptures.[164]

Judicial proceedings were to be conducted twice a year by the magistrates. This Court of the Magistrates was to conduct trials of "weighty and capital cases" that were beyond the jurisdiction of the towns. The Court of the Magistrates was also to decide appeals from decisions of the town courts and was otherwise to summon inhabitants of the colony "to account for the breach of any laws" and for "other misdemeanors."[165] Because the Fundamentals made no provision for juries, New Haven was alone among the New England colonies not to grant a right to trial by jury.[166]

THE UNIFICATION OF THE CONNECTICUT COLONIES

The restoration of Charles II to the throne in 1660 elevated the concerns of the Connecticut colonists regarding the legal status of their colony. Unlike

Massachusetts Bay, Connecticut had no royal charter legitimizing its foundation, and although thought had been given to petitioning the Long Parliament, no action to obtain a charter had been taken.[167]

To remedy the colony's uncertain status, the general court in Connecticut authorized a petition for a royal charter, which was transmitted to England in June 1661 by John Winthrop, Jr. On May 10, 1662, the charter received the great seal.

Like other charters before it, the Connecticut charter established the colony as a body corporate and politic. Also as noted, the charter confirmed the form of government established by the colonists under the Fundamental Orders of 1639.[168]

There was to be a general assembly comprised of two elected representatives from each town, the governor and at least six assistants. This general assembly was authorized to admit freemen and to elect colonial officials.[169] Later, in 1698, the general assembly divided into two houses: an "upper house," consisting of the governor and the assistants, and a "lower house," of the representatives of the towns. The consent of both houses was required to enact or repeal a law.[170] The broad power of the general assembly to enact "all manner of wholesome, and reasonable laws" that were "not contrary to the laws" of England was also confirmed, as was the assembly's authority to establish "needful" colonial offices and to erect "judicatories." The assembly was further authorized to defend the colony and "upon just causes" to "invade and destroy the natives and other enemies of said colony."[171]

The grant of Connecticut's royal charter accelerated the dissolution of the New Haven colony, which has been described as having been at best a "loose confederacy of towns, scattered and lacking unity."[172] Indeed, soon after the charter was received in 1662, the towns of Greenwich, Guilford, Southold, and Stamford withdrew from the New Haven colony and affiliated with Connecticut.

In 1664, the former Dutch colony of New Netherland, which bordered New Haven, was given over to the king's brother, James, the Duke of York. Fearing that they would be incorporated into York's proprietary colony, the remaining towns of Branford, Milford, and New Haven accepted shares in Connecticut, passing a formal act of submission on January 5, 1665, and with that, the New Haven Colony passed into history.[173]

THE PROTOFEDERALISM OF THE UNITED COLONIES OF NEW ENGLAND

The westward expansion from Massachusetts Bay into New Hampshire, Connecticut, and Rhode Island included the establishment of trading posts along with agricultural communities. As early as 1630, merchants from Massachusetts Bay joined the westward migration, and by 1640, those mercantile interests extended to Connecticut in the west, Long Island in the south, and Maine in the north.[174]

Inevitably, there were conflicts between the colonies concerning boundaries and trading rights, particularly with the native peoples. To address these conflicts, commissioners were appointed by the Massachusetts Bay and Plymouth colonies to negotiate these disputes, which eventually led to agreements on boundaries. Similar conflicts with Dutch and French traders, as well as conflicts with the native peoples also caused the colonies to look for common ground.[175]

On May 19, 1643, representatives of the New England colonies, not including Rhode Island which was considered to be part of the Plymouth colony,[176] adopted articles of confederation creating the United Colonies of New England, "for mutual help and strength in all our future concernments," in order that "in nation and region, so in other respects, we be and continue one according to the tenor and true meaning of the ensuing articles."[177]

The stated purpose of this confederation was to "enter into a firm and perpetual league of friendship and amity for the offence and defence, mutual advice and succor . . . both for preserving and propagating the truth and liberties of the Gospel for their own mutual safety and welfare." The articles specifically provided, however, that the union would not affect a colony's internal governance, and it was stipulated that two colonies could not join in one jurisdiction without the consent of the other colonies.[178]

The government formed by the articles was one of strictly limited authority. However, the articles upon which the union was grounded represent the earliest experiment in federalism in America and, like the Articles of Confederation 130 years later, the union of colonies was an attempt to address matters of common concern requiring concerted action, while recognizing and preserving the unique independence and sovereignty of the member colonies.

The articles created a general court composed of two representatives from each of the member colonies, who were to meet at least annually in regular session. The articles provided for mutual defense of the colonies and accordingly, the general court was given authority to determine questions of "war, or peace, leagues, aids, charges, and number of men for war, division of spoils and whatsoever is gotten by conquest." The general court also was to exercise jurisdiction over the "receiving of more confederates for plantations into combination with any confederates, and all things of like nature, which are the proper concomitants or consequences of such a Confederation for amity, offence and defense." However, in keeping with the strict limitations on political jurisdiction of the United Colonies, the general court was explicitly foreclosed from "intermeddling with the government of any jurisdictions," which, under the articles, was "preserved entirely to themselves."[179]

Despite the limitation on authority over internal colonial matters, the general court was authorized to "frame and establish agreements and orders" to prevent differences among the colonies and "for preserving peace among themselves." These agreements and orders were to concern, "speedy passage of justice in every direction," the movement of persons from one colony to another "without due certificates," and relations of the colonies with the native peoples, "that they neither grow insolent nor be injured without due satisfaction, lest war break in upon the confederates through such miscarriage," the return of servants who had fled from their masters, and the extradition of fugitive criminals.[180]

Thus, individually and as a group, the New England colonies followed a path of development very different from that of Virginia. Unlike the enterprise colonies that preceded them in Virginia, the New England colonies were intended from the outset to be permanent colonies that were both self-sustaining and self-governing. Also unlike the settlers of Virginia, the New England colonies were founded on a common bond of faith, which informed the colonists' conception of the societies they had come to create. Their lack of reliance on England for subsistence and the almost complete absence of crown involvement and supervision during this formative period allowed the New England settlers much greater liberty to find their own way in structuring their communities and in governing themselves.

As they gave effect to these structures, the settlers drew upon the religious traditions and solemnized their agreements in written covenants and foundational documents that authoritatively defined the jurisdiction and structure of their governments and secured certain fundamental liberties that they believed necessary to bound the powers of the governments they were creating.

In part, these constitutional documents were the product of the colonists' religiosity and their separatist inclinations. In part, they responded to the harsh circumstances of their alien land. In part, they were the product of the imperatives of defining a social and political structure in the absence of established governmental institutions.

These fundamental documents were constitutions of their governments. They created governments with authority to enact and enforce laws, to provide for the common defense, and to undertake public works for the benefit of the colony as a whole. These powers were apportioned between local, town governments, and the colonial government and were to be exercised by an elected executive and legislature, which over time became bicameral to harmonize the interests of both. Provisions were also made for an elected executive and a judiciary.

Also found in those statements of first principles were guarantees of personal liberties that were secure from encroachment by the state. Liberty of conscience in matters of religion, the right to vote, freedom of speech and of debate in the legislature, due process for those accused of crime, including the right to trial by jury, all found expression in the early New England constitutions. For these reasons, the constitutionalism of New England was uniquely American.

The colonies of the mid-Atlantic followed yet a different path. They were "palatine" colonies, so called because virtually unrestrained authority to govern those colonies was entrusted to individuals as a reward for loyalty and service to the crown. Although this proprietary form of government was in many ways medieval, over time, the settlers asserted their own interests and imperatives to erect their own institutions of government founded on fundamental principles of their own. In this way, the settlers of the palatine colonies too made their own contribution to the emerging constitutional tradition.

NOTES

1. Appleby, "War, Politics, and Colonization, 1558–1625," in Canny, ed., *The Oxford History of the British Empire*, 72; Middleton and Lombard, *Colonial America*, 59.
2. Story, *Commentaries on the Constitution of the United States*, vol. 1: 34; Andrews, *The Colonial Period of American History*, vol. 1: 251; Sarson, *British America 1500–1800*, 122: Meinig, *The Shaping of America*, 37.
3. Haven, *History of Grants Under the Great Council of New England*, 16.
4. Osgood, *The American Colonies in the Seventeenth Century*, vol. 1: 98–102.
5. Thorpe, *The Federal and State Constitutions*, vol. 3: 1827–29.
6. Thorpe, *The Federal and State Constitutions*, vol. 3: 1832.
7. Thorpe, *The Federal and State Constitutions*, vol. 3: 1833.
8. Thorpe, *The Federal and State Constitutions*, vol. 3: 1838–39.
9. Thorpe, *The Federal and State Constitutions*, vol. 3: 1833–36.
10. Osgood, *The American Colonies in the Seventeenth Century*, vol. 1: 1835–36.
11. Sarson, *British America 1500–1800*, 125.
12. Middleton and Lombard, *Colonial America*, 85.
13. Andrews, *The Colonial Period of American History*, vol. 1: 252.
14. Andrews, *The Colonial Period of American History*, vol. 1: 258.
15. Osgood, *The American Colonies in the Seventeenth Century*, vol. 1: 105–6.
16. John E. Pomfret, *Founding the American Colonies* (New York: Harper & Row, 1970), 107–8.
17. Pomfret, *Founding the American Colonies*, 108; Andrews, *The Colonial Period in American History*, vol. 1: 261.
18. Middleton and Lombard, *Colonial America*, 80.
19. Andrews, *The Colonial Period of American History*, vol. 1: 261–68; Pomfret, *Founding the American Colonies*, 111; Sarson, *British America 1500 – 1800*, 123.
20. Andrews, *The Colonial Period in American History*, vol. 1: 272; Pomfret, *Founding the American Colonies*, 109–13; Virginia DeJohn Anderson, "New England in the Seventeenth Century," in Canny, ed., *The Oxford History of the British Empire*, 193.
21. Middleton and Lombard, *Colonial America*, 80–82.
22. Thorpe, *The Federal and State Constitutions*, vol. 3: 1841.
23. James Truslow Adams, *The Founding of New England* (New York: Atlantic Monthly Press, 1921), 98.
24. Sarson, *British America 1500 – 1800*, 124.
25. Donald S. Lutz, "The Mayflower Compact," in Stephen L. Schecter, ed., *Roots of the Republic: American Founding Documents Interpreted* (Madison: Madison House, 1990), 20–21 (emphasis original).
26. Story, *Commentaries on the Constitution of the United States*, vol. 1: 38.

27. Osgood, *The American Colonies in the Seventeenth Century*, vol. 1: 109; Andrews, *Trade, Plunder and Settlement*, 330.
28. Osgood, *The American Colonies in the Seventeenth Century*, vol. 1: 109.
29. Andrews, *The Colonial Period of American History*, vol. 1: 290–91.
30. Andrews, *The Colonial Period in American History*, vol. 1: 272–73.
31. Osgood, *The American Colonies in the Seventeenth Century*, vol. 1: 111–12.
32. Oscar Handlin, "The Significance of the Seventeenth Century," in James Morton Smith, ed., *Seventeenth Century America: Essays in Colonial History* (Chapel Hill: North Carolina University Press, 1959), 8; Pomfret, *Founding the American Colonies*, 114; Middleton and Lombard, *Colonial America*, 83–84.
33. Osgood, *The American Colonies in the Seventeenth Century*, vol. 1: 117-118; Andrews, *The Colonial Period in American History*, vol. 1: 293–94.
34. Story, *Commentaries on the Constitution of the United States*, vol. 1: 39; Rodick, *American Constitutional Custom*, 15–16.
35. Thorpe, *The Federal and State Constitutions*, vol. 3: 1842.
36. Story, *Commentaries on the Constitution of the United States*, vol. 1: 40.
37. Andrews, *The Colonial Period of American History*, vol. 1: 297.
38. Lutz, *Colonial Origins of the American Constitution*, 60.
39. Lutz, *Colonial Origins of the American Constitution*, 61–63.
40. Lutz, *Colonial Origins of the American Constitution*, 62–63.
41. Lutz, *Colonial Origins of the American Constitution*, 63.
42. Lutz, *Colonial Origins of the American Constitution*, 63–64.
43. Osgood, *The American Colonies in the Seventeenth Century*, vol. 1: 295–300.
44. Osgood, *The American Colonies in the Seventeenth Century*, vol. 1: 130–31; Andrews, *The Colonial Period of American History*, vol. 1: 346–73; Charles M. Andrews, *Our Earliest Colonial Settlements* (Ithaca: Cornell University Press, 1933), 64–65; Clarence L. Ver Steeg, *The Formative Years 1607–1763* (New York: Hill & Wang, 1968), 35; Sarson, *British America 1500–1800*, 126; Pomfret, *Founding the American Colonies*, 153.
45. Thorpe, *The Federal and State Constitutions*, vol. 3: 1852–53.
46. Pomfret, *Founding the American Colonies*, 154; Andrews, *The Colonial Period of American History*, vol. 1: 375.
47. Story, *Commentaries on the Constitution of the United States*, vol. 1: 46.
48. Thorpe, *The Federal and State Constitutions*, vol. 3: 1857–58.
49. Lutz, *Colonial Origins of the American Constitution*, 37; Osgood, *The American Colonies in the Seventeenth Century*, vol. 1: 146; Osgood emphasized his view that of greater significance than the removal of the charter to Massachusetts was the relocation of the governor, the deputy governor, and the assistants to the colony. Herbert L. Osgood, "The Corporation as a Form of Colonial Government II," *Political Science Quarterly*, vol. 11: 505–6; Andrews, *The Colonial Period of American History*, vol. 1: 354–91; Ver Steeg, *The Formative Years*, 36.
50. Andrews, *The Colonial Period of American History*, vol. 1: 371.
51. Osgood, *The American Colonies in the Seventeenth Century*, vol. 1: 143; Pomfret, *Founding the American Colonies*, 155; Middleton and Lombard, *Colonial America*, 88.
52. Story, *Commentaries on the Constitution of the United States*, vol. 1: 50.
53. Virginia de John Anderson, "New England in the Seventeenth Century," in Canny, ed., *The Origins of Empire*, 193.
54. Ver Steeg, *The Formative Years*, 37.
55. Middleton and Lombard, *Colonial America*, 88.
56. Osgood, *The American Colonies in the Seventeenth Century*, vol. 1: 142; Ver Steeg, *The Formative Years*, 36; Pomfret, *Founding the American Colonies*, 155.
57. Osgood, *The American Colonies in the Seventeenth Century*, vol. 1: 151; Andrews, *The Colonial Period of American History*, vol. 1: 432–33.
58. Ver Steeg, *The Formative Years*, 39.
59. Andrews, *The Colonial Period of American History*, vol. 1: 435–36.
60. Ver Steeg, *The Formative Years*, 39.
61. Lutz, *Colonial Origins of the American Constitution*, 50.
62. Lutz, *Colonial Origins of the American Constitution*, 50.

63. Lutz, *Colonial Origins of the American Constitution*, 50.
64. Lutz, *Colonial Origins of the American Constitution*, 50.
65. Story, *Commentaries on the Constitution of the United States*, vol. 1: 53; Osgood, *The American Colonies in the Seventeenth Century*, vol. 1: 158.
66. Lutz, *Colonial Origins of the American Constitution*, 50.
67. Haven, *History of Grants Under the Great Council for New England*, 3.
68. Thorpe, *The Federal and State Constitutions*, vol. 3: 1860–61.
69. Sarson, *British America 1500–1800*, 195.
70. Middleton and Lombard, *Colonial America*, 102.
71. Lutz, *Colonial Origins of the American Constitution*, 70–87.
72. H. D. Hazeltine, "The Influence of Magna Carta on American Constitutional Development," *Columbia Law Review*, Vol. 17 (1917), 10.
73. Lutz, *Colonial Origins of the American Constitution*, 90–94.
74. Lutz, *Colonial Origins of the American Constitution*, 95.
75. Lutz, *Colonial Origins of the American Constitution*, 95–99.
76. Lutz, *Colonial Origins of the American Constitution*, 109–15.
77. Lutz, *Colonial Origins of the American Constitution*, 106–9, 132–33.
78. Lutz, *Colonial Origins of the American Constitution*, 123–24.
79. Lutz, *Colonial Origins of the American Constitution*, 123–24.
80. Lutz, *Colonial Origins of the American Constitution*, 130–34.
81. Lutz, *Colonial Origins of the American Constitution*, 119, 125.
82. Lutz, *Colonial Origins of the American Constitution*, 131.
83. Lutz, *Colonial Origins of the American Constitution*, 119.
84. Lutz, *Colonial Origins of the American Constitution*, 129.
85. Andrews, *The Colonial Period of American History*, vol. 1: 461.
86. See, for example, Lutz, *Colonial Origins of the American Constitution*, 35 (Salem Covenant), 38–39 (Watertown Covenant), 68 (Deadham Covenant).
87. Middleton and Lombard, *Colonial America*, 89–90.
88. Robert M. Bliss, *Revolution and Empire: English Politics and the American Colonies in the Seventeenth Century* (Manchester: Manchester University Press, 1990), 147.
89. Lutz, *Colonial Origins of the American Constitution*, 158–60.
90. Middleton and Lombard, *Colonial America*, 136–37.
91. Winfred T. Root, "The Lords of Trade and Plantations," *American Historical Review* (October 1917), vol. 23: 20–41; Louise Phelps Kellog, *The American Colonial Charter: A Study of English Administration in Relation Thereto, Chiefly after 1688* (New York: Da Capo Press, 1971), 24.
92. Sarson, *British America 1500–1800*, 142; McFarlane, *The British in the Americas 1480–1815*, 201; Richard S. Dunn, "The Glorious Revolution in America," in Canny, *The Oxford History of the British Empire*, 450; Middleton and Lombard, *Colonial America*, 136–37, 182–83; Viola F. Barnes, *The Dominion of New England: A Study in British Colonial Policy* (New Haven: Yale University Press, 1923), 14–15.
93. Adams, *The Founding of New England*, 314–26.
94. Mary L. Lustig, *The Imperial Executive in America* (Madison, NJ: Farleigh Dickinson University Press, 2002), 135.
95. Bliss observed that the crown "imposed autocratic rule in New England as if the colonists were still little more than species of English local government." Bliss, *Revolution and Empire*, 244.
96. Lustig, *The Imperial Executive in America*, 134–69; Barnes, *The Dominion of New England*, 15; Richard S. Dunn, "The Dominion of New England," in James K. Martin, ed., *Interpreting Colonial America: Selected Readings*. 2nd ed. (New York: Harper & Row, 1973), 205; Sarson, *British America 1500–1800*, 301; Anderson, "New England in the Seventeenth Century," in Canny, ed., *The Origins of Empire*, 445; Dunn, "The Glorious Revolution in America," in Canny, ed., *The Origins of Empire*, 445; McFarlane, *The British in the Americas 1480–1815*, 201.
97. Thorpe, *The Federal and State Constitutions*, vol. 3: 1870–86.
98. Labaree, *Royal Government in America*, 7–8.

99. Andrews, *The Colonial Period of American History*, vol. 2: 4; Ver Steeg, *The Formative Years*, 47–49; Anderson, "New England in the Seventeenth Century," in Canny, ed., *The Origins of Empire*, 202–3.

100. Lutz, *Colonial Origins of the American Constitution*, 161.

101. Lutz, *Colonial Origins of the American Constitution*, 161–62; Andrews, *The Colonial Period of American History*, vol. 1: 8; Osgood, *The American Colonies in the Seventeenth Century*, vol. 1: 336–37.

102. Pomfret, Founding the American Colonies, 193; Anderson, "New England in the Seventeenth Century," in Canny, ed., *The Origins of Empire*, 203; Ver Steeg, *The Formative Years*, 49–50; Andrews, *The Colonial Period of American History*, vol. 2: 8; Osgood, *The American Colonies in the Seventeenth Century*, vol. 1: 341–43.

103. Lutz, *Colonial Origins of the American Constitution*, 163–64.

104. Andrews, *The Colonial Period of American History*, vol. 2: 9–10; Osgood, *The American Colonies in the Seventeenth Century*, vol. 1: 343.

105. Lutz, *Colonial Origins of the American Constitution*, 166–67.

106. Thorpe, *The Federal and State Constitutions*, vol. 6: 3207–8.

107. Lutz, *Colonial Origins of the American Constitution*, 172–73; Andrews, *The Colonial Period of American History*, vol. 2: 10–11; Osgood, *The American Colonies in the Seventeenth Century*, vol. 1: 344–45.

108. Thorpe, *The Federal and State Constitutions*, vol. 6: 3209–11; Andrews, *The Colonial Period of American History*, vol. 2: 23–25; Osgood, *The American Colonies in the Seventeenth Century*, vol. 1: 354–55; Pomfret, *Founding the American Colonies*, 219.

109. Andrews, *The Colonial Period of American History*, vol. 2: 15.

110. Lutz, *Colonial Origins of the American Constitution*, 176–77; Osgood, *The American Colonies in the Seventeenth Century*, vol. 1: 345–52.

111. Lutz, *Colonial Origins of the American Constitution*, 176–77; Osgood, *The American Colonies in the Seventeenth Century*, vol. 1: 345–52.

112. The royal charter of 1663 ratified the government framed by the 1647 Acts and Orders, and following independence, Rhode Island, like Connecticut and Massachusetts, retained the charter, with references to the king redacted, as its constitution until 1842. Lutz, *Colonial Origins of the American Constitution*, 178; Osgood, *The American Colonies in the Seventeenth Century*, vol. 1: 355–57.

113. Lutz, *Colonial Origins of the American Constitution*, 178.

114. Lutz, *Colonial Origins of the American Constitution*, 179–80, 194–95.

115. Lutz, *Colonial Origins of the American Constitution*, 179–80, 182.

116. Lutz, *Colonial Origins of the American Constitution*, 179–80.

117. Lutz, *Colonial Origins of the American Constitution*, 180, 194–95.

118. Lutz, *Colonial origins of the American Constitution*, 182–84.

119. Lutz, *Colonial Origins of the American Constitution*, 186, 198–202.

120. Lutz, *Colonial Origins of the American Constitution*, 204–5; Andrews, *The Colonial Period of American History*, vol. 2: 34–36; Pomfret, *Founding the American Colonies*, 224.

121. Thorpe, *The Federal and State Constitutions*, vol. 6: 324; Andrews, *Colonial Self-Government*, 63–68. The boundary dispute continued for a number of years, however. Andrews, *The Colonial Period of American History*, vol. 2: 52–54; Osgood, *The American Colonies in the Seventeenth Century*, vol. 1: 369–70.

122. Charles M. Andrews, *Colonial Self-Government 1652–1689* (New York: Harper Brothers, 1907), 68.

123. Thorpe, *The Federal and State Constitutions*, vol. 6: 3214–16.

124. Thorpe, *The Federal and State Constitutions*, vol. 6: 3215.

125. Thorpe, *The Federal and State Constitutions*, vol. 6: 3218.

126. Story, *Commentaries on the Constitution of the United States*, vol. 1: 85.

127. Lutz, *Colonial Origins of the American Constitution*, 207–8.

128. Middleton and Lombard, *Colonial America*, 93–97.

129. Thorpe, *The Federal and State Constitutions*, vol. 4: 2433–36; Jere R. Daniell, *Colonial New Hampshire: A History* (Millwood: KTO Press, 1981), 21–22; Anderson, "New England in

the Seventeenth Century," in Canny, ed., *The Origins of Empire*, 202; Meinig, *The Shaping of America*, vol. 1: 90.

130. David E. Van Deventer, *The Emergence of Provincial New Hampshire 1623–1741* (Baltimore: Johns Hopkins University Press, 1976), 5–6.

131. Van Deventer, *The Emergence of Provincial New Hampshire*, 7-8; Daniell, *Colonial New Hampshire*, 36; Sarson, *British America 1500–1800*, 132, Middleton, *Colonial America*, 102; Anderson, "New England in the Seventeenth Century," 202.

132. Thorpe, *The Federal and State Constitutions*, vol. 4: 2445; Lutz, *Colonial Origins of the American Constitution*, 3–4.

133. Van Deventer, *The Emergence of Provincial New Hampshire*, 11–12.

134. Daniell, *Colonial New Hampshire: A History*, 57.

135. Philip S. Haffenden, "The Crown and the Colonial Charters, 1675–1688: Part I," *The William and Mary Quarterly* (1958), vol. 15: 301.

136. Lutz, *Colonial Origins of the American Constitution*, 5.

137. Lutz, *Colonial Origins of the American Constitution*, 25.

138. Lutz, *Colonial Origins of the American Constitution*, 17.

139. Lutz, *Colonial Origins of the American Constitution*, 10, 29.

140. Osgood, *The American Colonies in the Eighteenth Century*, vol. 3: 191.

141. Osgood, *The American Colonies in the Seventeenth Century*, vol. 1: 301–2.

142. Andrews, *The Colonial Period of American History*, vol. 2: 67–68; Pomfret, *Founding the American Colonies*, 232–33.

143. Middleton and Lombard, *Colonial America*, 97.

144. Andrews, *The Colonial Period of American History*, vol. 2: 68–78.

145. William DeLos Love, *The Colonial History of Hartford* (Hartford: self-published, 1914) 65–66; Andrews, *The Colonial Period of American History*, vol. 2: 78–79.

146. Andrews, *The Colonial Period of American History*, vol. 2: 92; Osgood, *The American Colonies in the Seventeenth Century*, vol. 1: 304–6; Love, *The Colonial History of Hartford*, 68–70.

147. Pomfret, *Founding the American Colonies*, 242; Andrews, *The Colonial Period of American History*, vol. 2: 94–96.

148. Lutz, *Colonial Origins of the American Constitution*, 210; Story, *Commentaries on the Constitution of the United States*, vol. 1: 72, Andrews, *The Colonial Period of American History*, vol. 2: 309. Pomfret did not share this view, however. Pomfret, *Founding the American Colonies*, 246.

149. Andrews, *The Colonial Period of American History*, vol. 2: 102.

150. Thorpe, *The Federal and State Constitutions*, vol. 1: 519–20; Lutz, *Colonial Origins of the American Constitution*, 211–12.

151. Thorpe, *The Federal and State Constitutions*, vol. 1: 520–22; Lutz, *Colonial Origins of the American Constitution*, 212–14.

152. Donald S. Lutz, "The Fundamental Orders of Connecticut 1639," in Stephen L. Schecter, ed., *Roots of the Republic*, 28.

153. Andrews, *The Colonial Period of American History*, vol. 2: 109.

154. Lutz, *Colonial Origins of the American Constitution*, 217–19.

155. Lutz, *Colonial Origins of the American Constitution*, 241–49.

156. Andrews, *The Colonial Period of American History*, vol. 2: 145–53; Pomfret, *Founding the American Colonies*, 256–60.

157. Lutz, *Colonial Origins of the American Constitution*, 209.

158. Andrews, *The Colonial Period of American History*, vol. 2: 154–56; Pomfret, *Founding the American Colonies*, 261–62.

159. Thorpe, *The Federal and State Constitutions*, vol. 1: 523; Lutz, *Colonial Origins of the American Constitution*, 221; Andrews, *The Colonial Period of American History*, vol. 2: 157; Pomfret, *Founding the American Colonies*, 262.

160. Thorpe, *The Federal and State Constitutions*, vol. 1: 523–26; Lutz, *Colonial Origins of the American Constitution*, 221–26.

161. Andrews, *The Colonial Period of American History*, vol. 2: 158–65.

162. Thorpe, *The Federal and State Constitutions*, vol. 1: 526–27; Lutz, *Colonial Origins of the American Constitution*, 235–36; Pomfret, *Founding the American Colonies*, 266.

163. Thorpe, *The Federal and State Constitutions*, vol. 1: 527; Lutz, *Colonial Origins of the American Constitution*, 236.

164. Thorpe, *The Federal and State Constitutions*, vol. 1: 527; Lutz, *Colonial Origins of the American Constitution*, 236.

165. Thorpe, *The Federal and State Constitutions*, vol. 1: 527–28; Lutz, *Colonial Origins of the American Constitution*, 236.

166. Andrews, *The Colonial Period of American History*, vol. 2: 166–67.

167. Pomfret, *Founding the American Colonies*, 251.

168. Thorpe, *The Federal and State Constitutions*, vol. 1: 530.

169. Thorpe, *The Federal and State Constitutions*, vol. 1: 531.

170. Lutz, *Colonial Origins of the American Constitution*, 253.

171. Thorpe, *The Federal and State Constitutions*, vol. 1: 534.

172. Andrews, *The Colonial Period of American History*, vol. 2: 166.

173. Andrews, *The Colonial Period of American History*, vol. 2: 186–93.

174. Bailyn, *The New England Merchants in the Seventeenth Century* (Cambridge, MA: Harvard University Press, 1979), 23–29.

175. Osgood, *The American Colonies in the Seventeenth Century*, vol. 1: 392–95.

176. Story, *Commentaries on the Constitution of the United States*, vol. 1: 91.

177. Thorpe, *The Federal and State Constitutions*, vol. 1: 77; Lutz, *Colonial Origins of the American Constitution*, 366; Osgood, *The American Colonies in the Seventeenth Century*, vol. 1: 396–400.

178. Thorpe, *The Federal and State Constitutions*, vol. 1: 77–78; Lutz, *Colonial Origins of the American Constitution*, 366–67.

179. Thorpe, *The Federal and State Constitutions*, vol. 1: 79; Lutz, *Colonial Origins of the American Constitution*, 368.

180. Thorpe, *The Federal and State Constitutions*, vol. 1: 79–80; Lutz, *Colonial Origins of the American Constitution*, 368–69.

Chapter Three

The Proprietary Colonies of the Mid-Atlantic

It is fair to say that when the colonies of Virginia and New England were settled, before the restoration of the House of Stuart in 1660, England had no coherent colonial policy.[1] While as Ken MacMillan has argued, from the time of their inception, the crown maintained oversight of the American colonies before the Restoration, there is general agreement that during this formative period of English colonization in North America, the governing authority over the colonies was remanded to nongovernmental parties (chartered companies in Virginia and New England and an individual in Maryland).[2] As Edmund Burke observed in 1757, "The settlement of our colonies was never pursued upon any regular plan; but they were formed, grew, and flourished, as accidents, the nature of climate, or the disposition of private men happened to operate."[3] Indeed, Jack P. Greene has suggested that the American settlements were viewed by English officials as "subordinate political communities" and as a "series of economic units intended to contribute to the prosperity of England and to provide it with a solid claim to a portion of the vast riches of the New World," rather than as "colonies of England organized into separate or auxiliary societies overseas."[4]

The colonies, particularly in New England, exploited this official indifference and came to view themselves as autonomous states with only vague ties to England. In that regard, during the Interregnum following the execution of Charles I in 1649, Massachusetts Bay declared itself a commonwealth and petitioned Oliver Cromwell for recognition as such.[5]

This absence of official engagement in the internal affairs of the American colonies has been attributed to a variety of circumstances. Those circumstances included the lack of sufficient crown resources to administer distant territories; the distraction of more pressing political concerns both domestically and in Europe; and the perception that in view of their poverty, the colonial settlements did not represent a significant financial resource.[6]

With the restoration of Charles II came a greater commitment to administering the North American enterprise and to incorporating the colonies into the English commonwealth to realize their commercial and strategic advantages.[7] Also, the British conception of the American colonies became one of permanent, primarily agricultural, settlements rather than distant commercial enterprises for the exploitation of resources, and perhaps in reaction to the independence of the New England colonies, the colonization of the mid-Atlantic territory was of a different character. Rather than rely on chartered enterprises to conduct local affairs (the Virginia colony had been remanded to control of the crown in 1625 and New England was becoming progressively problematic), Charles favored proprietary charters similar to that fashioned by his father for the Maryland colony often as an expression of royal favor or as a reward for services to the crown. Vast grants of land were made to one or more individuals in whose loyalty Charles was confident.[8] By 1640, proprietary colonies predominated in America such that roughly half of the population resided on proprietary lands. It was under such proprietary grants that the colonies of Maryland, New York, New Jersey, Pennsylvania, and the Carolinas were founded.

Virtually plenary powers were conferred on the proprietors. As was said of Maryland, the first proprietary under a grant from Charles I,

> The entire area was a palatine or great barony, within which, standing within a feudal relationship with the proprietor, were lords of the manors and the free-holders with their tenements. . . . They set the stamp of a decentralized and royal plantation system upon the colony, organized on a manorial plan and imitating as nearly as possible the features of an English barony.[9]

These charters allowed the proprietor and his heirs to conduct the affairs of the colony without the constraints and revenue demands that had hobbled the Virginia Companies. Although hardly democratic in origin, the proprietors granted concessions to the settlers that allowed greater participation in the government and the development of democratic institutions. Every colony had a legislative chamber of elected representatives.[10]

The restoration of Charles II also brought with it a change in official attitude toward the American colonies. By this time, England considered itself to be a trading nation and the colonies were viewed as being important economically, fiscally, and strategically.[11] The colonies represented an expanding sector of English overseas commerce as a source of raw materials and as a market for English goods.[12] This change in attitude was accompanied by greater attention to the administration of the colonies and to the partners with whom the colonies would trade.

By 1650, parliament had declared the colonies subordinate to parliament's laws and in 1651, parliament enacted the first of the Navigation Acts restricting colonial commerce and requiring the transportation of goods on English ships. After the Restoration, parliament reenacted similar legislation, but the acts were largely ineffectual because the institutions for enforcement and for oversight of the colonies were largely non-existent (leading G. E. Aylmer to characterize the Stuart colonial policy as being like Lewis Carroll's Cheshire Cat, which all but faded away save for its grin).[13] In that regard, the Stuart reliance on local authorities, the proprietors in the mid-Atlantic, to carry out administrative duties (what MacMillan described as the "weak state" model) continued under Charles II.[14] However, as England's imperial vision emerged under Charles and more so his brother, James II, royal policy trended toward centralization of control over the colonies (the "strong state" model).[15] The instruments of this movement toward centralization were a succession of committees of parliament and the privy council charged with oversight of trade and plantations.

The American colonies were initially under the care of the privy council, which had filled a similar role with respect to the Scottish borders, Wales, the Channel Islands, and Ireland. As membership of the council grew under the Stuarts, committees were formed to address specific areas of the council's responsibilities. In May 1660, shortly after his assumption of the throne, Charles II appointed a Committee for Foreign Plantations with responsibility for the colonies. The committee proved to be ineffectual, which allowed the American colonies to pursue their own course unfettered. The committee was abolished in December 1674 and in February 1675, a second committee of the privy council was formed that became known as the Lords of Trade and Plantations. The committee's objective was to impose crown rule on the colonies, and this committee proved to be more forceful and adroit at meeting the demands of the crown's imperial aspirations.[16]

England's imperial aims matured under James II who assumed the crown in 1685. James had revealed his preference for a centralized structure of administration when, as the Duke of York, he was the proprietor of the New York colony. Charter governments were declared to be prejudicial to sound colonial policy after reports were received of the murder the customs collector in Maryland; complaints were made that the governments of Connecticut and Rhode Island had enacted laws that were contrary to the laws of England and had violated the Navigation Acts; and it was reported that trade in New York had declined following the loss of control over the territories of New Jersey and Delaware.[17]

The Lords of Trade directed that *quo warranto* proceedings be instituted against Connecticut, New Jersey (East and West), New York, and Rhode Island, as well as against Massachusetts Bay and Plymouth. As noted, these colonies together with New Hampshire were to be the initial gambit of the centralization initiative, the short-lived Dominion of New England.

While James II had intended to direct the implementation of the imperial colonial policy, his attention was distracted by other domestic and international issues. Because of the "erratic nature of the king's guidance," as well as the removal of senior officials and their replacement with persons who "evidenced no outstanding abilities," the Lords of Trade suffered a loss of effectiveness that "helped to ensure that the schemes for empire which James had endorsed should never become more than a promise." Thus, "because there was no other person of sufficient importance to watch over the cause of centralization, the schemes languished, failed to achieve fruition, and largely perished in the turmoil which accompanied the overthrow of the Stuarts in 1688."[18]

After the Glorious Revolution, William III abandoned the strategy of centralization in favor of control of the individual colonies by executives appointed by the crown. A new charter was issued to Massachusetts in 1691. In 1694, Pennsylvania was returned to William Penn. This colonial policy was not a complete success, however. Greene described William's "campaign for a consolidated empire" as "desultory, sporadic, unsustained, and, at best, only modestly successful." Greene explained that

> the ideological commitment to limited governance and to the sanctity of private and corporate rights, a commitment which was reinforced by the conception of the British polity confirmed by the Glorious Revolution, obviously served as a powerful restraint upon metropolitan behavior toward the colonies.[19]

Nevertheless, by 1700, with the exception of Connecticut and Rhode Island, the executive power in each of the colonies was in the hands of the king's appointed representative who was invested with broad civil, military, and judicial powers.

THE MARYLAND PALATINE

The Maryland colony was intended to provide a haven for English Catholics who had been subject to increasing discrimination and persecution by the Protestant majority in England, particularly after the excommunication of Elizabeth I by the Holy See in 1570. The failed Gunpowder Plot of Guy Fawkes to murder James I on the opening of parliament in 1605, the perceived war of Catholic Spain on Protestant Europe, and the refusal by many Catholics to take the Oath of Supremacy acknowledging the English crown as the rightful head of the church, caused Protestants to view the Catholic minority with deep suspicion and resentment.[20]

George Calvert was from a prominent family with close ties to the Catholic aristocracy. Although his parents were Catholic, Calvert was not and after graduating from Trinity College, Oxford, Calvert served as clerk to the privy council and as a member of parliament from 1609 to 1624. Calvert was made the first Lord Baltimore in 1625, which was also the year of his conversion to Catholicism.

Calvert's relative, the Earl of Warwick, interested him in the opportunities presented by the American colonies. Calvert joined Warwick in the Council for New England and funded a small settlement in Newfoundland with a view toward profiting from the fisheries there. Calvert visited the settlement in 1627 but found the winter too harsh and the soil too barren to support agriculture.

Calvert's interests turned to Virginia and Warwick persuaded him to invest in the Virginia Company. Calvert and his family journeyed to Virginia intending to settle there in 1629, but he was refused entry because, as a Catholic, he refused to take the Oath of Supremacy.[21]

After returning to England, Calvert sought his own charter to found a colony on Chesapeake Bay. As the format for his charter, Calvert drew upon the patent that had been granted to the Bishops of Durham in the fourteenth century for the settlement of the frontier between England and Scotland.[22] The patent created a palatine, which was, Meinig wrote, "a medieval concept designed to give quasi royal powers to a noble proprietor in return for settling and stabilizing some dangerous frontier zone."[23]

Calvert died before receiving the charter, which was granted by Charles I on June 30, 1632 to Calvert's son Cecilius, the second Lord Baltimore.[24]

Under the charter, Baltimore and his heirs were constituted "the true and absolute Lords and Proprietors of the Region," which was to be "erected into a Province" named Maryland. For "the good and happy Government of said Province," Baltimore was granted "free, full and absolute Power . . . to Ordain, Make and Enact Laws, of what kind so ever, according to their sound Discretions whether relating to the Public State of the said Province, or the private Utility of Individuals."[25] This charter "conferred on Lord Baltimore a princely domain,"[26] but it has been noted, however, "The instrument creating Maryland was unique even among proprietary charters in that it represented a type of government and land holding that England itself had largely outgrown."[27]

As extensive and comprehensive as Baltimore's powers were, the charter gave the settlers a voice in the affairs of their colony. All laws were to be enacted "with the advice, assent, and approbation of the freemen," acting through their elected representatives, who were to be summoned by Baltimore "for the framing of laws" at such times "as need shall require."[28] This grant of legislative authority was somewhat ironical in that, "the Stuart kings by no means looked upon the exercise of this right by the people with pleasure and called their representatives together in parliament as seldom as their own needs would allow."[29] Remarkably, there was no provision in the charter that required transmission of colonial laws to the king or providing for his assent.[30]

The charter conferred full executive authority on Baltimore and left to him the determination of how the government of the colony was to be structured.[31] Baltimore was to appoint other officers to fulfill the administrative and judicial needs of the colony. Baltimore was authorized to punish offenders, including by "privation of member or life" as well as to pardon and remit offenders who had been convicted of crimes.[32]

It was left to Baltimore's discretion whether and when to call the legislative assembly into session. In times of emergency, Baltimore himself could adopt ordinances for the "conservation of the peace" and for the "better government of the people" before the legislature could be summoned.[33]

Recalling the mutinies that had troubled the neighboring Virginia colony, Baltimore was empowered to impose martial law, as well as to raise and equip an army to wage war. Anyone refusing to serve would be subject to harsh punishment under martial law.[34]

Also as befit his noble status, and to ensure the loyalty of those around him, Baltimore was given "free and plenary power" to bestow "favors, rewards, and honors" on the citizens of the province as well as to "adorn them whatsoever titles and dignities they shall appoint." In this same connection, Baltimore could "erect parcels of land into manors and there to hold courts," and to "incorporate towns into boroughs, and boroughs into cities with suitable privileges and immunities." Harbors and ports were to be constructed and Baltimore was "to enjoy the taxes and subsidies payable," there from.[35] In this, Maryland was unique, and Baltimore created in excess of sixty manors not including his own and those of his family.[36]

Baltimore's intention that the colony would serve as a refuge for English Catholics foundered because for the most part, it was the Protestants who were drawn to settle in America. Protestants were not inclined to invest in a Catholic venture, however. Baltimore sought to assure would-be investors that all Christian denominations were welcome in Maryland, and eventually twenty-five investors, mostly Catholic, signed on to the venture along with servants, artisans, and laborers, who were predominantly Protestant.[37]

On November 22, 1632, two ships, the *Ark* and the *Dove*, sailed from Portsmouth bound for Maryland. They were joined by another ship en route, the *Dragon*, and together the ships arrived in Maryland on March 13, 1634. In all, approximately two hundred settlers made the voyage.[38]

Baltimore did not accompany the settlers and did not visit the colony before his death in 1675. Instead, Baltimore sent his brother Leonard to serve as governor. Leonard served in that capacity until his death in 1647.

Before Leonard sailed, Baltimore gave him written instructions for the governance of the colony. Among those instructions, Leonard was directed to convene a general assembly of the settlers' representatives. Leonard was also to empanel a council with whom he was to consult.[39]

From the outset, there were controversies over the proprietor's authority. A Virginian, William Claiborne, had obtained a commission from the crown to develop Kent Island as a trading post. Despite Kent Island being situated within the boundaries of Baltimore's grant, Claiborne refused to acknowledge Baltimore's control of the island under the charter. The issue was only resolved in 1635 when Baltimore's forces took the island by force.[40] Despite this defeat, Claiborne continued to challenge Baltimore's authority for the next two decades.

The general assembly met on February 25, 1638, and adopted rules governing its own proceedings. The governor (referred to as the Lieutenant General) was to preside over the assembly. All laws required the assent of "the greater part of the house" and the assent of the governor "in the name of the proprietary." If either the house or the governor withheld their assent, the bill was effectively vetoed.[41]

Baltimore objected to the initiation of legislation by the assembly and in 1638, Baltimore directed Leonard to inform the assembly that the laws that had been adopted to date were void. The freemen ultimately prevailed on Baltimore to reconsider, and in 1639, Baltimore authorized the governor to assent on his behalf to the laws originated by the representatives.[42]

In the meantime, the assembly adopted other legislation in 1638 giving greater definition to the colonial government. A procedure was adopted for the election of representatives to the assembly under which the freemen in each "hundred" were to elect "able and sufficient men" by majority vote to represent them. The assembly was to be convened at least every three years "to consult on the affairs and the public good of this province and for enacting of laws and ordinances for the better government of the same." Twelve or more members of the assembly, of which the governor and the secretary of the province had to be two, could enact legislation, which with the assent of the governor would become law as if the "lord proprietary and all the freemen of this province were personally present and did assent and approve the same."[43]

During this same period, the assembly enacted laws securing religious liberty. The 1638 Act for Church Liberties extended "rights, liberties and immunities safe, whole and inviolable" to the Catholic Church. The Act for the Liberties of the People in that same year reiterated the charter's pledge that Christian inhabitants of the province would enjoy "all such rights, liberties, immunities, privileges and free customs within this Province as any natural born subject of England hath or ought to have or enjoy in the realm of England by force or virtue of the common law or statute law of England."

The act guaranteed that no Christian inhabitant would be imprisoned, exiled, or have property seized except "according to the laws of this province saving to the lord proprietor and his heirs all rights and prerogatives by reason of his dominion and seigniory over this province." These laws were only to remain in effect until the end of the next assembly, however.[44]

The history of the Maryland province was tumultuous, due largely to the hostility between the Catholic settlers in Maryland and the Protestant settlers of Virginia. The 1640s were marred by a two-year period of upheaval known as the "plundering time," during which Protestant Virginians, under Claiborne's leadership, attempted to take control of Kent Island. Additionally, in the anti-Catholic ferment following the impeachment and execution of Charles I, the English parliament threatened to seize the land holdings of the Catholic settlers.[45]

To meet the threat posed by parliament and to counter the charge that Maryland was a haven for "Popery," on April 21, 1649, the general assembly passed the Act Concerning Religion, which declared that no one "professing to believe in Jesus Christ" would in any way be "troubled, molested, discountenanced" because of the exercise of religion in the colony , nor would be "in any way compelled to the belief or exercise of any other religion against his or her consent."[46]

In 1652, the Council of State in England reduced to subjection all of the colonies on Chesapeake Bay, including Virginia and Maryland, and as a consequence, Baltimore lost control of his colony. A commission was sent by parliament to seize the colonies, and among the commissioners were Claiborne and Richard Bennett, the Puritan leader of a settlement on the Severn River. On the strength of that authority, Claiborne and Bennett asserted control over Maryland "in the name of the keepers of liberties in England." Violent conflict resulted between the Puritan and proprietary factions for the next six years.

Claiborne and Bennett were successful in deposing Baltimore's governor, William Stone (a Protestant) and in his place installed their own appointee, William Fuller, intending to establish a Puritan commonwealth patterned after Massachusetts Bay, in which Catholics and Anglicans would be excluded. On instructions from Claiborne and Bennett, governor Fuller called for a meeting of the general assembly, taking care that no Catholic was elected as a representative. The assembly met on October 20, 1654, and as its first action, the assembly repudiated the Act Concerning Religion and in its place, the assembly announced that "none who profess and exercise the Popish religion . . . can be protected in this province.[47]

In England, however, Oliver Cromwell, the Lord Protector, had little sympathy for the radical Puritans in Maryland, and after Baltimore pressed his claim with Cromwell, the Committee of Trade in England ordered that the Act Concerning Religion be restored. Finally, on November 30, 1657, an agreement was reached, following the intervention of Edward Diggs, governor of Virginia, and Baltimore's patent for the colony was again secured.[48]

By this time, the assembly had divided itself into two houses. In 1650, the three-member council that Baltimore had formed in 1637 to advise the governor became the upper chamber while the elected assembly remained the lower chamber. In time, the number of councilors increased and after Baltimore's son Charles (who became the third Lord Baltimore following his father's death in 1675) became governor in 1661, the membership of the upper house, all of whom were manor lords, grew to fifteen and were known either as the Council of State or the privy council.[49]

In the years following the restoration of Charles II, tensions grew between the Protestant majority and the favored Catholic elite. In 1669, the assembly adopted a statement of grievances complaining of the proprietor's arbitrary vetoing of legislation and levying of taxes and fees without their consent. Charles responded by charging the assembly with mutiny and by limiting the right to vote. Charles also reduced the number of representatives from each county.[50]

Distrust of the Catholic proprietary government continued to build, aggravated by Bacon's Rebellion led by Nathaniel Bacon in Virginia in 1676 and fears of a Catholic takeover of the English government. Coinciding with these events was a decline in the price of tobacco, a cash crop in Maryland as in Virginia. In 1682, the assembly insisted on being allowed to conduct their affairs as the House of Commons did in England. Baltimore replied that he was the absolute authority in the colony and the colonists enjoyed only the rights that he conferred on them.

In 1684, Baltimore was compelled by events to return to England to answer charges that he had defrauded the royal customs and to defend his interests in a border dispute with the neighboring proprietary in Pennsylvania. Although Baltimore planned to remain in England for only a few months, he never returned to Maryland.[51]

On October 31, 1684, the man that Baltimore had left to oversee the colony, George Talbot, murdered Charles Rousby, the royal tax collector. Talbot then fled his post. At the request of James II, *quo warranto* proceedings were commenced to vacate Baltimore's charter.

Conditions remained volatile in the colony and in April 1689, Baltimore decided against calling a general assembly. By then, William and Mary had succeeded James II to the throne of England, but Baltimore did not declare his loyalty. In mid-July 1689, John Coode, a former militia officer whom Baltimore had charged in 1680 with mutiny and sedition (Coode was acquitted), led a force against the capital. After the assembly affirmed the colony's loyalty to William and Mary and expressed solidarity with England to "stop Popery," Coode relinquished his temporary control to a committee that Coode led.

In 1690, Coode carried another statement of grievances and charges to England, where they were favorably received. In 1691, the Lords of Trade and Plantations concluded that governmental authority over Maryland should be returned to the crown. Baltimore was allowed to retain his property interests in the colony, however, and in 1715, the proprietary was restored to the Calvert family.[52]

THE PROPRIETARY COLONIES OF THE RESTORATION

The proprietary colonies of the mid-Atlantic: New York, New Jersey (East and West), Pennsylvania, Delaware (which broke away from Pennsylvania in 1701), and the Carolinas have been referred to as the "Restoration Colonies," and their establishment in the years following the restoration of Charles II to the English throne has been said to reflect a renewal of England's interest in the colonization of North America.[53]

Unlike the colonies of Virginia, New England, and Maryland, which were populated by settlers who had come directly from England, the settlers of the mid-Atlantic colonies came primarily from other colonies.[54] New York had an established Dutch population that predated the colony's acquisition by the British. Thus, the development of the governing structures of the colonies were shaped to a great extent by the expectations of the colonists based on their previous colonial experiences, including guarantees of religious and political rights.[55] The governance of the colonies was also shaped to a significant extent by the legacy of the English Civil War.[56]

The Carolina Palatine

A second palatine was created by Charles II in the territory of what are now the Carolinas and Georgia. Although the powers conferred under the royal grant were the same as those of Lord Baltimore, unlike the Maryland palatinate, those powers were conferred on a consortium of nobles led by Sir John Colleton, and this diffusion of powers profoundly affected the society that emerged in the Carolinas.

Colleton was a successful planter in Barbados to which he, a royalist, had repaired following the execution of Charles I. By the beginning of the 1660s, Colleton was looking for new entrepreneurial opportunities. When Charles II was restored to the throne, Colleton returned to England with the hope of reward for his loyalty to the crown. With the endorsement of Lord Berkeley, under whom Colleton had served in the loyalist army during the civil war, Colleton was knighted and appointed to the Council for Plantations.[57]

Colleton's service on the council had brought him into contact with Sir William Berkeley (Lord Berkeley's brother), the former governor of Virginia; Sir Anthony Ashley Cooper (later Lord Cooper), another Barbados planter who was to become Chancellor of the Exchequer; Edward Hyde, Earl of Clarendon; and Sir George Carteret. When, during this time, Colleton formulated his plans for a colony in Carolina, he turned to these colleagues, as well as to his relative, George Monck, Duke of Albemarle, and to William, Earl of Craven. Together, they petitioned for a royal charter to found a proprietary colony in Carolina, which was granted on March 24, 1663.[58] The charter was modeled after the grant made to Lord Baltimore for the Maryland proprietary.[59]

The charter granted to the eight proprietors the territory generally encompassing North Carolina, South Carolina, and Georgia.[60] This territory was enlarged in a second charter granted on June 30, 1665, to include part of Spanish Florida and all of Albemarle Sound (including a settlement of Virginia colonists). The territory was to extend from the Atlantic Ocean to the "South Seas."[61]

Under this charter, as in Maryland, the proprietors were granted virtually absolute governmental powers over their territory, "To have, use, exercise and enjoy, and in as ample manner as any Bishop of Durham in our Kingdom of England, ever heretofore have held, used or enjoyed, or of right ought or could have, use or enjoy," as the "true and absolute lords proprietors of the country aforesaid."[62] As Story noted, "The grantees were created absolute Lords Proprietors, saving the faith, allegiance, and supreme dominion of the crown, and invested with as ample rights and jurisdictions as the Bishop of Durham possessed in his palatine diocese."[63]

The territory was declared to be the Province of Carolina and "for the good and happy government of the said province," the proprietors were empowered "to ordain, make, enact, and under their seals to publish any laws whatsoever, either appertaining to the public state of the said province, or to the private utility of particular persons, according to their best discretions." However, also like Maryland, the proprietors' legislative authority was subject to "the advice, assent and approbation of the freemen of the said province, or of the greater part of them, or of their delegates or deputies."[64] The coexistence of a democratic assembly and the autocratic proprietary was intrinsically contradictory and for that reason, "The history of the Carolina region throughout the proprietorship and for many years afterward shows a struggle between a democratic assembly representing the people and an appointed governor nearly always representing an outside authority."[65] Also, although the charter granted to the proprietors "full power and authority from time to time to make and ordain fit and wholesome orders and ordinances," such orders and ordinances were to be "reasonable, and not repugnant or contrary, but as near as may be, agreeable to the laws and statutes of this our Kingdom of England."[66]

The proprietors were invested with the judicial power of the province. They were to establish "justices unto courts, sessions and forms of judicature and manners of proceedings therein do belong" and "to appoint and establish any judges or justices, magistrates or officers whatsoever, within the said province, at sea or land." In furtherance of their judicial power, the proprietors could exercise penal jurisdiction, including capital punishment. Here again, however, those powers were subject also to the constraint of being "consonant to reason, and as near as may be conveniently, agreeable to the laws and customs of this our Kingdom of England,"[67] In addition to their authority to raise and equip an armed force, to construct fortifications and to make war, the proprietors could impose martial law, "in case of rebellion, tumult, or sedition."[68]

The proprietors were given plenary authority over the disposition of land within the territory, including the incorporation of cities, boroughs, towns, and villages. Like the palatine of Maryland, the Carolina proprietors were given "full power and authority" to confer "marks of favor and titles of honor," to establish manors, and "to have and to hold a court baron." The proprietors could undertake the construction of "churches, chapels and oratories," and "erect and constitute . . . such and so many seaports, harbors, creeks and other places, for the discharge and unloading of merchandises."[69]

The charter secured certain individual rights of the settlers. As in previous charters, the settlers were to enjoy generally "all liberties, franchises and privileges of this our kingdom of England." However, the charter also made specific provision for "indulgencies and dispensations" to be granted by the proprietors to those inhabitants of the province who "cannot in their private opinions, conform to the public exercise of religion, according to the liturgy, form and ceremonies of the Church of England, or take and subscribe the oaths and articles, made and established in that behalf." This toleration of dissent, however, was predicated on "fidelity, loyalty, obedience" to the crown, obedience to civil and ecclesiastical laws, and abstention from disturbing the peace or reproach of the church's liturgy and ceremonies.[70]

Lastly, the charter sought to avoid conflict between the new province and the other established colonies, as had been the case between Maryland and Virginia. The broad territorial grant included the fledging settlement of Virginians on Albemarle Sound. But additionally, the charter specifically provided that Carolina was not to be "held or reputed a member or part of any colony whatsoever in America, or elsewhere, now transported or made, or hereafter to be transported or made . . . but be absolutely separated and divided from the same."[71]

Six months after receiving their charter, the proprietors issued "A Declaration and Proposals of the Lord Proprietor of Carolina," on August 25, 1663. In that document, the proprietors established the form of government for the province and granted a degree of autonomy to the settlers in matters of their own governance.[72]

The administration of the colony was to be in the hands of a governor and council. The proprietors directed those who were to undertake the first settlement of the province (which was to be on the Charles River near Cape Fear) to select thirteen people from among whom the proprietors would select one to be the governor (for a term of three years) and six others to serve as the governor's council. The remaining six were to be alternates in the event of death or removal of a councilor (in like fashion, a councilor was to succeed to the governorship should the governor die or be removed prior to fulfilling his term). Succeeding governments were to consist of thirteen persons chosen by the freeholders (at least four of whom were to have been in the government at the time of their election) from whom, again, the proprietors would select the governor and council.[73]

The declaration further provided that a majority of the freeholders or their elected representatives were empowered to "make their own laws," with the "advice and consent of the governor and council." These laws were not to be contrary to the laws of England and were to be presented to the proprietors for ratification within one year of enactment.[74]

The proprietors' declaration also established a scheme under which land was to be allocated during the first five years of the settlement to settlers and to their male and female servants after the period of their indenture had expired. Provision was made for the collection of public moneys for the construction of courthouses and other public buildings and for the conscription of "one armed man . . . for every fifty acres" granted pursuant to the declaration.[75]

Lastly, the declaration granted "freedom and liberty of conscience in all religious or spiritual things," in "as ample manner" as the settlers "shall desire."[76]

Greater detail concerning the structure of government was provided by the proprietors in their Concessions and Agreements of the Proprietors of Carolina with the Prospective Settlers, which they issued on January 7, 1664. In the Concessions and Agreements, the proprietors enumerated certain powers of the assemblies of the northern and southern counties as well as the powers of the governor and council.

The assembly in each county was to "enact and make all such laws, acts and constitutions as shall be necessary for the well government of the county," subject to the requirement that such acts be "consonant and consistent" with the laws of England. The assembly was to constitute judicial courts; levy taxes and assessments on lands other than the lands owned by the proprietors; erect baronies and manors; raise and train armies and erect fortifications; incorporate cities, boroughs, towns and villages; confer citizenship on qualified persons coming into the colony; and to alot land "to every head, free servant, male and female."

The governor was to choose between six and twelve councilors with whose advice and consent he was to govern. He was also to appoint other government officers who would serve at the pleasure of the proprietors. With the council, the governor was to appoint judges and oversee the judiciary; deploy military forces; reprieve, pardon or execute penal sentences in criminal cases; conduct elections in the event of the death or removal of an elected member of the assembly; and to "make warrants and seal grants of land" according to the advice of the assembly. The governor and council were also authorized to "act and do all other thing or things that may conduce to the safety, peace and well government of the said counties" that were not otherwise contrary to law.

The Concessions and Agreements gave specific assurance with regard to the practice of religion in the colony that "no person . . . at any time shall be in any ways molested, punished, disquieted or called in question for any differences in opinion or practice in matters of religious concernment who do not actually disturb the peace."[77]

The early years of the colony were not a success. The settlement established by immigrants from New England at the mouth of the Cape Fear River was abandoned after several months. In 1665, the proprietors granted the right to settle on the river to a group of adventurers from Barbados, but they too abandoned their efforts at settlement in 1667.[78] Also at this time, settlers from Virginia, who had migrated to the northern shore of Albemarle Sound over the proceeding ten years, chose William Drummond in October 1664 to be the governor of their separate Province of Albemarle, which would later become the colony of North Carolina.[79]

Anthony Ashley Cooper (later Earl of Shaftsbury) assumed control of the proprietors on April 26, 1669. At his urging, the proprietors increased their financial commitment to Carolina, and by August 1669, a fleet of three ships carrying more than one hundred settlers prepared to sail from England.[80]

It was at this time that Cooper wrote the Fundamental Constitution of Carolina for the governance of the new colony.[81] Cooper was assisted in this effort by John Locke, Enlightenment political philosopher, who was Cooper's personal physician and confidant.[82] Locke is believed to have been the principal author, however.[83]

The Fundamental Constitutions was an attempt to establish what has been described as "a variant form of manorial system" in the palatine colony.[84] To that end, the Fundamental Constitutions set up a pyramid landholding structure divided into two provinces: Clarendon in the south (which would become South Carolina) and Albemarle in the north (which would become North Carolina). Under this system, each proprietor owned twelve thousand acres in each county, landgraves were to receive four baronies of twelve thousand acres each, and two caciques would each be given two baronies. The landgraves and caciques were to constitute the nobility. There were also to be lords of the manor, each of whom would receive between three thousand and twelve thousand acres of land. The remainder of the land (approximately 60 percent of the colony) was to be allotted to freeholders.[85]

The Fundamental Constitutions established an executive, legislative, and judicial framework for the colony's government. A series of courts, usually comprised of a proprietor and six councilors, exercised the executive functions of the colony.[86] The judicial power of the colony was also exercised by a hierarchy of proprietary and nonproprietary courts.[87]

A unicameral parliament was established that included the proprietors, other nobles (landgraves and caciques), and one freeholder from each of the precincts. The members were to "sit together in one room and have every member one vote." However, all legislation was subject to review by the Grand Council, composed of the eight proprietors and forty-two councilors of the proprietary courts. The consent of the palatine and three of the proprietors was required for an enactment of the parliament to become law.[88]

The Fundamental Constitutions made provision for local governments as well.[89]

A degree of religious pluralism was allowed, although no one could be a freeman who did not acknowledge that "God is publicly and solemnly to be worshipped" and no one older than the age of seventeen years who was not a member church could enjoy the benefit of law. Although the Church of England was the official church and received public support, seven or more people could establish a church so long as they recognized the existence of God who was to be publicly worshipped and that there was "a duty to bear witness to the truth." Slaves were entitled to be church members.[90]

Otherwise, the Fundamental Constitutions provided that no one could be excluded from the colony on grounds of religious belief, "that civil peace may be maintained amidst diversity of opinions, and our agreement and compact with all men may be duly and faithfully observed" (and also that "by having an opportunity of acquainting themselves with the truth and reasonableness of its doctrines" those not belonging to the Church of England might "be won over to embrace and unfeignedly receive the truth"). It was further provided that "no man shall use any reproachful, reviling or abusive language against any religion," and that "No person whatsoever shall disturb, molest, or persecute another for his speculative opinions in religion, or his way of worship."[91]

It has been said that the Fundamental Constitutions represented Cooper's version of a "balance of government," between "aristocracy and democracy."[92] Not everyone shares this view, however.[93] In all events, the constitution proved to be largely aspirational and was never fully implemented in the colony.[94]

Nevertheless, the Fundamental Constitutions represented the attempt to set forth a coherent scheme of government in which executive, judicial, and legislative authorities were distributed in a single written document setting forth the enumerated powers of the various governmental bodies. The ultimate failure of the Fundamental Constitutions was in many ways a cautionary lesson that the constitution of government must ultimately arise from the experience of the governed, rather than being imposed from without by a distant and unengaged power. As Story wrote,

> It is easy to perceive, that it was ill adapted to the feelings, wants, and the opinions of the colonists. The introduction of it, therefore, was resisted by the people, as much as it could be; and indeed, in some respects it was found impracticable. Public dissatisfaction increased; and after a few years' experience of its ill arrangements, and its mischievous tendency, the proprietaries, upon application of the people, (in 1639) abrogated the constitution and restored the ancient form of government.[95]

Ultimately, the proprietors' plan proved to be unworkable. The enterprise of the landgrave or cacique, a central feature of the plan, was beyond the means of most grantees. Even when the freemen were provided a head right of fifty acres in exchange for a quitrent of one penny per acre, most settlers resisted paying even so modest an amount.[96]

South Carolina

The internal affairs of the colony came to be dominated by a group of Barbadian expatriates who settled along Goose Creek, a tributary of the Cooper River. Known as the "Goose Creek Men," they formed the nucleus of the opposition to the authority of the lords proprietors and their policy of religious toleration.[97]

Between 1674 and 1682, the colonists regularly ignored the proprietors' instructions.[98] In England, Lord Cooper was imprisoned in the Tower of London in 1682 on charges of treason for his opposition to Charles II. Cooper was allowed to escape from his imprisonment and he fled to Amsterdam where he died.[99]

In 1687, the Goose Creek Men challenged the legality of the government of James Colleton (brother of the lord proprietor, Sir Peter Colleton) who had been appointed provincial governor after the lords proprietors repudiated the Fundamental Constitutions of 1669 (in favor of an unratified amendment of the Fundamental Constitutions in 1682). Parliament passed a "Charter Bill" contending that only the royal charter of 1665 was the legitimate basis of government, thereby denying the constitutionality of the proprietors' subsequent actions. The bill was rejected by the Grand Council and Colleton refused to call the colonial parliament into session again.[100]

After war broke out between England and France, Governor Colleton declared martial law on February 26, 1690. The opposition of the Goose

Creek Men became open and they supported the claim of Seth Sothel who had purchased the Clarendon proprietary interest and had served as governor of Albemarle until the assembly had forced him to leave for corruption and malfeasance. Sothel became governor of the southern colony in 1690.[101]

Parliament was reconvened in 1690. Among the first actions of the parliament was the barring of Colleton and four other proprietary men from holding public office. The support of the proprietors was withdrawn when they learned of the banishment of Colleton (even though the proprietors apparently had agreed that martial law was not warranted) and Sothel was removed as governor in November 1691. What remained of the Fundamental Constitutions was also suspended and several significant changes were made in the governmental structure.

In the place of the council comprised of the governor, deputies, and five elected members, the proprietors appointed a council of only deputies.[102] The elected representatives of the freemen in the parliament comprised a separate chamber making the parliament a bicameral legislature.[103]

Thereafter, the introduction of rice as a staple cash crop, together with the suppression of pirate activity and the regularization of the trade with the native peoples, produced a period of economic prosperity and political stability. During this time, the "Commons House" in the provincial parliament grew in stature as the forum for the grievances and aspirations of the settlers. The commons assumed the authority to initiate legislation (a prerogative that was formally accepted by the proprietors in the revision of the Fundamental Constitutions issued in 1698). By the end of the seventeenth century, the commons had secured to itself the right to determine its own membership (as evidenced by the refusal to seat the sheriff of Colleton County on the grounds that its rules prohibited sheriffs from standing for election to the assembly).[104]

There was a resumption of factionalism in the eighteenth century. This factionalism centered on conflicts between adherents of the Church of England and the dissenters who had been drawn to Carolina by the promise of religious tolerance.[105]

Ultimately, the authority of the proprietors was overthrown. In part this was due to the proprietors' inability to prevent abuses in the trade with the native peoples, which led to a series of uprisings. Notably, the Yamasee War came close to wrecking the colony both physically and financially and gave rise to the perception that the proprietors were incapable of supporting the colonists in their defense.

As early as 1715, there was an expressed sentiment that the colony should be taken out of the hands of the proprietors and remanded to the direct control of the crown. The commons became the principal organ of this sentiment, and in 1716 and 1717, petitions were sent by the commons to the crown remonstrating against the proprietors. In an irony of history, the petitioners relied on the writings of John Locke, to the effect that the proprietors had breached their social contract with the settlers by endangering them and their property to justify the dissolution of the proprietary government that Locke had played a major part in creating. The proprietors dismissed these sentiments as being nothing more than the "Business of Faction and Party."[106]

By December 1719, the colony was in open rebellion against the proprietors. The commons styled itself a "Convention delegated by the People, to prevent the utter Ruin of this Government, if not the Loss of the Province, until His Majesty's Pleasure be known." The commons petitioned the Board of Trade to be made a royal colony and elected a provisional governor to assume control of the government from the proprietors. When the governor appointed by the proprietors attempted to dismiss the militia, which had assembled on December 21, they refused.[107]

The Board of Trade recommended that the privy council assume responsibility for Carolina and on August 11, 1720, the council did so. The privy council appointed Francis Nicholson, who had served as governor of Maryland, New York, Nova Scotia, and Virginia, as the first royal governor.[108] Although control of the Carolina colony in fact had passed to the crown, it was not until the financial terms had been resolved that the charter was ultimately surrendered in 1729.[109]

North Carolina

The course of the Albemarle colony, known after 1691 as North Carolina, ran somewhat differently. Although subject to the Fundamental Constitutions and expected to adhere to its principles, little attention was paid by the Carolina proprietors to North Carolina. Nevertheless, what involvement by the proprietors there was in the affairs of the colony was not welcomed by the inhabitants.[110]

Ignored by the proprietors, largely bereft of religious institutions, and reliant on subsistence farming, principally of tobacco and corn, life in the North Carolina colony was hard scrabble.[111] Enforcement of the Navigation Acts threatened to restrict trade with New England, and when one of the oldest, preproprietary settlers, George Durant, and a Boston trader, Zachariah Gilliam, were arrested for transporting a cargo of goods to be exchanged for North Carolina tobacco, there was a popular revolt resulting in a revolutionary government being established. Eventually, peace was restored and Durant was appointed governor.[112]

Durant was succeeded by Seth Sothel who in six years as governor appears to have alienated both the proprietors and the colonists. Sothel was charged by the former with having disregarded the Fundamental Constitutions and by the latter with arbitrary conduct toward individuals. As a consequence of his having imprisoned Durant and others, a group of insurgents rose up against Sothel and imprisoned him until he renounced the government. The proprietors immediately relieved Sothel of his duties, and after several months, Sothel left Albemarle for South Carolina were he attempted to resume the governorship. He was expelled from South Carolina a year later in 1691.[113]

Albemarle became the independent proprietary colony of North Carolina in 1691. In 1710, North Carolina attained equivalent stature with South Carolina when the proprietors appointed Edward Hyde as governor of the independent colony. Unfortunately, Hyde's weakness as an administrator and his alignment with the Anglican Church (against the dissenters) led to another insurrection and an attempt to overthrow his government by force. Although the uprising was put down by a show of armed force from Virginia, the charges against the insurgents were not sustained by the palatine court in England.[114]

The civil disorder occasioned by the rebellion coupled with war with the Tuscarora and frequent outbreaks of fever caused an even greater loss of interest on the part of the proprietors in the North Carolina colony. Nevertheless, because there was no popular demand for conversion to a crown colony once peace had been restored, North Carolina continued as a proprietary colony even after control of South Carolina had been taken over by the privy council.

However, after 1718, North Carolina was effectively under the control of the crown. The financial settlement reached with the proprietors extinguished their interest in North Carolina as well, and thus, North Carolina became a royal colony in 1729.[115]

The New York Palatine

The Dutch first came to what would become the New York Colony in 1609, when the English explorer, Henry Hudson, sailed to present-day Albany in search of a northwest passage on behalf of the Dutch East India Company. The Dutch established their first trading post there in 1613. Eventually, Dutch trading interests in North America would extend from Cape Cod on Massachusetts Bay to Cape Henlopen on Delaware Bay, reflecting the Dutch strategy of focusing on trade rather than settlement.[116]

The impending war with Spain in 1620 focused Dutch attention on the strategic value of fortified settlements. A small group under the sponsorship of the Dutch West India Company settled Fort Nassau, near what is now Philadelphia, while others settled first on Governors Island at the mouth of the Hudson River and in 1625, at New Amsterdam on Manhattan Island. In keeping with Dutch policy, the land for the settlements was acquired from the native peoples by purchase rather than conquest.[117]

Like the Virginia Company, settlers came to the colony effectively as servants of the company for a period of seven years. Governing authority was in the hands of the company, with little, if any, participation by the settlers. However, unlike the Virginia enterprise, the Dutch settlers were expected only to grow food for sale to the company, and thus, the settlements were self-sufficient virtually from the beginning.[118]

The appointment of Peter Stuyvesant in 1646 led to changes in the governance of the colony. Although he was criticized for being autocratic, Stuyvesant, albeit briefly, allowed elected representatives of the settlers to advise concerning taxes. Of greater significance, in 1652, New Amsterdam became a municipality with local courts that were subordinate to the Director General and his council.[119]

In contrast to the English colonies of the time, New Amsterdam and the other Dutch settlements were pluralistic societies. Drawn by greater religious tolerance, Germans, French Huguenots, English Quakers, New England Protestants, and Scandinavians immigrated to North America along with the Dutch.[120] However, because these settlements were neither socially cohesive nor fiscally robust, they were vulnerable to their English rivals.[121]

Tensions between the Dutch and the English had grown from their mutual interests along the Connecticut River and on Long Island, where the New Haven Colony had established settlements at Southold and Southampton. Although nominally at peace after the 1650 Treaty at Hartford, the larger strategic rivalries of England and Holland only aggravated those tensions slightly below the surface in America.[122]

In January 1664, the Council for Plantations in England issued a report endorsing the seizure of the Dutch colony of New Amsterdam. Four months later, the king made his intentions known. Richard Nicholls, who had been one of the royal commissioners sent to investigate conditions in New England, led a force of four hundred troops, several frigates and a bomb vessel, against the New Amsterdam settlement. Nicholls arrived at New Amsterdam on August 18, 1664, where he was joined by another force from Connecticut under the command of John Winthrop, Jr. Although Stuyvesant urged the colonists to resist the British, because Stuyvesant did not enjoy either the political or financial support of the burghers, New Amsterdam surrendered to the British on August 26. The British then proceeded to capture the Dutch trading posts in what would become New Jersey and Delaware.[123]

Nicholls named the captured territory New York in honor of the Duke of York, upon whom the charter for the territory had been conferred previously by his brother Charles II on March 12, 1664. The charter gave York "full and absolute power and authority to correct, punish, govern, and rule the territory" extending from northern New England and Canada to Delaware Bay. This charter has been called "the briefest and most hastily executed of all the seventeenth century colonial charters," as well as having been the only charter issued to a member of the royal family and heir to the throne.[124] The grant of territory was unique in that "The lands were widely scattered, the boundaries almost grotesque in their contours, and the territory without symmetry or uniformity of race, religion, or products of the soil."[125]

Like Lord Baltimore in Maryland, York was given absolute legislative authority to "make, ordain and establish all manner of laws, directions, instructions, forms, ceremonies of government and majesty fit and necessary for and concerning the government of the territories," subject only to the qualification that those laws be "agreeable" to the laws of England. York was also empowered to establish administrative offices, including a governor, and other officers, ministers, deputies, and commissioners as "shall seem good."

The charter also conferred judicial jurisdiction over all civil and criminal cases, subject to the right to appeal any judgment or sentence to the king. In cases of mutiny or insurrection, York was to impose martial law and he was authorized to defend the colony by force of arms.[126]

York's relationship with the colony has been described as "authoritarian permissiveness." On the one hand, the powers under the charter were complete, and it has been noted that York "yielded concessions only grudgingly and slowly." On the other hand, York was an absentee proprietor, never visiting the colony, and as a consequence, York was not able to exercise personal influence over the colony.[127]

Nicholls had been named deputy governor by York on April 2, 1664, before the territory had been secured from the Dutch. Shortly after taking office, Nicholls promulgated an extensive compendium of laws for the regulation of the colony, which Nicholls had drawn from the various bodies of law in the New England colonies. This code, which came to be known as the "Duke's Laws," was written without consultation of the settlers to whom the laws applied and has been said to have been "the most authoritarian form of colonial rule in Anglo-America." Thus, it has been said in light of the Duke's Laws that "James had decided to create an absolutist government in his colony."[128]

Like the foundational codes in New England, the Duke's Laws defined a variety of criminal offenses; established civil and criminal judicial proceedings; regulated commerce with the native peoples; provided for collection of revenues to defray the costs of the colony and the church; designated the administrative offices for the colony; set forth the structure of local governments; set down rules for the maintenance of the church, including the qualification of ministers; required the recording of births, marriages, and deaths; and provided for the common defense of the colony.[129]

Unlike the Maryland proprietary, York's charter made no provision for participation by the free settlers in the legislative process. However, shortly after the Dutch surrender, Nicholls stated his intention to summon representatives of the settlers "to propose and give their advice in all matters tending to the peace and benefit of Long Island." In February 1665, Nicholls published a letter to the settlers on Long Island in which Nicholls called for a meeting of representatives who were to be elected by a majority of the freemen. This meeting was held in Hempstead, on Long Island, on March 1, 1665, but because the charter did not provide for such an assembly, Nicholls simply presented the Duke's Laws to the delegates at the meeting.[130]

Nicholls was succeeded by Major Edmund Andros. In 1678, Andros attempted to consolidate his control over the colony and to raise revenue by ordering the ports of Southampton and Southold to be closed to foreign trade and requiring that all overseas trade had to pass through New York City, where the merchants paid substantial fees for their monopoly and trading privileges. The colonists' reaction was bitter, particularly among the merchants in the Long Island and Albany settlements. As a consequence, in 1680, merchants refused to pay import duties and took Andros's collector of customs to court. A grand jury in the colony demanded that York put the colonists "upon equal ground with our fellow Brethren and subjects of the realm of England," meaning that the colonists should be represented in a legislative assembly.[131]

Faced with the revolt of the merchants and the loss of revenue, York relented. York's agreement was conditional however, on the settlers' pledge of support and their promise to repay the revenue lost since the controversy began.[132]

Under a newly appointed governor, Thomas Dugan, an assembly of seventeen representatives was convened on October 17, 1683. Although other legislation was enacted during that legislative session, by far the most significant was the Charter of Franchises and Liberties.[133]

The charter incorporated civil rights secured for Englishmen in Magna Carta, the Confirmation of Charters, the Petition of Right, and the Navigation Acts.[134] The framework of government in the charter was similar (although different in several material respects) to those that had developed elsewhere in the colonies.

The "Supreme Legislative Authority," conferred on York by the charter of 1664 was to "forever be and reside in a governor, council and the people met in General Assembly," which was to be the sole legislative body of the colony. Executive power was to be exercised by the governor with the advice and consent of at least four members of the governor's appointed council.[135]

The general assembly was to meet at least every three years at times set by the representatives. Representation in the assembly was to be proportional and representatives were to be elected by a majority vote of the freeholders in each city and county. The assembly was to be the sole judge of the qualifications of its members (the assembly had the authority to "purge their house"). As would be provided in the federal Constitution, members of the assembly were to be immune from arrest while going to or coming from sessions of the assembly.[136]

Legislation required the assent of the governor and council and once given, legislative acts were to be "Esteemed and accounted the laws of the province," until repealed by the governor, council, and assembly. The assessment of taxes and other charges required the consent of the governor, council, and assembly as well.[137]

The charter guaranteed certain civil liberties to the colonists. These liberties included the right to indictment by a grand jury, due process, trial by jury, bail, inheritance, and the devise of property (including the rights of dower and coverture); the prohibition against quartering the military in private homes during peacetime; and freedom of conscience in the exercise of religion.[138]

The Charter of Franchises and Liberties was conveyed to England in December 1683 and received York's seal on October 4, 1684. However, before the charter was returned to New York, Charles II died and was succeeded by James II, his brother and the former Duke of York. As a consequence, the New York colony was transmogrified from a ducal proprietary to a royal colony, and as king, James rejected the charter that he had approved as duke, apparently on the recommendation of the Lords of Trade that the colonies, including the New York proprietary, be brought under closer royal control. The privy council formally disallowed the charter in May 1686.[139]

The discontent of the English settlers was reignited by the revocation of the Charter of Franchises and Liberties. Then, in 1688, it was announced that New York was to be annexed to New England, and although a lieutenant governor and council would govern New York separately, the New York officials would be answerable to the governor of New England, Edmund Andros, in Boston.

When news arrived of the abdication of James II and the uprising in Boston that culminated in the arrest of Andros, the English settlers of Long Island joined the Dutch population of Queens and Westchester Counties and rose up in support of William and Mary. In May, the city militia repudiated the authority of its commander after Colonel Francis Nicholson, the Lieutenant Governor appointed in 1688 to bring order to the colony, was reported to have said that he would burn New York City rather than tolerate further insubordination. Nicholson was recalled to England, and the colony proclaimed its loyalty to William and Mary on June 3, 1689.

Although the rebellion was ultimately unsuccessful and its leaders, Joseph Leisler and Jacob Milbourne, were hanged for treason, the compromise that brought the conflict to a close ended the proposal of merging New York into the Dominion of New England and assured that New York would continue to have a representative assembly. However, because New York did not have a long tradition of elected assemblies and because the population remained divided, royal governors were able to exploit the lack of unity to undermine the assembly's effectiveness.[140]

THE NEW JERSEY PROPRIETARIES

On June 24, 1664, just three months after he had received the royal patent from his brother, Charles II, the Duke of York conveyed the land bordered by the Hudson and Delaware Rivers as far south as Cape May to Lord Berkeley and Sir George Carteret, who had been allies and supporters of York during his exile following the execution of his father.[141] This conveyance was accomplished by a "lease and release," which conferred the "royalties, profits, commodities and hereditaments . . . in as fully and ample manner as the same is granted to the said Duke of York by the before-cited Letters Patents."[142] The colony was named New Jersey in honor of Carteret's birthplace, the Isle of Jersey.[143] However, because their grant was not from the crown, there has been a question historically whether the proprietors of the New Jersey colony had the legal rights of government.[144] For, although Berkeley and Cateret assumed they had been granted palatine rights, in fact, the 1664 charter conferred only rights to the soil, but it did not specifically bestow rights of government. In any event, York could not delegate powers that belonged exclusively to the crown.[145]

The fundamental plan of the government of the colony was laid out in the Concession and Agreements of the Lords Proprietors.[146] Like the Concession and Agreements of the Carolina proprietors, the plan put forward by Berkeley and Carteret provided for a governor and a council of at least six but not more than twelve members with whose advice and consent he was to govern. There was also to be a secretary of the colony (who was to keep "fair books of all public affairs," including conveyances and leases of land) and a surveyor general (who was to "survey, lay out and bound all such lands as shall be granted from the lords to the planters" and who was to certify such surveys to the secretary).[147]

Provision was made for the establishment of a general assembly of freemen, and as soon as "parishes, divisions, tribes and other distinctions are made," there were to be annual elections of representatives. This general assembly was to join the governor and council "for the making of such laws, ordinances and constitutions as shall be necessary for the present good and welfare of the said Province."[148]

Broad powers were conferred on the assembly "to enact, constitute and ordain all such . . . laws and constitutions as shall or may be necessary for the good, prosperity and settlement of the said Province." Such legislation, however, was subject to the limitations that they be "agreeable" to English law and that they were not contrary to the interests of the Lords Proprietors or "repugnant" to the "liberty of conscience" specifically provided for the in the Concession and Agreements. All laws enacted by the assembly had to be confirmed by the proprietors before becoming law.[149]

The Concession and Agreements directed the assembly to constitute judicial courts with specified powers and jurisdiction. Similarly, in accordance with the provisions securing the liberty of conscience in religious worship, the assembly was authorized "to constitute and appoint such and so many ministers or preachers as they shall think fit."[150]

The assembly had the exclusive authority "to lay equal taxes and assessments . . . to raise moneys or goods upon lands," except the lands of the proprietors. These revenue measures were to be adopted "as oft as necessary shall require" and to be "in such manner as to them shall seem most equal and easy for the said inhabitants."[151]

The assembly was given jurisdiction over the political division of land. The assembly was to erect "such and so many manors, with their necessary courts, jurisdictions, freedoms, and privileges, as to them shall be meet and convenient." The assembly was also to divide the colony into "hundreds, parishes, tribes or other such divisions and districts, as they shall think fit." Allotments of land "to every head, free or servant, male or female" were to be made according to rules adopted by the assembly.[152]

Further, the assembly was granted broad authority over the affairs of the colony. Legislation was to be adopted providing for the defense of the colony, including the erection and provisioning of fortifications. When necessary, there was to be legislation suppressing mutinies and rebellions and legislation for making war "with all Indians, strangers, and foreigners" on land and sea.[153]

The governor and council were to oversee "all ministers and officers civil and military." They were also to appoint judges and other members and officers of the courts. In the event of a criminal conviction, the governor and council were authorized to grant reprieves of sentences until the lords proprietors had determined the appeal, if any.[154]

Lastly, the governor was given command of the colony's armed forces (including the conscription of freeholders and non-freeholders alike) and with the council was to prosecute war and to suppress rebellion. The governor and council were authorized to order elections for the replacement of representatives who died or were removed and they were authorized to affix the seal to grants of land according to the advice of the general assembly.[155]

The 1664 Concession and Agreements served as the constitution for the government of New Jersey during the entire proprietary period. Attracted by the liberal provisions respecting self-government and freedom of conscience, the colony was populated by émigrés from England, Finland, Holland, Sweden, and from New England.[156]

Largely as a result of the autocratic rule of the proprietary governor, Philip Carteret (possibly a brother or cousin of the proprietor, Sir George),[157] rebellion broke out in 1672.[158] In response, on December 6, 1672, the lords proprietary issued a Declaration of True Intent and Meaning of the Concession of 1664. The proprietors' declaration concentrated power in the governor and council.[159]

After a brief reoccupation by the Dutch in 1673, the New Jersey colony was restored to the English by the Treaty of Westminster in 1674, and the proprietary grant was reissued to the Duke of York. Apparently after a falling-out with Carteret, Lord Berkeley sold his interest in the New Jersey colony to Edward Byllynge and John Fenwick, both of whom were Quakers.[160] As a consequence, Carteret became the sole owner of the eastern half of New Jersey.[161] It appears that the Duke of York did not approve this transaction and may have sought to defeat the reconveyance (York did not recognize the sale until August 6, 1780). In any event, the lease and release issued by York in 1674 divided the colony in two parts: East New Jersey and West New Jersey.[162] The boundaries were finally settled by "quintipartite deed" on July 1, 1676.[163]

West New Jersey

In 1676, the proprietors and freeholders of West New Jersey agreed to a statement of fundamental rights and privileges. Among these rights and privileges were: an explicit statement of freedom of conscience in religious matters; the right to a trial by a jury; the right to be notified prior to an arrest for debt together with the right to a hearing in court and the right to have the debt discharged by delivery "of such estate, goods, and chattels which he . . . hath for his . . . use" (i.e., bankruptcy); the requirement of three justices at every trial to assist the jury in matters of law; the requirement of sworn testimony by "two honest and reputable persons" (with provision for the punishment of false witness); the right to a public trial; and the right of a complainant "to forgive the person or persons offending against him or herself."[164]

On August 6, 1680, Byllynge received a grant from the Duke of York recognizing Byllynge's title to the proprietary of West New Jersey and conferring on Byllynge the authority to govern the province.[165] Samuel Jennings was sent as governor. On November 21, 1681, Jennings met with the assembled representatives who informed Jennings that they would recognize his authority as governor if Jennings, in turn, would consent to a bill placing limits on his gubernatorial authority. On November 25 Jennings assented to an Agreement of Fundamentals.[166]

The agreement provided that there would be an assembly every year (without prorogation by the governor) "to consider of the affairs of the said Province, and to make and ordain such acts, and laws, as shall be requisite and necessary for the good government and prosperity of the free people of the said Province." With respect to such legislation, it was agreed that the governor would not "suspend or defer the signing, sealing and confirming of such acts and laws." It was further agreed that the governor and council would not "make or enact any law or laws for the said Province, without the consent, act and concurrence of the General Assembly," and if they were determined to have done so, the act would have no force or effect.[167]

The agreement also restored to the legislature the prerogatives that had been granted in 1664. No taxes or assessments could be levied without the "consent and concurrence" of the assembly, and all such laws were to be effective for one year only. All officers of the government were to be elected by the assembly and were to be accountable to the assembly. Additionally, the foreign relations of the province, including the sending of ambassadors as well as the making of treaties and alliances, were to be conducted with the consent of the assembly. The agreement concluded with a reiteration of the guaranty of "Liberty of conscience in matters of worship towards God."[168]

Ownership and control over the West New Jersey proprietary changed hands several times following the death of Byllynge in 1687 and there followed a period of confusion and disorder. As a consequence, in 1702, the proprietary was returned to the crown.[169]

East New Jersey

In the meantime, by letter dated November 23, 1683, Charles II recognized the grant of East New Jersey by the Duke of York to twenty-four grantees, including William Penn, who had purchased Carteret's interest following his death. They became known as the "twenty four proprietors."[170] The letter established the twenty-four "as absolute Proprietors and Governors thereof (who have sole power and right derived under his Royal Highness from his said Majesty, to settle and dispose of the said Province upon such terms and condition as to them shall seem good)." The letter further attested to the authority of "their deputy or deputies, agents, lieutenants, and officers lawfully commissioned by them according to the powers and authorities granted to them." The letter directed "due compliance with this his royal will and pleasure, from all persons as well without the Province as within same . . . as they will answer to the contrary thereof at their peril."[171]

Previously, the proprietors had received a deed of release from the Duke of York dated March 14, 1683. On that basis, a plan of government, titled The Fundamental Constitutions for the Province of East New Jersey in America, was transmitted to the colony over the signatures of sixteen of the twenty-four proprietors. However, the plan was never given effect.[172]

After the accession to the throne by James II, there was movement within the British government to consolidate the northern colonies under crown rule. In early 1688, *quo warranto* proceedings were threatened against the East New Jersey proprietors to determine their authority to govern the province. Rather than subject themselves to this proceeding, the proprietors offered up their claim of government. Although these powers were restored to the proprietors, there followed a period of disorder resulting in the "virtual disintegration of proprietary authority." As a consequence, the Board of Trade recommended in 1701 that the province be remanded to the direct rule of the crown and on April 15, 1702, the proprietors surrendered their powers to Queen Anne and the province became a royal colony along with the West New Jersey proprietary. However, although the proprietors formally surrendered their powers of government to the crown, they retained their lands.[173]

THE PENNSYLVANIA PROPRIETARY

William Penn, the founder of the Pennsylvania proprietary, was the scion of a prominent British family. His father, Admiral Penn, had been a leading naval officer and an intimate of both Charles II and his brother James, the Duke of York. William Penn was also a Quaker, having undergone a religious conversion after meeting Thomas Loe in 1666 while visiting his father's estates in Ireland.[174]

Penn was desirous of establishing a colony in America that would shelter the Quakers from their persecution in England. Penn had been involved previously in American colonization after Edward Byllynge, a fellow Quaker, had transferred his rights in the New Jersey proprietary to Penn and to other Quakers, Gawan Lawrie and Nicholas Lucas, who with Byllynge had been signatories in the Quintipartite Deed of 1676. Four years later, Penn was one of the twelve Quakers (including Byllynge and Lawrie) who had purchased the interests of Sir George Carteret following Carteret's death in 1680.[175]

Finding the New Jersey colony unsatisfactory for his proprietary purposes, Penn petitioned Charles II in June 1680 for a tract of land north of Maryland on which to found his own colony. Charles II had borrowed heavily from Penn's father and apparently the grant was seen as a means of repayment of the debt.[176] The charter was signed on March 4, 1681.[177] Penn named his colony Pennsylvania in honor of his father.[178]

Like the proprietary charters for Maryland, New York, and the Carolinas, Penn's authority over his territory was extensive. Unlike Lord Baltimore in Maryland, Penn was not a feudal palatine, but like the New York and Carolinas proprietaries, Pennsylvania was ultimately under the control of the crown, reflecting the British government's evolved view of the American colonies.[179] Nevertheless, "free, full, and absolute power" was conferred on Penn "to ordain, make, and enact . . . any laws whatsoever, for the raising of money for the public use of the said Province, or for any other end, appertaining either unto the public state, peace or safety of the said Country, or unto the private utility of particular persons, according until their best discretions. . . ." This broad legislative power was subject, however, to the "advice, assent and approbation of the Freemen of the said country," and to that end, the charter provided that "Delegates or Deputies" were to be assembled "for the enacting of the said Laws" and that Penn was to assemble the deputies for that purpose. In emergent circumstances, when the deputies could not be assembled, Penn was authorized "to make and constitute fit and wholesome Ordinances . . . for the preservation of the peace, as for the better government of the people there inhabiting," subject to the limitation that such ordinances could not "bind, charge or take away the right or interest of any person or persons, for or in their life, members, freehold, goods or chattels." In the meantime, the "general course" of the laws of England was to be in effect.[180]

Copies of all laws were to be forwarded to the privy council for review within five years of their enactment. If within six months thereafter, the laws were found to be either "inconsistent with the Sovereignty or lawful Prerogatives" of the crown, or to be "contrary to the Faith and Allegiance due by the legal government of this Realm," the laws would be "adjudged and declared to be void. . . ." Otherwise, after the six-month review period, the laws were to "stand in full force, according to the true intent and meaning thereof."[181] It has been suggested that retention of this authority to veto legislation by the privy council represented a reaction by Charles II to the prerogatives claimed by the assembly of Massachusetts Bay.[182]

Penn was given authority to establish a judicial system for the adjudication of "what causes so ever," both criminal and civil, including the probate of wills and the granting of administration. The power to pardon offenses, other than treason and willful murder, was also conferred, as was the power to grant reprieves of sentences. The right to appeal to the crown was specifically reserved.[183]

Penn was empowered to take the actions necessary for the physical and economic development of the colony. He had the authority to divide the territory into towns, hundreds, and counties; to construct ports and harbors; to convey land; to erect manors; and to hold a "court baron"; and to import and export goods and merchandise. Penn was also to have the benefit of customs and duties assessed on merchandise brought into the colony, and the king agreed not to impose any tax or contribution on the colonists without the consent of the proprietary.[184]

Penn was to provide for the defense of the colony through the raising and outfitting of a militia. Authority was given to make war against "robbers" and enemies on land and at sea. However, Penn was specifically enjoined from making war or committing any act of hostility against "any other king, princes or state, or any of their subjects, who shall be in league or amity with us. . . ."[185]

Penn was to constitute and appoint an agent residing in or near London, who would be available "to appear in any of our Courts at Westminster, or Answer for any Misdemeanors that shall be committed, or by any willful default or neglect permitted by the said William Penn . . . ." Penn was to be responsible for the payment of any damages and failing to do so would be subject to such forfeitures and penalties established by acts of parliament. The crown would have the right "to seize and Resume the government of the said Province" until payment was made but in that event, the ownership of land or the property of anyone other than the offender was not to be in "any way be affected or molested thereby."[186]

The king's affection toward Penn was also reflected in the charter provision that enjoined all officers and ministers, "upon pain of our high displeasure," not to "presume at any time to attempt anything to the contrary of the premises, or that do in any sort withstand the same" but instead that "they be at all times aiding and assisting, as fitting unto the said William Penn. . . ." The charter further stated that in the event "any doubts or questions should arise, concerning the true Sense and meaning" of a provision of the charter, "such interpretation be made thereof, and allowed in any of our Courts whatsoever, as shall be adjudged most advantageous and favorable unto the said William Penn. . . ."[187] It is interesting, as Story noted, that unlike the charters of all the other colonies at the time, Penn's charter did not provide that the settlers were to be deemed to be British subjects and entitled to all of the privileges and immunities of English citizenship.[188]

Penn began immediately to launch the colony. On July 11, 1681, Penn issued his concessions setting forth how he proposed to divide the territory.[189] Although not a frame of government, the concessions contained several provisions concerning the regulation of conduct within the colony. There was, for example, a consumer protection law that required the sale of goods to be conducted in a public market in which the goods "shall pass public stamp, or mark." The law further provided that if "bad ware, and prized as good, or deceitful in proportion or weight" were offered, the seller would "forfeit the value, as if good and full weight and proportion." Similarly, goods to be sold to the native peoples were to be sold in the market place, "as it is usual with planters to over-reach the poor natives of the country, in trade, by goods not being good of the kind, or debased with mixtures, with which they are sensibly aggrieved."[190]

The concessions contained other provisions concerning relations with the native peoples. First, it was stated that "no man shall, by any ways or means, in word or deed, affront, or wrong any Indian" and if so, the offender would "incur the same penalty of law, as if he had committed it against his fellow planter." In the event that a settler claimed to have been abused, "he shall not be his own judge upon the Indian, but he shall make his complaint to the governor of the province." Disputes between the native population and the planters were to be resolved by a jury comprised of six settlers and six "natives." Native peoples were also guaranteed the "liberty to do all things relating to improvement of their ground, and providing sustenance for their families, that any of the planters shall enjoy." The concessions directed that measures be taken for the conservation of land, requiring" that "in clearing the ground, care be taken to leave one acre of trees for every five acres cleared."[191] Thus, commenting on Penn's concessions, Story remarked that "Under his benign and enlightened policy a foundation was early laid for the establishment of a government and laws which have been justly celebrated for their moderation, wisdom, just protection of the rights and liberties of the people."[192]

Penn appointed his cousin William Markham as his representative in the colony and soon, surveyors were sent to layout cities and towns.[193] After much labor, on April 25, 1682, Penn issued his Charter of Liberty, in which he laid out the framework for the government of the colony.[194]

Penn had previously expressed his vision of colonial government in the 1676 Fundamental Laws of West New Jersey, of which Penn had been one of the authors.[195] Andrews described the Fundamental Laws as "the broadest, sanest, and most equitable charter drafted for any body of colonists up to this time."[196] In his Charter of Liberty for Pennsylvania, Penn expanded on those views.

There were to be annual elections of freemen to serve in the provincial council for a staggered term of three years. After service of one term, a freeman would be ineligible for reelection for a year. The governor was to preside over the provincial council and was to exercise a "treble vote."[197]

The provincial council was charged with proposing legislation to be enacted by the general assembly. For matters of moment (i.e., proposed legislation, judgments in criminal trials, and the selection of officers), two-thirds of the members were required for a quorum and of them, the vote of two-thirds was required for action. Otherwise, in matters of "lesser moment," twenty-four members were needed for a quorum and the assent of twenty-four attendees was required for action.[198] In this regard, the provincial council has been viewed as functioning more in the nature of an upper house of the legislature rather than a privy council advising the governor,[199] and it has been said that the council under the Charter of Liberties was a direct precursor of the US Senate.[200]

The council was to be divided into four committees. The Committee on Plantations was to situate ports, market towns, and highways and was to decide all suits relating to plantations. The Committee on Justice and Safety was to punish maladministration by those who subverted justice to the prejudice of both public and private interests. The Committee on Trade and Treasury was to regulate trade and stimulate manufacturing and other economic growth. Lastly, the Committee on Manners Education was charged with the training of youth in "Virtue and useful Knowledge and Arts."[201]

The governor and provincial council were given a variety of responsibilities. They were to "take care that all Laws, Statutes and Ordinances . . . be duly and diligently executed." They were to "have care for the peace and safety of the colony." They were to inspect the management of the public treasury and to punish the use of funds for purposes other than those directed by the governor, provincial council, and general assembly. The governor and provincial council were also responsible for the erection of public schools and the encouragement of "useful Science and Laudable Inventions."[202]

The governor and provincial council were further charged with establishing courts of justice. The council was to elect and present annually for the governor's selection, "a double number of persons or serve for Judges, Treasurers, Masters of the Rolls" for the following year.[203]

The freemen were also to elect deputies to represent them in the general assembly that was to meeting annually. The deputies were to confer with each other and as appropriate with one or more of the committees of the provincial council to secure the legislation proposed for consideration by the general assembly. The assembly was to enact the legislation "they shall think fit to pass" and to "Impeach criminals fit there to be Impeached." The general assembly was also to submit to the governor twice the number of persons to serve as sheriffs, justices of the peace, and coroners. In all these matters, a quorum of two-thirds of the deputies was necessary for the assembly to act.[204]

All elections and votes of the provincial council and general assembly were to be by means of ballot. Also, any amendment to the Charter of Liberty required the consent of the governor and of six-sevenths of the provincial council and general assembly respectively.[205] This has been considered to be the first formal amendment process.[206]

The Charter of Liberty, together with certain "laws agreed upon in England," was reprised by Penn in his Frame of Governmenton May 5, 1682.[207] In his introductory comments, Penn invoked the derivation of earthy government from the divine. Thus, he wrote, "government seems to me a part of religion itself, a thing sacred in its institution and end . . . an emanation of the same Divine Power, that is both author and object of pure religion." Penn also spoke to the basis of government, writing that "Any government is free to the people under it (whatever be the frame) where the laws rule, and the people are a party to those laws, and more than this is tyranny, oligarchy, or confusion." Penn appreciated the human element of government when he wrote that "some say, let us have good laws, and no matter for the men that execute them: but let them consider, that though good laws do well, good men do better: for good laws may want good men, and be abolished or evaded by ill men: but good men will never want good laws, nor suffer ill ones." In this, Penn explained that it was his intention "To support power in reverence with the people, and to secure the people from the abuse of power."[208] Thus, it has been written that to Penn, "forms of government signified little, but rather the character of men whom the management of its affairs was entrusted."[209]

In keeping with Penn's intention, the laws that were agreed on in England and appended to the April 1682 Charter of Liberty were more in the nature of a bill of rights than they were a codification of laws and regulations. These laws established the qualifications of a freeman (based on land ownership or the payment of "scot and lot" to the government), provided for the election of representatives, enumerated individual liberties in criminal matters, addressed rights in property, and secured freedom of religious worship.[210]

The laws addressed corruption in elections. In regard to the election of representatives, the law disqualified anyone who either offered or accepted "any reward or gift, in meat, drink, monies or otherwise" in connection with an election. The laws also established qualifications for election to public office that unlike the other colonies were not wealth-based. To hold public office, a candidate was to be at least twenty years of age, not have been convicted of "ill fame, or unsober and dishonest conversation," and "possessed of faith in Jesus Christ." Persons chosen for public office were limited to holding one office only.[211]

The laws enumerated a variety of individual rights in judicial proceedings. These rights included: a public trial; the right to defend oneself or to be represented by counsel; short, simple pleadings "in English;" testimony under oath (with penalties for willful falsehood); judgment by a jury of "twelve men, and as near as may be, peers or equals, and of the neighborhood;" the right to bail; imposition of fees and fines that were established by the provincial council; incarceration in prisons that were "work houses," in which food and lodging were provided at no charge; double damages against the prosecutor or "informer" for wrongful prosecution or imprisonment; and compensation for victims of crime by the offender."[212]

The laws made provision for the devise of lands, the quieting of title to land; and the registry of wills, conveyances, births, and deaths. Penalties were also imposed for falsification of registry entries as well as for bribery, extortion, and defamation.[213]

It was Penn's intention that there would be no state-church but rather his colony would be a "holy experiment" in which all Christians would live in society with mutual respect.[214] In keeping with that vision, the laws set forth a variety of guarantees respecting the freedom of worship. Those who acknowledged God "to be the Creator, Upholder and Ruler of the world," were not to be "molested or prejudiced for their religious persuasion, or practice" nor were they to be "compelled, at any time, to frequent or maintain any religious worship, place or ministry whatever." The law exempted the first day of the week ("the Lord's Day") from "common daily labour."

The laws identified certain "offences against God" which were to be "discouraged and severely punished." These offenses included crimes of violence such as murder, rape, incest, and sedition, but also included offenses such as swearing, cursing, and using obscene words; drunkenness; stage plays, card games, masques, and revels; and other similar activities that would "excite the people to rudeness, cruelty, looseness, and irregulation."[215]

Penn came to the colony in October 1682. Almost immediately, Penn directed that elections be held to designate freemen to serve in the assembly. On December 4, the assembly convened and adopted the "Great Law," which included the laws agreed on in England that had been annexed to the Charter of Liberties.[216] On December 7, the assembly passed the Act for Freedom of Conscience that reiterated the requirement that only Christians could be elected to public office.[217]

The colony experienced rapid growth. Drawn by the generous distribution of land in the concessions, six hundred Welsh and English settlers, known as the "First Purchasers" came almost immediately.[218] By 1685, the population of the colony had grown from one thousand to more than eight thousand. The population of the colony was diverse with only approximately half of the settlers being English.[219]

Nevertheless, Penn and Markham were of the view that the council and assembly were too large to be sustained by the colony. During this time also, fifty-four members of the council withdrew to form a lower house.

As a consequence, the assembly requested that a new charter of government be written. Thereafter, a new frame of government was agreed upon on February 2, 1683, and announced to the colony on April 8.[220] Significantly, the new charter was the work of the assembly and not of the proprietary.[221]

Not surprisingly, the frame of government remained in broad outline as it had been in the charter of 1682.[222] The size of the council was reduced from seventy-two to eighteen and the general assembly was reduced from two hundred to thirty-six (although provision was made to restore the council and the assembly to seventy-two and two hundred members, respectively).

The powers of the governor were also somewhat curtailed. The governor no longer had a "treble vote" in the council and the revised charter made it explicit that the governor "shall at no time, therein perform any public act of state whatsoever, that shall, or may, relate unto the justice, trade, treasury or safety of the province and territories as aforesaid, but by and with the advice and consent of the provincial council thereof."[223]

The first assembly under the revised frame of government met in May 1684. A short time later, in August, Penn returned to England to defend against Lord Baltimore's claims to the southern boundary of Pennsylvania before the Lords of Trade. Penn was ultimately successful in holding on to the lower counties and was successful in avoiding the *quo warranto* proceedings instituted by the crown against the other proprietary and charter colonies in 1685 and in 1688. Penn was also able to obtain an exemption for Pennsylvania when Sir Edmund Andros was made governor of the New England, New York, and New Jersey colonies.[224]

Penn's influence at court did not survive the Glorious Revolution and the ascension of William and Mary to the throne. Penn's close ties to James II and his liberal views on matters of religion, led to suspicion if not outright disfavor in the court of William and Mary. In addition to suffering financial reverses, on three occasions Penn was charged with treason. There was also dissension in the colony which resulted in the loss of Penn's proprietary rights between 1692 and 1694 "by reason of great neglects and miscarriages in the government," during which time the colony was governed as a dependency of New York.[225]

The colony was restored to Penn on August 12, 1694. Finding that the frame of government under the Charter of Liberties was "not deemed, in all respects, suitably accommodated to our present circumstances," a new frame of government was promulgated "with the advice and consent of the freemen of the said province and territories," on November 1, 1696.[226]

Under the 1696 plan, the membership of the council and the assembly was again reduced and the members were to be elected annually. To qualify for election, a candidate had to be at least twenty-one years of age and possess either fifty acres of land (at least ten of which were "seated and cleared") or have fifty pounds "lawful money," a "clear estate," and to have been resident for the two years preceding the election. Perhaps most significantly, under this revised frame of government, the assembly was given the authority to initiate legislation.[227]

Penn returned to the colony in 1699 and a further revision of the Charter of Privileges was made on October 28, 1701.[228] By referring only to the "approbation of freemen in general assembly," the 1701 charter effectively wrote the council out of the legislative process. It has been observed that this made Pennsylvania unique by having a unicameral legislature (which would be continued in Pennsylvania's state constitution after independence). Penn retained the power to veto legislation, however, and laws continued to be subject to the review of the privy council.[229]

This charter remained the constitution of the Pennsylvania colony, which continued as a proprietary until independence.[230] Also at that time, Penn executed a proviso to the charter revisions allowing the Delaware counties to separate.[231]

THE DELAWARE PROPRIETARY

The three Delaware counties—New Castle, Kent, and Sussex—had been settled by colonists from Sweden. The Swedish colony was overthrown by the Dutch in 1655, but the colony later came under English dominion after the defeat of the Dutch by Duke of York in 1664. Although Lord Baltimore claimed the territory under his palatine grant, York asserted that because the Dutch had occupied the territory before Baltimore's grant, York's claim was superior.[232]

Penn, whose grant extended only to twelve miles north of New Castle, was desirous of having access to Delaware Bay and the ocean, Penn made a personal application to York to add the three counties to his holdings, and on August 24, 1682, York executed two leases in favor of Penn conferring on him the land as far south as Cape Henlopen.[233]

Although Penn claimed that these leases conferred governmental authority, it is by no means clear that they did so. Sir Robert Carr overthrew the Dutch in Delaware in the name of Charles II, not his brother York, and at the time of the conveyance to Penn, York had not received a grant from his brother for the territory. Moreover, after York finally received a royal grant for Delaware on March 22, 1683, York did not make a further conveyance to Penn. After the Lords of Trade rejected Baltimore's claim, although he appeared inclined to grant the territory to Penn, York (now James II) fled from England in the Glorious Revolution before making the grant. Thus, it has been said that "Penn's title always remained defective."[234]

Compounding Penn's difficulties, there were substantial differences between the main Pennsylvania colony and the "Lower Counties," as Delaware was known. The predominantly Anglican and Calvinist Delaware counties resented Quaker rule. Also, because they did not enjoy the same level of economic development as the more prosperous Pennsylvania, there was a fear among the Delaware settlers of political and economic domination by Pennsylvania. As a consequence, there was a strong separatist ethos in the Lower Counties.[235]

Despite the questions concerning the legitimacy of his authority, Penn issued his Charter of Liberties, Franchises and Privileges for the Freemen, Planters and Adventurers of Delaware in 1682. Like his Charter of Liberty for Pennsylvania, Penn ensured a degree of religious tolerance such that those acknowledging one God would not be "molested or prejudiced" by virtue of "their conscious persuasion or practice," nor would they be "compelled to frequent or maintain and religious worship . . . contrary to their religious persuasion." But consistent with Penn's belief that Christian principles were the foundation liberty, Penn's charter provided that only Christians could serve in public office.[236]

The plan of government for the Lower Counties set forth in the charter provided for direct election of a representative assembly with the power to enact laws, impeach criminals, and redress grievances, and to have those powers "as is usual in any of the King's plantations in America." Such laws were subject to confirmation by the colonial governor.[237] Penn sought to assure the inhabitants that they would enjoy the same privileges as the settlers of Pennsylvania, and shortly after taking possession of Delaware, Penn authorized the calling of an election for representatives to the assembly that was to convene in Chester.[238]

Other individual rights were established in the charter. These included rights to mount a defense in criminal cases and the assurance that no complaint involving property was answerable except in the "ordinary course of justice." The charter further provided that the property of a person committing suicide was not to be forfeit to the governor but was to pass to the heirs by the ordinary rules of descent and distribution.[239]

Also as he had in Pennsylvania, Penn made provision for amendment of the charter. However, like Pennsylvania, the charter could not be altered without the consent of the governor and the approval of six-sevenths of the members of the assembly. No alteration could be made in any event to the first article of the charter that guaranteed liberty of conscience.[240]

The charter did not ameliorate the dissension in the Lower Counties, however. Even as the charter was being put into effect, representatives of the Delaware counties lodged formal complaints with the Board of Trade in England concerning their treatment by the Pennsylvania assembly. Ultimately, Penn prevailed and the privy council recognized Penn's right to appoint a governor for Pennsylvania, including the Delaware counties, though Penn had to specify that this was not to be construed in derogation of the crown's authority over the counties.

As noted, in 1701, Penn issued a proviso to the Pennsylvania charter that allowed the inhabitants of the Delaware counties to separate from Pennsylvania for purposes of legislation while assuring them that they would continue separately to enjoy "all other liberties, privileges and benefits" granted to them by the Pennsylvania charter. Delaware continued to exist without a royal charter and its ambiguous constitutional standing lasted until independence, so much so that Penn's heirs persisted in their claims to Delaware as late as 1814.[241]

THE GEORGIA TRUSTEESHIP

The founding of the Georgia colony was not in the mainstream of American colonial development. Unlike the other corporate, covenant, and proprietary colonies, the Georgia colony was not intended to serve commercial or religious ends, but rather the colony represented both a social welfare experiment and a strategic initiative on the part of the British government. The colony was to provide a place where indigents who might otherwise be confined in debtors prisons could migrate[242] and was to provide a buffer between Carolina and Spanish Florida, ostensibly as a defense against aggression by the native peoples.[243] For that reason, the founding of the Georgia colony was not in the mainstream of British colonial development.[244]

The colony's anomalous nature was revealed in the charter itself. The charter created a corporation of twenty named individuals to serve as trustees. It has been suggested that the appointment of trustees rather than creating either a proprietary or a trading company indicated a shift in the attitude toward the British colonial enterprise away from the "crude profiteering in the manner of the seventeenth century."[245]

Although the charter contained the common language of incorporation—that the company was "one body corporate and politic" with perpetual succession, able to sue and be sued—the grant of powers to the trustees was to terminate by operation of the charter in twenty-one years, after which the governance of the colony was to be remanded to the crown.[246] On June 9, 1732, King George II granted the charter to the trustees to found a colony between the Savannah and Altamaha Rivers, a territory that had formerly been part of South Carolina.

Despite its fixed duration, the charter conferred broad powers on the trustees for the governance of the colony. The trustees were given authority to "form and prepare laws, statutes and ordinances, fit and necessary for and concerning the government of said colony." These laws were subject to the limitations that they not be "repugnant to the laws and statutes of England," and that were subject to "approbation or disallowance" by the crown.[247]

The corporation was empowered to make grants of land to those willing to "live under our allegiance in the said colony." To avoid the creation of large estates, leading to the disparities in wealth experienced in the other colonies, such grants were limited individually to not more than five hundred acres and there was the further restriction that "no grants shall be made of any part of the said lands unto any person in trust, for the benefit of any member of the said corporation."[248]

The corporate proprietors were to "erect and constitute judicatories and courts of record, or other courts . . . for hearing and determining of all manner of crimes, offences, pleas, processes, plaints, actions, matters, causes and things whatsoever." Authority was also given to appoint judges and magistrates, and to administer oaths "for the discovery of truth."[249]

The corporation was to appoint governors and other civil and military officers and ministers. A militia was to be raised and equipped to defend the colony against "persons as shall at any time hereafter, in any hostile manner, attempt or enterprise the destruction, invasion, detriment or annoyance of our said colony." Evidencing the defensive purpose of the colony, the charter provided that command of the Georgia militia should be in the hands of the "governor and commander in chief of the province of South Carolina."[250]

Reminiscent of the earlier charters of the Virginia Companies, the Georgia charter provided a framework for the governance of the corporation. There was to be a president and a common council with a chairman. The work of the corporation was to be carried out by the common council, which was authorized to disburse corporate funds, contract on behalf of the corporation, and to appoint "a treasurer or treasurers, secretary or secretaries, and such other officers, ministers and servants" as the council deemed "proper or requisite for the good management of their affairs" and to set "such reasonable salaries, perquisites and other rewards, for their labor or service." The president and members of the council were initially appointed by the king but thereafter, they were to be elected by the members of the corporation who were to meet annually to elect new members and to replace members who either had resigned or who had died. The president, chairman of the council and the members of the council were to serve without compensation and conversely, no one employed by the corporation could be a member of the corporation.[251]

The charter provided for royal oversight of the corporation's activities and finances. Reports of the colony's progress were to be made "from time to time" by the corporation to "one of the principal secretaries of state, and to the commissioners of trade and plantations." Additionally, the rents and profits of the corporation were to be expended in a way to "most improve and enlarge said colony, and best answer the good purposes herein before mentioned, and for defraying all other charges about the same." The corporation was required annually to provide a written accounting to the Chancellor of the Bank of England and to the Lord Chief Justice of all receipts and expenditures for "the carrying on of the good purposes aforesaid."[252]

Lastly, the charter contained a guaranty of "a liberty of conscience . . . in the worship of God." The settlers were to enjoy "free exercise of their religion, so they be contented with the quiet and peaceable enjoyment of the same." However, specifically excluded from this "liberty of conscience" were "papists."[253]

The governing structure of the colony under the charter has been described as "paternalistic,"[254] and it has been suggested that the limited independence of the corporation and the absence of a charter provision authorizing a constituent assembly prevented development of self-government in the colony.[255] Nevertheless, in June 1743, an order was issued by the corporation establishing a president of the colony with four assistants. Thus, a government was formed with a provincial governor and council but no provincial assembly. This remained the form of government for the remainder of the corporate period.[256]

Although the Georgia colonial experiment enjoyed some initial success, the trustees' prohibition of slavery and their limitation on landholding caused dissension between the trustees and the settlers, particularly those settlers from South Carolina who believed that large-scale farming supported by slave labor was the only means by which the colony would grow and prosper. Eventually, in 1742, the trustees allowed individual land holdings of up to two thousand acres, and in 1750, the ban on slavery was lifted.[257]

The trustees' concession on slavery was their last act. Although the degree of involvement of the members in the affairs of the corporation and the colony was low,[258] according to Joseph Story, "At length the trustees, wearied with their own labours, and the complaints of the people." Consequently, the trustees surrendered the charter to the crown in June 1751.[259]

On August 6, 1754, John Reynolds was commissioned as royal governor of the Georgia Colony, with broad powers over the structure of government, the establishment of a judiciary, the regulation of commerce, and the defense of the colony. In this, the governor was to be assisted by a seven-member council appointed by the crown. Significantly, the extensive and detailed instructions accompanying his commission directed Reynolds to call a representative assembly of the freemen and planters of the colony. Representation in the assembly was to be proportional, as specified in the instructions, and representatives were to hold at least five hundred acres of land to qualify for election (this was subsequently reduced by the governor and council). Representatives were to be elected by majority vote of their county or district. With the advice and consent of the council and the assembly, the governor was to adopt laws and ordinances "for the public peace, welfare, and good government" of the colony.[260] The first meeting of the assembly was called for November 7, 1754.[261]

NOTES

1. McFarlane, *The British in the Americas 1480–1815*, 189; Jack P. Greene, *Negotiated Authorities: Essays in Colonial Political and Constitutional History* (Charlottesville: University of Virginia Press, 1994) 43; Barnes, *The Dominion of New England*, 1.

2. Ken MacMillan, *The Atlantic Imperial Constitution: Center and Periphery in the English Atlantic World* (New York: Palgrave Macmillan, 2011), 11–29. The Maryland palatine, which differed dramatically from the corporate colonies of Virginia and New England, reflected Charles's preference for domestic administration by nobility and gentry. Kevin Sharpe wrote that "The king attached great importance to the role of the nobility and gentry in the governance of the localities," and "The re-establishment of authority in the localities in the hands of the most important local families, was a central beam of his social reconstruction." Kevin Sharpe, "The Personal Rule of Charles I," in Howard Tomlinson, ed., *Before the English Civil War: Essays on Early Stuart Politics and Government* (London: Macmillan Press, 1984), 61.

3. Edmund Burke, *An Account of the European Settlements in America* (London: J. Dodsley, 1770), vol. 2: 288.

4. Greene, *Negotiated Authorities*, 43. John Miller described the conduct of government by Charles II as being "characterized by indolence and cynicism." Although Charles's government "took pains to exact obedience on matters affecting revenue," in the execution of policy, "Charles's regime left to those in control of local administration largely to their own devices." John Miller, "The Later Stuart Monarchy," in J. R. Jones, ed., *The Restored Monarchy 1660–1688* (London: Macmillan, 1979), 37, 44.

5. McFarlane, *The British in America 1480–1815*, 189–94. Barnes noted that after the monarchy was restored, Massachusetts almost refused to recognize Charles II. Barnes, *The Dominion of New England*, 2.

6. McFarlane, *The British in America 1480–1815*, 194; MacMillan, *The Atlantic Imperial Constitution*, 8; Barnes, *The Dominion of New England*, 6. As George L. Beer pointed out, "At the outset of the colonial movement, not only was the cost of transportation very high, but furthermore considerable time was recognized before a living could be secured from America's virgin soil. Hence the settlement of an individual in the colonies implied the expenditure of a considerable sum of money." Beer, "The Early English Colonial Movement I," *Political Science Quarterly*, Vol. 23: 92. Beer suggested that in addition to strategic interests, the early colonization movement, particularly in Virginia, was viewed as a means of relieving perceived overpopulation and congested conditions by resettling the poor and unemployed in the colonies.

7. MacMillan, *The Atlantic Imperial Constitution*, 170.

8. Ken MacMillan, "Bound by Our Regal Office: Empire, Sovereignty and the American Colonies in the Seventeenth Century," in Stephan Foster, ed., *Oxford History of the British Empire: British North America in the Seventeenth and Eighteenth Centuries* (Oxford: Oxford University Press, 2013), 88; Ned C. Landsman, "The Middle Colonies: New Opportunities for Settlement, 1660–1700," in Canny *The Oxford History of the British Empire*, 371.

9. Andrews, *The Colonial Period of American History*, vol. 2: 293.

10. McFarlane, *The British in the Americas 1480–1815*, 197; Greene, "Empire and Identity from the Glorious Revolution to the American Revolution," in P. J. Marshall and Alaine Low, eds. *The Oxford History of the British Empire: Volume 2: The Eighteenth Century* (Oxford: Oxford University Press, 1998), 218; Barnes, *The Dominion of New England*, 2.

11. Stephen Conway, "Britain and the Revolutionary Crisis, 1763–1791," Marshall and Low, eds., *The Eighteenth Century*, 325.

12. Lustig, *The Imperial Executive in America*, 135; Greene, "Empire and Identity from the Glorious Revolution to the American Revolution," in Marshall and Low, eds., *The Eighteenth Century*, 218.

13. Foster, "British North America in the Empire," in Foster, ed., *British North America in the Seventeenth and Eighteenth Centuries*, 30.

14. MacMillan, *The Atlantic Imperial Constitution*, 170. MacMillan wrote that "the crown turned predominantly to proprietary charters, hoping that these would allow the weak-state model while offering better political mechanisms than the 'popular' methods used by trading companies. This system, initiated under the early Stuarts, continued into the Restoration and characterized many of the Atlantic colonies planted after 1660."

15. MacMillan, *The Atlantic Imperial Constitution*, 166–67. MacMillan attributes this movement to a strong state model to the demands of the expanded empire and to the "fiscal-military state" that had developed from the European conflicts of the late seventeenth century.

16. MacMillan, "Bound by Our Regal Office," in Foster, ed., *British North America in the Seventeenth Century*, 97–101; Hillary McD Beckles, "The Hub of the Empire: The Caribbean and Britain in the Seventeenth Century," in Canny, *The Oxford History of the British Empire*, 236; Root, "The Lords of Trade and Plantations," *American Historical Review*, vol. 23: 20–24.

17. Philip S. Haffenden, "The Crown and the Colonial Charters 1675–1688 Part II," *The William and Mary Quarterly* (1958), vol. 15: 452–54.

18. Haffenden, "The Crown and the Colonial Charters 1675–1688 Part II," *William and Mary Quarterly*, Vol. 15: 454–59.

19. Greene, *Negotiated Authorities*, 85.

20. Middleton and Lombard, *Colonial America*, 120.

21. Theodore C. Gambrell, *History of Early Maryland* (New York: Thomas Wittaker, 1893), 44–46; William Hand Bowne, *Maryland, The History of a Palatinate* (Boston: Houghton Mifflin, 1904), 4–11; Andrews, *The Colonial Period of American History*, vol. 2: 274–78; Ver Steeg, *The Formative Years*, 42–43; Sarson, *British America 1500–1800*, 60; Middleton and Lombard, *Colonial America*, 120–21.

22. Middleton and Lombard, *Colonial America*, 121; William J. Braddick, "The English Government, War, Trade, and Settlement, 1625–1688," in Canny, ed., *The Oxford History of the British Empire*, 297; Newton D. Mereness, *Maryland as a Proprietary Province* (New York: Macmillan, 1901), 6–8.

23. Meinig, *The Shaping of America*, 151.

24. Mereness, *Maryland as a Proprietary Province*, 5–6, 11–12; Bowne, *Maryland, The History of a Palatinate*, 17; Andrews, *The Colonial Period of American History*, vol. 2: 289–92; Aubrey C. Land, *Colonial Maryland: A History* (Millwood: KTO Press, 1981), 4–6.

25. Thorpe, *The Federal and State Constitutions*, vol. 3: 1679.

26. Land, *Colonial Maryland*, 6.

27. Pomfret, *Founding the American Colonies*, 78.

28. Thorpe, *The Federal and State Constitutions*, vol. 3: 1679.

29. Gambrell, *History of Early Maryland*, 34.

30. Story, *Commentaries on the Constitution of the United States*, vol. 1: 94.

31. Osgood, *The American Colonies in the Seventeenth Century*, vol. 2: 59.

32. Thorpe, *The Federal and State Constitutions*, vol. 3: 1679.

33. Thorpe, *The Federal and State Constitutions*, vol. 3: 1680; Osgood, *The American Colonies in the Seventeenth Century*, vol. 2: 59.

34. Thorpe, *The Federal and State Constitutions*, vol. 3: 1682.

35. Thorpe, *The Federal and State Constitutions*, vol. 3: 1683–85.

36. Pomfret, *Founding the American Colonies*, 83–87.

37. Middleton and Lombard, *Colonial America*, 122.

38. Andrews, *The Colonial Period of American History*, vol. 2: 286–88; Land, *Colonial Maryland*, 8–9; Pomfret, *Founding the American Colonies*, 80–81; Story, *Commentaries on the Constitution of the United States*, vol. 1: 94.

39. Andrews, *The Colonial Period of American History*, vol. 2: 299–301; Osgood, *The American Colonies in the Seventeenth Century*, vol. 2: 65.

40. Middleton and Lombard, *Colonial America*, 123.

41. Lutz, *The Colonial Origins of the American Constitution*, 297–98.

42. Pomfret, *Founding the American Colonies*, 88; Osgood, *The American Colonies in the Seventeenth Century*, vol. 2: 76–81; Land, *Colonial Maryland*, 34–36.

43. Lutz, *The Colonial Origins of the American Constitution*, 300–1.

44. Lutz, *The Colonial Origins of the American Constitution*, 302–8.

45. Andrews, *The Colonial Period of American History*, vol. 2: 302–9; Pomfret, *Founding the American Colonies*, 92; Middleton and Lombard, *Colonial America*, 124–25; Land, *Colonial Maryland*, 46–47; Gambrell, *History of Early Maryland*, 68–71.

46. Lutz, *Colonial Origins of the American Constitution*, 309–13; Andrews, *The Colonial Period of American History*, vol. 2: 310; Pomfret, *Founding the American Colonies*, 93–94; Bowne, *Maryland: The History of a Palatinate*, 67–71; Land, *Colonial Maryland*, 49–50.

47. Andrews, *The Colonial Period of American History*, vol. 2: 312–20; Pomfret, *Founding the American Colonies*, 97–98; McFarlane, *The British in America*, 98; Mereness, *Maryland as a Proprietary Province*, 24–25; Middleton and Lombard, *Colonial America*, 125.

48. Andrews, *The Colonial Period of American History*, vol. 2: 320–21; Land, *Colonial Maryland*, 52–53; Gambrell, *History of Early Maryland*, 70–71.

49. Andrews, *The Colonial Period of American History*, vol. 2: 328–29; Bowne, *Maryland: The History of a Palatinate*, 73–74.

50. Andrews, *The Colonial Period of American History*, vol. 2: 338–41; Middleton and Lombard, *Colonial America*, 194.

51. Andrews, *The Colonial Period of American History*, vol. 2: 342–56; Middleton and Lombard, *Colonial America*, 195.

52. Andrews, *The Colonial Period of American History*, vol. 2: 357, 363–76; Middleton and Lombard, *Colonial America*, 195–96; Gambrell, *History of Early Maryland*, 142–62.
53. John E. Pomfret, *Colonial New Jersey—A History* (New York: Scribner, 1973), 1.
54. Wesley Frank Craven, *New Jersey and the English Colonization of North America* (Princeton: Van Norstrand, 1964), 2–3.
55. Craven, *New Jersey and the English Colonization of North America*, 4.
56. Sarason, *British America 1500–1800*, 151.
57. M. Eugene Sirmans, *Colonial South Carolina: A Political History* (Chapel Hill: University of North Carolina Press, 1966), 4; Andrews, *Colonial Self-Government*, 132
58. Thorpe, *The Federal and State Constitutions*, vol. 5: 2743; Sirmans, *Colonial South Carolina*, 4–5; Robert M. Weir, *Colonial South Carolina-A History* (Millwood: KTO Press, 1983), 48–49; Andrews, *The Colonial Period of American History*, vol. 3: 183–87.
59. Andrews, *Colonial Self-Government*, 133.
60. Thorpe, *The Federal and State Constitutions*, vol. 5: 2744.
61. Thorpe, *The Federal and State Constitutions*, vol. 5: 2756; Story, *Commentaries on the Constitution of the United States*, vol. 1: 119–20; Sirmans, *Colonial South Carolina*, 5; Weir, *Colonial South Carolina-A History*, 49–50; Andrews, *The Colonial Period of American History*, vol. 3: 191.
62. Thorpe, *The Federal and State Constitutions*, vol. 5: 2744.
63. Story, *Commentaries on the Constitution of the United States*, vol. 1: 118.
64. Thorpe, *The Federal and State Constitutions*, vol. 5: 2745. Story observed that "The charter seems to have been copied from that of Maryland, and resembles in it many of its provisions." Story, *Commentaries on the Constitution of the United States*, vol. 1: 118.
65. Hugh T. Lefler and William S. Powell, *Colonial North Carolina—A History* (New York: Scribner, 1973), 33.
66. Thorpe, *The Federal and State Constitutions*, vol. 5: 2746.
67. Thorpe, *The Federal and State Constitutions*, vol. 5: 2745–46.
68. Thorpe, *The Federal and State Constitutions*, vol. 5: 2750–52.
69. Thorpe, *The Federal and State Constitutions*, vol. 5: 2749–51.
70. Thorpe, *The Federal and State Constitutions*, vol. 5: 2747, 2752–53.
71. Thorpe, *The Federal and State Constitutions*, vol. 5: 2752. The claims of Heath and the group of London adventurers who had invested in a colonial undertaking by a contingent of New Englanders was ultimately resolved in favor of the Carolina proprietors by the privy council in 1663. Andrews, *Colonial Self-Government*, 134; Andrews, *The Colonial Period of American History*, vol. 5: 191.
72. Thorpe, *The Federal and State Constitutions*, vol. 5: 2753; Andrews, *Colonial Self-Government*, 135. Story suggested that the proposed form of government was motivated at least in part by "the desire of the New England settlers within" the province. Story, *Commentaries on the Constitution of the United States*, vol. 1: 118.
73. Thorpe, *The Federal and State Constitutions*, vol. 5: 2754.
74. Thorpe, *The Federal and State Constitutions*, vol. 5: 2755.
75. Thorpe, *The Federal and State Constitutions*, vol. 5: 2755.
76. Thorpe, *The Federal and State Constitutions*, vol. 5: 2755; Weir, *Colonial South Carolina—A History*, 51; Osgood, *The American Colonies in the Seventeenth Century*, vol. 2: 204–5.
77. Kavenagh, *Foundations of Colonial History*, vol. 3: 1908–21.
78. Sirmans, *Colonial South Carolina*, 6; Lefler and Powell, *Colonial North Carolina—A History*, 38–43; Weir, *Colonial South Carolina—A History*, 50–51; Andrews, *The Colonial Period of American History*, vol. 3: 192–95; Osgood, *The American Colonies in the Seventeenth Century*, vol. 2: 202–7; Andrews, *Colonial Self-Government*, 137–38.
79. Andrews, *The Colonial Period of American History*, vol. 3: 196; see Lefler and Powell, *Colonial North Carolina—A History*, 45–46.
80. Sirmans, *Colonial South Carolina*, 7; Andrews, *The Colonial Period of American History*, vol. 3: 199–201.
81. Thorpe, *The Federal and State Constitutions*, vol. 5: 2772.
82. Sirmans, *Colonial South Carolina*, 7–9; Andrews, *Colonial Self-Government*, 139–40.

83. Story, *Commentaries on the Constitution of the United States*, vol. 21: 120–21; Andrews, *The Colonial Period of American History*, vol. 3: 212–13.

84. Sirmans, *Colonial South Carolina*, 9.

85. Thorpe, *The Federal and State Constitutions*, vol. 5: 2773–75; Middleton and Lombard, *Colonial America,* 151–52.

86. The courts were: the Palatine's Court (with authority to veto legislative enactments, disburse public funds, elect government officials, and pardon offenses); the Grand Council (which disbursed public funds and conducted relations with the native peoples); the Chancellor's Court (which maintained the palatine seal and oversaw communications with the native peoples); the Constable's Court (which oversaw the armed forces); the Admiral's Court (which oversaw naval matters including the maintenance of ports and navigable waters); the Treasurer's Court (which was responsible for the treasury and public revenue); the High Steward's Court (which was responsible for public works); the Steward's Court (which was responsible for public health, urban planning, and commerce); and the Chamberlain's Court (which was responsible for maintaining public records). Thorpe, *The Federal and State Constitutions*, vol. 5: 2777–78.

87. Thorpe, *The Federal and State Constitutions*, vol. 5: 2777, 2779–81.

88. Thorpe, *The Federal and State Constitutions*, vol. 5: 2779, 2781–82.

89. Thorpe, *The Federal and State Constitutions*, vol. 5: 2783.

90. Thorpe, *The Federal and State Constitutions*, vol. 5: 2783–85

91. Thorpe, *The Federal and State Constitutions*, vol. 5: 2785.

92. Sirmans, *Colonial South Carolina*, 10; see Weir, *Colonial South Carolina—A History*, 50.

93. Andrews, *The Colonial Period of American History*, vol. 3: 212–20; Osgood, *The American Colonies in the Seventeenth Century*, vol. 2: 208–10.

94. Andrews, *Colonial Self-Government*, 141.

95. Story, *Commentaries of the Constitution of the United States*, vol. 1: 122–23.

96. Middleton and Lombard, *Colonial America*, 152.

97. Sirmans, *Colonial South Carolina*, 18–19, 41–42; Weir, *Colonial South Carolina—A History*, 65.

98. Sirmans, *Colonial South Carolina*, 30.

99. Sirmans, *Colonial South Carolina*, 35.

100. Sirmans, *Colonial South Carolina*, 45–46; see Weir, *Colonial South Carolina—A History*, 66; Osgood; *The American Colonies in the Seventeenth Century*, vol. 2: 223–25.

101. Sirmans, *Colonial South Carolina*, 48; Weir, *Colonial South Carolina—A History*, 67; Middleton and Lombard, *Colonial America,* 218.

102. Weir, *Colonial South Carolina—A History*, 59; see Osgood, *The American Colonies in the Seventeenth Century*, vol. 2: 212.

103. Sirmans, *Colonial South Carolina*, 49–51.

104. Sirmans, *Colonial South Carolina*, 55–70.

105. Sirmans, *Colonial South Carolina*, 75–96; see Andrews, *The Colonial Period of American History*, vol. 3: 241–45.

106. Sirmans, *Colonial South Carolina*, 111–18, Andrews, *The Colonial Period of American History*, vol. 3: 245–46.

107. Sirmans, *Colonial South Carolina*, 118–28, Weir, *Colonial South Carolina—A History*, 101.

108. Sirmans, *Colonial South Carolina*, 129–31.

109. Andrews, *The Colonial Period of American History*, vol. 3: 246; Middleton and Lombard, *Colonial America*, 221.

110. Andrews, *The Colonial Period of American History*, vol. 3: 247–48; Osgood, *The American Colonies in the Seventeenth Century*, vol. 2: 233; Lefler and Powell, *Colonial North Carolina—A History*, 47.

111. Lefler and Powell, *Colonial North Carolina—A History*, 47–48; Andrews, *The Colonial Period of American History*, vol. 3: 249–50.

112. Lefler and Powell, *Colonial North Carolina—A History*, 49–52; Andrews, *The Colonial Period of American History*, vol. 3: 252–56; Osgood, *The American Colonies in the Seven-*

teenth Century, vol. 2: 239–41. As Andrews noted, "In the last analysis one is led to believe that it was neither the dislike of the 'plantation duty' that brought about the rebellion nor any deep-seated objection to the proprietary rule as such, for after all that rule rested very lightly on the colony, but rather the conviction that the Durant party was the most representative group of the planters in Albemarle and the only one that could be trusted with the colony's well being." Andrews, *The Colonial Period of American History*, vol. 3: 256–57.

113. Lefler and Powell, *Colonial North Carolina—A History*, 54; Andrews, *The Colonial Period of American History*, vol. 3: 257–58.

114. Andrews, *The Colonial Period of American History*, vol. 3: 258–63; Osgood, *The American Colonies in the Seventeenth Century*, vol. 2: 248–50.

115. Andrews, *The Colonial Period of American History*, vol. 3: 263–67; see Lefler and Powell, *Colonial North Carolina—A History*, 65–80.

116. Andrews, *The Colonial Period of American History*, vol. 3: 76–77; Middleton and Lombard, *Colonial America*, 113.

117. Middleton and Lombard, *Colonial America*, 115–16.

118. Middleton and Lombard, *Colonial America*, 113

119. Middleton and Lombard, *Colonial America*, 117.

120. Middleton and Lombard, *Colonial America*, 117–18.

121. Andrews, *The Colonial Period of American History*, vol. 3: 76–77.

122. Michael Kammen, *Colonial New York* (New York: Scribner, 1975), 71.

123. Pomfret, *Colonial New Jersey*, 4–5; Richard P. McCormick, *New Jersey from Colony to State* (Princeton: Princeton University Press, 1964), 16–17; Andrews, *Colonial Self-Government*, 76–81; Middleton and Lombard, *Colonial America*, 140–41.

124. Kammen, *Colonial New York*, 76; Pomfret, *Colonial New Jersey*, 5–6.

125. Andrews, *The Colonial Period of American History*, vol. 3: 57.

126. Thorpe, *The Federal and State Constitutions*, vol. 3: 1638–40.

127. Kammen, *Colonial New York*, 76.

128. John M. Murrin, "The New York Charter of Liberties 1683 and 1691," in Schecter, ed., *Roots of the Republic*, 48.

129. Commissioners of Statutory Revision, *The Colonial Laws of New York from Year 1664 to the Revolution* (Albany: James B. Lyon, 1894), 6–73.

130. *The Colonial Laws of New York*, xii–xiii; Lutz, *Colonial Origins of the American Constitution*, 254–55; Andrews, *Self-Government*, 84–85; Andrews, *The Colonial Period in American History*, vol. 3: 106–7; Osgood, *The American Colonies in the Seventeenth Century*, vol. 2: 159–60.

131. Middleton and Lombard, *Colonial America*, 144–47; Kammen, *Colonial New York*, 100.

132. Kammen, *Colonial New York*, 102.

133. Kammen, *Colonial New York*, 103; Andrews, *Colonial Self-Government*, 94–96; Andrews, *The Colonial Period of American History*, vol. 3: 112–17; Osgood, *The American Colonies in the Seventeenth Century*, vol. 2: 162–66.

134. Andrews, *Self-Government*, 96.

135. Lutz, *Colonial Origins of the American Constitution*, 256.

136. Lutz, *Colonial Origins of the American Constitution*, 257–58.

137. Lutz, *Colonial Origins of the American Constitution*, 258.

138. Lutz, *Colonial Origins of the American Constitution*, 259–61.

139. Kammen, *Colonial New York*, 104–105; Andrews, *Colonial Self-Government*, 96–98; Andrews, *The Colonial Period of American History*, vol. 3: 117–20; Osgood, *The American Colonies in the Seventeenth Century*, vol. 2: 167–68. On April 27, 1686, shortly before the revocation of the Charter of Franchises and Liberties, a charter for the City of New York was issued by governor Dugan on instructions from James II. This charter granted the citizens of New York City the liberties, franchises and privileges "As they have anciently had used, held and enjoyed." The city charter established a government including a mayor, six alderman and six assistants, who were to be elected by majority vote. The charter also provided for a court of common pleas. Schechter, *Roots of the Republic*, 91–105.

140. Middleton and Lombard, *Colonial America*, 189–94.

141. Berkeley and Carteret had been allies and supporters of York during his exile following the execution of his father, Charles I. Andrews, *Colonial Self-Government*, 102–4.

142. Thorpe, *The Federal and State Constitutions*, vol. 3: 2533–35; Story, *Commentaries on the Constitution of the United States*, vol. 1: 104–5; Andrews, *The Colonial Period of American History*, vol. 3: 138–39; Osgood, *The American Colonies in the Seventeenth Century*, vol. 2: 169–70.

143. Pomfret, *Colonial New Jersey-A History*, 7–8.

144. Osgood, *The American Colonies in the Seventeenth Century*, vol. 2: 169–73; Andrews, *The Colonial Period of American History*, vol. 3: 140; I. K. Steele, "The Board of Trade, The Quakers, and the Resumption of Colonial Charters, 1699–1702," *The William and Mary Quarterly* (1966), vol. 23: 603.

145. Pomfret, *Colonial New Jersey*, 22; McCormick, *New Jersey from Colony to State*, 35.

146. Thorpe, *The Federal and State Constitutions*, vol. 5: 2535; McCormick, *New Jersey from Colony to State*, 24; Pomfret; *Colonial New Jersey—A History*, 22–23; Craven, *New Jersey and the English Colonization of North America*, 48–49.

147. Thorpe, *The Federal and State Constitutions*, vol. 5: 2535–36.

148. Thorpe, *The Federal and State Constitutions*, vol. 5: 2535, 2537.

149. Thorpe, *The Federal and State Constitutions*, vol. 5: 2537–38.

150. Thorpe, *The Federal and State Constitutions*, vol. 5: 2538.

151. Thorpe, *The Federal and State Constitutions*, vol. 5: 2538.

152. Thorpe, *The Federal and State Constitutions*, vol. 5: 2538–39.

153. Thorpe, *The Federal and State Constitutions*, vol. 5: 2539.

154. Thorpe, *The Federal and State Constitutions*, vol. 5: 2539–40.

155. Thorpe, *The Federal and State Constitutions*, vol. 5: 2539–40, 2544.

156. Andrews, *Colonial Self-Government*, 104–9.

157. Pomfret, *Colonial New Jersey—A History*, 24 (cousin); Andrews, *Colonial Self-Government*, 107 (brother).

158. McCormick, *New Jersey from Colony to State*, 26–27; John E. Pomfret, *The Province of East New Jersey 1609–1702* (Princeton: Princeton University Press, 1962), 56–67.

159. Pomfret, *The Province of East New Jersey*, 67–68; Andrews, *The Colonial Period of American History*, vol. 3: 150; Osgood, *the American Colonies in the Seventeenth Century*, vol. 2: 180–81.

160. Middleton and Lombard, *Colonial America*, 174.

161. Pomfret, *Colonial New Jersey—A History*, 31, 36; Andrews, *The Colonial Period of American History*, vol. 3: 152.

162. Craven, *New Jersey and the English Colonization of North America*, 61–62; Andrews, *Colonial Self-Government*, 114–16.

163. McCormick, *New Jersey from Colony to State*, 27, 40; Andrews, *The Colonial Period of American History*, vol. 3: 152–53; Thorpe, *The Federal and State Constitutions*, vol. 5: 2551–60.

164. Thorpe, *The Federal and State Constitutions*, vol. 5: 2548–51; Osgood, *The American Colonies in the Seventeenth Century*, vol. 2: 192–93.

165. Thorpe, *The Federal and State Constitutions*, vol. 5: 2560–65.

166. Thorpe, *The Federal and State Constitutions*, vol. 5: 2565; Pomfret, *Colonial New Jersey—A History*, 45; McCormick, *New Jersey from Colony to State*, 46–47; Andrews, *Colonial Self-Government*, 122.

167. Thorpe, *The Federal and State Constitutions*, vol. 5: 2565–66.

168. Thorpe, *The Federal and State Constitutions*, vol. 5: 2566–67.

169. Pomfret, *Colonial New Jersey—A History*, 77–91; McCormick, *New Jersey from Colony to State*, 47–48; Andrews, *Colonial Self-Government*, 123–25; Osgood, *The American Colonies in the Seventeenth Century*, vol. 2: 199.

170. McCormick, *New Jersey from Colony to State*, 31; Story, *Commentaries on the Constitution of the United States*, vol. 1: 106–7; Pomfret, *the Province of East New Jersey*, 130–32.

171. Thorpe, *The Federal and State Constitutions*, vol. 5: 2567–73.

172. Thorpe, *The Federal and State Constitutions*, vol. 5: 2574–82; Pomfret, *The Province of East New Jersey*, 140.

173. Thorpe, *The Federal and State Constitutions*, vol. 5: 2584–90; Craven, *New Jersey and the English Colonization of North America*, 91–92; Andrews, *Colonial Self-Government*, 127; Story, *Commentaries of the Constitution of the United States*, vol. 1: 107; McCormick, *New Jersey from Colony to State*, 34–36; Pomfret, *The Province of East New Jersey*, 259–62, 336–64.
174. Andrews, *Colonial Self-Government*, 165–66; see Andrews, *The Colonial Period of American History*, vol. 3: 268–70; Wayland Fuller Dunaway, *A History of Pennsylvania* (New York: Prentice-Hall, 1935), 25–29.
175. Andrews, *The Colonial Period of American History*, vol. 3: 152–54; 272–75; Middleton and Lombard, *Colonial America*, 161.
176. Sidney G. Fisher, *The Quaker Colonies* (New York: United Publishers Association, 1919), 9; Middleton and Lombard, *Colonial America*, 176.
177. Thorpe, *The Federal and State Constitutions*, vol. 5: 3035; Dunaway, *A History of Pennsylvania*, 30–33; Andrews, *Colonial Self-Government*, 168–71; Andrews, *The Colonial Period of American History*, vol. 3: 275–81; Middleton and Lombard, *Colonial America*, 161–63.
178. Story, *Commentaries on the Constitution of the United States*, vol. 1: 109.
179. Middleton and Lombard, *Colonial America*, 176.
180. Thorpe, *The Federal and State Constitutions*, vol. 5: 3037–39.
181. Thorpe, *The Federal and State Constitutions*, vol. 5: 3039.
182. Gambrell, *History of Early Maryland*, 31.
183. Thorpe, *The Federal and State Constitutions*, vol. 5: 3037–38.
184. Thorpe, *The Federal and State Constitutions*, vol. 5: 3040–43.
185. Thorpe, *The Federal and State Constitutions*, vol. 5: 3042.
186. Thorpe, *The Federal and State Constitutions*, vol. 5: 3041; see generally, Andrews, *The Colonial Period of American History*, vol. 3: 283–85.
187. Thorpe, *The Federal and State Constitutions*, vol. 5: 3043.
188. Story, *Commentaries on the Constitution of the United States*, vol. 1: 111.
189. Thorpe, *The Federal and State Constitutions*, vol. 5: 3044.
190. Thorpe, *The Federal and State Constitutions*, vol. 5: 3046.
191. Thorpe, *The Federal and State Constitutions*, vol. 5: 3046; Andrews, *Colonial Self-Government*, 177–79.
192. Story, *Commentaries on the Constitution of the United States*, vol. 1: 111–12.
193. Dunaway, *A History of Pennsylvania*, 34; Andrews, *Colonial Self-Government*, 179–80; Middleton, *Colonial America*, 164.
194. Thorpe, *The Federal and State Constitutions*, vol. 5: 3047. Landsman, "The Middle Colonies: New Opportunities for Settlement, 1660–1700," 360.
195. Andrews described the Fundamental Laws as "the broadest, sanest, and most equitable charter drafted for anybody of colonists up to this time." Andrews, *Colonial Self-Government*, 121.
196. Andrews, *Colonial Self-Government*, 21.
197. Thorpe, *The Federal and State Constitutions*, vol. 5: 3048; Osgood, *The American Colonies in the Seventeenth Century*, vol. 2: 257.
198. Thorpe, *The Federal and State Constitutions*, vol. 5: 3048.
199. Fisher, *The Quaker Colonies*, 14.
200. Lutz, *Colonial Origins of the American Constitution*, 271.
201. Thorpe, *The Federal and State Constitutions*, vol. 5: 3049.
202. Thorpe, *The Federal and State Constitutions*, vol. 5: 3049.
203. Thorpe, *The Federal and State Constitutions*, vol. 5: 3050.
204. Thorpe, *The Federal and State Constitutions*, vol. 5: 3050–51.
205. Thorpe, *The Federal and State Constitutions*, vol. 5: 3051–52; Andrews, *The Colonial Period of American History*, vol. 3: 288.
206. Lutz, *Colonial Origins of the American Constitution*, 271.
207. Thorpe, *The Federal and State Constitutions*, vol. 5: 3052.
208. Thorpe, *The Federal and State Constitutions*, vol. 5: 3052–54.
209. Osgood, *The American Colonies in the Seventeenth Century*, vol. 2: 252.

210. Thorpe, *The Federal and State Constitutions*, vol. 5: 3060.
211. Thorpe, *The Federal and State Constitutions*, vol. 5: 3062–63; Lutz, *Colonial Origins of the American Constitution*, 281–85.
212. Thorpe, *The Federal and State Constitutions*, vol. 5: 3060–61; Lutz, *Colonial Origins of the American Constitution*, 282–84.
213. Thorpe, *The Federal and State Constitutions*, vol. 5: 3061–62; Lutz, *Colonial Origins of the American Constitution*, 283–85.
214. Middleton and Lombard, *Colonial America*, 176.
215. Thorpe, *The Federal and State Constitutions*, vol. 5: 3063; Lutz, *Colonial Origins of the American Constitution*, 285–86.
216. Dunaway, *A History of Pennsylvania*, 35–37; Andrews, *Colonial Self-Government*, 185–86.
217. Lutz, *Colonial Origins of the American Constitution*, 287–88.
218. Middleton and Lombard, *Colonial America*, 177.
219. Andrews, *Colonial Self-Government*, 189–90. Landsman, "The Middle Colonies—New Opportunities for Settlement, 1600–1700," 360.
220. Thorpe, *The Federal and State Constitutions*, vol. 5: 3064.
221. Andrews, *Colonial Self-Government*, 191–93.
222. Andrews, *Colonial Self-Government*, 193.
223. Thorpe, *The Federal and State Constitutions*, vol. 5: 3071–76.
224. Andrews, *Colonial Self-Government*, 194–95.
225. Dunaway, *A History of Pennsylvania*, 53–55; Andrews, *Colonial Self-Government*, 196–200; Andrews, *The Colonial Period of American History*, vol. 3: 311–15; see Osgood, *The American Colonies in the Seventeenth Century*, vol. 2: 261–69; Middleton and Lombard, *Colonial America*, 223
226. Thorpe, *The Federal and State Constitutions*, vol. 5: 3070; Dunaway, *A History of Pennsylvania*, 55–56; Osgood, *The American Colonies in the Seventeenth Century*, vol. 2: 257.
227. Thorpe, *The Federal and State Constitutions*, vol. 5: 3071–76; Andrews, *The Colonial Period of American History*, vol. 3: 317.
228. Thorpe, *The Federal and State Constitutions*, vol. 5: 3076.
229. Thorpe, *The Federal and State Constitutions*, vol. 5: 3079; Andrews, *The Colonial Period of American History*, vol. 3: 317. Osgood, *The American Colonies in the Seventeenth Century*, vol. 2: 276; Sarson, *British America 1500–1800*, 162; Middleton and Lombard, *Colonial America*, 223–24.
230. Story, *Commentaries on the Constitution of the United States*, vol. 1: 113; Dunaway, *A History of Pennsylvania*, 58; Andrews, *The Colonial Period of American History*, vol. 3: 319–23; Sarson, *British America 1500–1800*, 162.
231. Thorpe, *The Federal and State Constitutions*, vo. 1: 557.
232. Andrews, *The Colonial Period of American History*, vol. 3: 293–94; Fisher, *The Quaker Colonies*, 200–13.
233. Andrews, *The Colonial Period of American History*, vol. 3: 294.
234. Andrews, *The Colonial Period of American History*, vol. 3: 295–96; John A. Munroe, *Colonial Delaware: A History* (Millwood: KTO Press, 1978), 62–63, 92–93.
235. Andrews, *The Colonial Period of American History*, vol. 3: 321–22.
236. Thorpe, *The Federal and State Constitutions*, vol. 1: 558.
237. Thorpe, *The Federal and State Constitutions*, vol. 1: 559.
238. Munroe, *Colonial Delaware*, 84–85.
239. Carol E. Hoffecker and Barbara F. Benson, "*Festina Lente*: The Development of Constitutionalism in Delaware," in George E. Connor and Christopher W. Hammons, eds., *The Constitutionalism of American States* (Columbia: Missouri University Press, 2008), 168.
240. Thorpe, *The Federal and State Constitutions*, vol. 1: 559.
241. Andrews, *The Colonial Period of American History*, vol. 3: 326 n.1.
242. See James Oglethorpe, "Some Account of the Designs of the Trustees for Establishing the Colony of Georgia in America," in Kavenagh, ed., *Foundations of Colonial America*, 1833.
243. Thorpe, *The Federal and State Constitutions*, vol. 2: 765–66; Sarson, *British America 1500–1800*, 178–79; Middleton and Lombard, *Colonial America*, 438.

244. Osgood, *The American Colonies in the Eighteenth Century*, vol. 2: 36; Meinig, *The Shaping of America*, 182.
245. Middleton and Lombard, *Colonial America*, 438.
246. Thorpe, *The Federal and State Constitutions*, vol. 2: 766–77.
247. Thorpe, *The Federal and State Constitutions*, vol. 5: 770–72.
248. Thorpe, *The Federal and State Constitutions*, vol. 5: 773–74; Middleton and Lombard, *Colonial America*, 438.
249. Thorpe, *The Federal and State Constitutions*, vol. 5: 774.
250. Thorpe, *The Federal and State Constitutions*, vol. 5: 776.
251. Thorpe, *The Federal and State Constitutions*, vol. 5: 767–65, 772–73; Osgood, *The American Colonies in the Seventeenth Century*, vol. 2: 38.
252. Thorpe, *The Federal and State Constitutions*, vol. 5: 770–75. The Bank of England was the financial agent of the corporation and the accounts were submitted annually to the Lord Chancellor and the Lord Chief Justice. Osgood, *The American Colonies in the Seventeenth Century*, vol. 2: 43.
253. Thorpe, *The Federal and State Constitutions*, vol. 5: 773.
254. Middleton and Lombard, *Colonial America*, 439.
255. Osgood, *The American Colonies in the Eighteenth Century*, vol. 2: 35.
256. Osgood, *The American Colonies in the Eighteenth Century*, vol. 2: 69.
257. Middleton and Lombard, *Colonial America*, 440–41.
258. Osgood, *The American Colonies in the Seventeenth Century*, vol. 2: 39.
259. Story, *Commentaries on the Constitution of the United States*, vol. 1: 130; Middleton and Lombard, *Colonial America*, 441; Meinig, *The Shaping of America*, 182.
260. Kavenagh, *Foundations of Colonial America*, vol. 3: 2028–57.
261. Kavenagh, *Foundations of Colonial America*, vol. 3: 2058–61.

Chapter Four

The Emergence of the American Constitutional Tradition in the Age of the Imperium

The conception of a written national constitution as the statement of the supreme and fundamental law has been seen as an American invention.[1] Before the federal convention of 1787, a constitution of government, like that of Great Britain, was considered to be comprised of substantive principles "embedded in the institutions of a nation," with an existence that was neither independent of nor precedent to the development of those institutions.[2]

However, as remarkable as the achievement of the 1787 convention was, the craftsmanship of the Constitution's writers was very much the product of two hundred years of history and experience that began with the earliest charters for the exploration and settlement of North America. Out of this history and the experiences of their predecessors emerged a tradition of constitutionalism that was uniquely American.

One effect of the corporate and proprietary charters was that they created largely autonomous political and social entities which, although nominally part of Britain and loyal to the king, were created as their own body politic and were functionally independent of the crown government.[3] One can readily see the genesis of the colonists' self-conception of independence in the creation of these micro-societies planted in a distant land and left to survive largely by their own devices without the direct involvement of the crown.

The colonies that were established under direct grants from the crown relied on the specified powers and authority enumerated in their charters to give legitimacy to the framework of their governments. The colonial governments crafted by the palatine proprietors similarly drew their legitimacy from the "concessions" propounded by the proprietors rather than from acts of parliament.

The charters granted to Gilbert and Raleigh, and later to the Virginia Company, established the colonial enterprises as their own body politic, invested with broad authority to adopt laws and to put them into execution, as well as to establish governmental structures of governors, councils, and legislative bodies. In New England, the Plymouth Colony, although lacking a formal royal charter of government, was founded on a written covenant to act as a "civil body politic" thereby to "enact, constitute, and frame, such just and equal laws, ordinances, acts, constitutions and offices, from time to time, as shall be thought most meet and convenient for the general good of the colony," to which the signatories pledged "all due submission and obedience."[4] In like fashion, the expatriate settlers from Massachusetts Bay who established the Connecticut, New Hampshire, New London, and Rhode Island settlements, also without the imprimatur of royal authority, relied on written mutually agreed on covenants to lay down the principles and structures of their governments.

Thus, from its beginnings, the constitutional tradition of America diverged fundamentally from its British antecedent. First, American constitutional law derives from the construction and interpretation of a single document on which the legitimacy of governmental institutions and actions depend. Although construction and interpretation may draw on a variety of sources, it is this single document around which the entirety of constitutional discourse revolves. Although custom may provide insight and legislation may provide practical application, it is the Constitution alone that is authoritative. Thus, regardless of how broadly or narrowly the provisions of the Constitution are construed, the authority of the federal government to act in its several spheres arises from the Constitution and from no other source.

The charters, together with the covenants and statements of fundamental law that emerged from them, served as the constitutions-in-fact of the various colonies. Importantly, they also established both the practice and the expectation among the colonists that the powers of their governments and the rights of the body politic vis-à-vis those governments should be solemnized in a writing that was commonly understood and readily available for consultation and interpretation.[5]

Second, unlike British constitutionalism, the American constitutional tradition is one of enumerated governmental powers. This conceptualization of a government founded on powers specifically set forth in a written constitution also had its beginnings in the colonial charters. The charters established the legitimacy of political power in British America and the charters established, in broad outline, the manner and the means by which that power would be exercised.

These foundational charters and agreements were the source of the government's authority in the colonies. It was under the charter of the Virginia Company in 1618 that the first representative assembly of the settlers was established through which the consent of the freemen of the colonies was expressed to the laws and ordinances for their governance. Over time, the colonists, acting through their assemblies, adopted their own written plans of government, including executive, legislative, and judicial functions, as they did in the 1634 Massachusetts Agreement on Legislation; the 1636 Plymouth Agreement; the Fundamental Orders of 1639 in Connecticut; the Fundamental Articles of 1639 in New Haven; the Act and Orders of 1647 in Rhode Island; the Concessions and Agreement of 1664 in New Jersey; the Fundamental Constitution of 1669 in Carolina; the General Laws and Liberties of 1680 in New Hampshire; the Charter of Liberty of 1682 in Pennsylvania; and the Charter of Franchises and Liberties of 1683 in New York.

Other foundational documents served as authoritative guarantees of fundamental individual and civic rights. For example, the 1641 Massachusetts Body of Liberties was an extensive statement of civic rights and liberties, many of which were later enshrined in the federal Bill of Rights. The edicts of the proprietors, such as the 1676 Statement of Rights and Privileges in New Jersey; the 1682 Charter of Liberty in Pennsylvania; and the 1683 Charter of Franchises and Liberties in New York, similarly included statements of rights and liberties that anticipated the federal Constitution a century later.

As reflected in the charters of the Virginia, New England, and Maryland colonies, the early Stuarts (particularly Charles I) pursued a "weak state" colonial policy in which the *imperium* was centered in the metropole of London and Westminster but administration of the colonies was left to the corporate body politic or to the proprietor. As MacMillan observed, because the early Stuarts lacked coercive power, they had to rely on peripheral elites to carry out policy and the farther away from the metropole the people or the institutions resided, the more independent and distinct they became.[6]

The later Stuarts, Charles II and his brother James II, acting through the privy council and the Committee on Trade, sought to assert royal authority over the colonies through centralization of the government of the American colonies into dominions. However, as the experience with the Dominion of New England (which was failing even before the Glorious Revolution)[7] demonstrated, the crown lacked both the focus and the resources to achieve the centralized authority over the American colonies that they sought.

The charters had particular significance in two respects during this weak-state era. First, the charters imparted legitimacy and authority for the colonial governments to establish laws and erect institutions. Second, the charters made explicit the relationship of the colonists to the crown. That is, the charters acknowledged that the colonists remained subjects of the king to whom they owed their allegiance, and in exchange for (or in consequence of) their allegiance, the colonists were endowed with the birth rights of English citizens (such as rights to due process and trial by jury and to freedom from arbitrary imprisonment and freedom of association).[8]

William III did not share the same imperial vision as Charles and James. Barnes noted that the change in imperial policy was signaled by the recommendation of the Lords of Trade in February 1689 that Governor Andros be recalled from New England and that a new charter be granted for Massachusetts.[9] The new charter, which was issued in 1691, differed significantly from the prior charter by providing for liberty of religious worship (thus undermining the Puritan theocracy) and for increased powers of the royal governor with respect to the legislature.

The domination of the royal governor over colonial affairs became the principal means by which the metropole sought to control the administration of the colonies. In 1696, the Lords of Trade were replaced by the Lords Commissioners of Trade and Plantations, known as the Board of Trade.[10] In 1701, the board recommended the forfeiture of all private charters and consolidation of the American colonies. Although parliament rejected the board's recommendation, all of the colonies were soon under the effective control of royal governors and their councils, and although conflict in the colonies arose from parliament's rejection of colonial claims of autonomy, a more relaxed and stable relationship between the metropole and the colonies ensued that lasted until mid-century.[11]

However, this new policy toward the American colonies would have significant implications later for the colonists' relations with the metropole.[12] As Sarson observed, after 1689, "the orientation of political antagonism in Britain shifted on its axis," to a "collusive relationship between the executive and legislature," such that there was less "vertical conflict" between the king and the parliament than there was "horizontal conflict" among the legislators.[13]

This was not the case in the American colonies. Unlike the relations between parliament and the crown following the Glorious Revolution, no "principal or practice of coordination" had evolved between the executive (the royal governor) and the colonial legislatures. As a consequence, "the primary axis of political antagonism remained the vertical one" resulting in polarized confrontations between the legislatures and the governors.[14]

With the conclusion of the Seven Years' War (and the American analog, the French and Indian War) in 1763, the wealth and population of the American colonies came to be viewed by the metropole as a source of revenue for the depleted treasury. David J. Hulsebosch has written that for the metropole, the end of the war, "was an opportunity to exercise greater control over the colonies and to force them to shoulder some of the expenses of the war and of maintaining the military in the colonies." An additional and "even more ambitious goal" of the metropole was to use the revenue from the colonies to free the royal administrators from dependence on the colonial legislatures for their salaries and for the fees for their services.[15]

To accomplish those goals, parliament enacted a variety of measures to raise funds and to assert its authority over the colonies beginning in April 1764 with the American Revenue Act (also known as the Sugar Act). These measures set in motion a series of events that would result in armed insurrection a decade later.

During this period, the colonial charters assumed an additional significance in the context of colonial petitions and grievances, a tradition as old as the colonies themselves.[16] Stephan Foster and Evan Haefeli noted that after 1689, "the colonies developed various semi-formal grievance mechanisms that, whatever the verdict rendered in any particular case, became an integral part of their constitution as that term was then understood."[17]

The right to petition was claimed by the colonists as being among their rights as English citizens, evidenced in the charters. That is, the charters provided that the colonies were an extension of the realm of England and the settlers could enjoy the liberties, franchises, and privileges of English citizens (although what that meant was a subject of dispute).[18] Greene observed in this regard that for those migrating to the American colonies, English law and liberties were "crucial to their ability to maintain their identity as English people." For that reason, "it is scarcely surprising that among English colonists all over America the attempt to establish English law and the rights and liberties of Englishmen was constantly pursued from the first settlements to the American Revolution." This assertion of English rights and liberties was not accepted by the metropole, which "remained skeptical about not whether, but to what extent English colonists were entitled to English law and liberties."[19]

Notwithstanding the skepticism of the metropole, the charters provided a basis for challenging what were perceived to be arbitrary actions by the crown governors and later by parliament itself.[20] The colonists and the revolutionaries relied on the charters not as the source of rights and liberties (because the crown could withdraw the charters at any time, and with them the colonists' English rights and liberties), but instead, the charters were regarded as a memorialization of those rights and liberties. In this regard, John P. Reid has argued, "What importance the charter had was not as substance but as symbols. People thought of them as they thought of another charter, an ancient English charter, permitting American whigs to frame an argument for colonial rights within one of the strongest, most persistent dogmas of English constitutionalism: the tradition of Magna Carta embodying the fundamental constitutional concept that individuals had rights limiting the power of government."[21]

Grievances were generally expressed as violations of rights, and the most common grievances were constitutional and asserted violations of colonial civil rights. Framed as complaints against the king and the metropole, the grievances grounded on the charters, particularly in the revolutionary era, were also statements of American rights.[22] Indeed, as Pauline Maier has made clear, Jefferson's preamble to the 1776 Virginia Constitution (and later the Declaration of Independence) as well as George Mason's Declaration of Rights for Virginia drew heavily from the English Declaration of Rights that ended the reign of James II,[23] the benefit of which the revolutionaries claimed by virtue of their charters.

When the crown provincial governments were withdrawn in the spring of 1775 and the newly independent states were compelled to confront the necessity of adopting their own constitutions for the structuring of their governments and the ordering their societies, the charters and the enactments of the colonial legislatures provided templates and first principles for the revolutionary state constitution writers.

Thus, by the time the Founders gathered to write the federal Constitution in 1787, Americans had become accustomed to an authoritative written document that provided the source of the rights and authorities that in Britain was comprised of the common law and parliamentary enactments. Accordingly, although the federal Constitution was firmly rooted in British constitutional principles, there was a continuity of American constitutional thought that stretched back to these foundational documents, representing the American constitutional tradition.

NOTES

1. Merrill D. Peterson, "The Idea of a Written Constitution in the Thought of the Founders," in Howard, ed., *The United States Constitution*, 43.
2. McIlwain, *Constitutionalism*, 14.
3. See Evarts Boutell Greene, *Political America, 1690–1740* (New York: Harpers, 1905), 63.
4. Lutz, *Colonial Origins of the American Constitution*, 32.
5. Hockett, *The Constitutional History of the United States, 1776–1826*, 117–18.
6. MacMillan, *The Atlantic Imperial Constitution*, 12–13.
7. As Barnes observed, the failure of the Dominion of New England "was due partly to the omission of a representative assembly, for which the king was responsible, and partly to certain blunders committed by the Lords of Trade in drawing up the details of Andros's instructions and by Andros in carrying out these instructions too strictly." Barnes, *The Dominion of New England*, 44.
8. MacMillan, *The Atlantic Imperial Constitution*, 27.
9. Barnes, *The Dominion of New England*, 262.
10. Among the responsibilities conferred on the Board of Trade were: to inquire into the state and conditions of the general trade of England; to consider methods for employing the poor of the kingdom; to inform themselves of what naval stores might be furnished by the colonies; to examine the instructions given to royal governors; and to examine the legislation

enacted by the colonial legislatures and to report on the "usefulness or mischief thereof." Greene, *Great Britain and the American Colonies*, 129–30.

11. Sarson, *British America 1500–1800*, 200–6; MacFarlane, *The British in the Americas 1480–1815*, 202–4; Greene, *Negotiated Authorities*, 48–62, 87–90; Richard R. Johnson, "Growth and Mastery: British North America 1690–1748," in Marshall and Low, eds., *The Eighteenth Century*, 297. As Lawrence H. Leder observed, "Out of the maelstrom of revolutions [against the dominions in Massachusetts, New York, and Maryland] emerged several lessons for imperial administrators. The Dominion was dead as a device to curb the individuality of the colonies, and future schemes for imperial unification met with chilled responses from Whitehall. Colonial cooperation replaced imperial coercion as the established goal in the first half of the eighteenth century." Lawrence H. Leder, "The Glorious Revolution and the Pattern of Imperial Relationships," in Martin, ed., *Interpreting Colonial America*, 220.

12. Leder further observed that, "From 1689 on each royal colony—and conversion of colonies to royal status became a fixed principle of policy—had a standard set of governmental institutions: a royal governor, an appointed council, and an elected assembly. This uniformity of institutional organization carried with it the premise that the rights of Englishmen followed the flag to the far corners of the empire and future arguments over governmental power and imperial relations would be predicated upon the implications of this touchstone of political faith." Leder, "The Glorious Revolution and the Pattern of Imperial Relationships," in Martin, ed., *Interpreting Colonial America*, 220.

13. Sarson, *British America 1500–1800*, 216–17.

14. Sarson, *British America 1500–1800*, 217–18.

15. Daniel J. Hulsebosch, "The American Revolution (II): The Origin and Nature of Colonial Grievances," in Foster, ed., *British North America in the Seventeenth and Eighteenth Centuries*, 304–5.

16. Hulsebosch observed that, "As soon as the colonists settled in America, they began to complain about the structure and the nature of imperial governance." Hulsebosch, "The American Revolution (II): The Origin and Nature of Colonial Grievances," in Foster, ed., *British North America in the Seventeenth and Eighteenth Centuries*, 289.

17. Stephan Foster and Evan Haefeli, "British North America in the Empire," in Foster, ed., *British North America in the Seventeenth and Eighteenth Centuries*, 32.

18. Mary S. Bilder has argued that the principles embodied in the charters of repugnancy and divergence of colonial laws *viz.* the laws of England—that is, the provisions of the charters to the effect that colonial legislatures could enact laws that differed from the laws of England to meet their individual circumstances (i.e., divergence) so long as those laws were "consonant with reason" and were neither repugnant nor contrary to the laws, statutes and rights of England (i.e., repugnance)—bound the American colonies as an extension of the realm of England. These twin principles formed the basis of a transatlantic constitution, which arguably included Magna Carta, that encompassed the dual authorities of the English empire in America, the metropole and the colonial legislatures. Mary S. Bilder, *The Transatlantic Constitution: Colonial Legal Culture and the Empire* (Cambridge: Harvard University Press, 2004), 1.

19. Greene, "Empire and Identity from the Glorious Revolution to the American Revolution," in Marshall and Low, eds., *The Eighteenth Century*, 222.

20. For example, in his pamphlet, "A Defense of the New-England Charters," written in 1712–1713 but published in 1721, Jeremiah Dummer argued that the inhabitants of the charter colonies "have the more need of their charters to make them amends; for people must have some encouragement to sit down on a cold and barren soil." Among other grievances, Dummer declaimed at length concerning the abuses of their offices by the royal governors who "are apt to abuse their power and grow rich by oppression." Drummer argued that the charters were necessary to restrain such abuses because "to enlarge the power of the governors is to give them greater power to oppress; and to vacate the charters is to enlarge their powers, the government in that case of course devolving upon them; as we see in those plantations which never had any charters." Greene, *Great Britain and the American Colonies, 1660–1763*, 165–71.

21. John Phillip Reid, *Constitutional History of the American Revolution* (Madison: University of Wisconsin Press, 1986), 166. For example, arguing the rights of colonists, Samuel Adams wrote in 1772, "That the colonists are well entitled to all the essential rights, liberties,

and privileges of men and freemen born in Britain is manifest not only from the colony charters in general, but as acts of the British Parliament." Samuel Adams, *The Rights of the Colonists: The Report of the Committee of Correspondence to the Boston Town Meeting*, Old South Leaflets No. 173 (Boston: Directors of Old South Works, 1906) vol. 7: 421.

22. Reid, *Constitutional History of the American Revolution*, 169–72. Reid also noted that the imperial representatives understood the colonists' grievances to be grounded on the British constitution and the charters. Reid quoted General Thomas Gage as having informed the metropole that, "There are three fundamentals on which the people of this colony endeavor to establish the political doctrines they have promulgated within these few years. These are *Charter Rights, British Constitution*, and the laws of God and Nature." Reid, *Constitutional History of the American Revolution*, 214 (emphasis original).

23. Pauline Maier, *American Scripture: Making the Declaration of Independence* (New York: Alfred A. Knopf, 1997), 51, 55, 126.

Part II

Revolutionary Constitutionalism, 1775 to 1784

Chapter Five

The Quest for a Federal Union

American constitutionalism also was influenced by the various proposals and plans for a colonial union government that were put forward in the roughly century and a half preceding the adoption and ratification of the federal Constitution. Although each of these initiatives was unsuccessful in its own time, these plans advanced a conception of federalism that sought to harmonize the sovereign interests of the constituent states with the necessity and advantages of collective action by a representative government when the interests involved transcended purely local concern.

Attempts were made on at least six occasions to fashion a union government of colonies. The earliest of these efforts was the confederation of the Connecticut, Massachusetts Bay, New Haven, and Plymouth Colonies, as discussed in Part I, styled as the United Colonies of New England. The articles under which the United Colonies were formed provided for mutual defense and the creation of a representative governing body, composed of two delegates from each of the member colonies, which was to resolve disputes among the members and to moderate the relations of the members with each other and with the native peoples.[1] As would be the case with later attempts at union, the articles of the United Colonies of New England forbade the governing body from "intermeddling" with the internal affairs of the member colonies. Formed primarily for mutual defense, active engagement in the confederation declined following the restoration of the English monarchy and the conversion to royal colonies under direct supervision of the crown. By the time the charter of the Massachusetts Bay Colony was recalled in 1684, the United Colonies of New England had become moribund.

Nevertheless, plans for broader unions of the colonies continued to be proposed. The first of these proposals was made by William Penn in 1697 as an alternate to the recommendation by the Lords of Trade and Plantations for the consolidation of all military forces in the colonies under the command of the King. Later, following a call by the Lords for a federation of the northern colonies to meet the military threat posed by the French, a proposal authored by Benjamin Franklin that became known as the Albany Plan of Union was submitted to the Crown government in 1754. Still later in 1774, as the movement for independence from Britain gained momentum, a plan of union was submitted to the Continental Congress by Joseph Galloway, a loyalist, in an effort to thwart a general rebellion of the colonies against the crown government. However, instead of Galloway's proposal, the Continental Congress adopted Articles of Association in reaction to the "Intolerable Acts." Although primarily commercial in nature, the Articles of Association represented a significant step toward concerted action by the colonies. Lastly, to meet the exigent demands of war with Britain, the newly independent states adopted the Articles of Confederation and Perpetual Union in November 1777. These Articles of Confederation served as the basis for the national government until they were replaced by the Constitution in 1787.

Each of these experiments in achieving a national structure of government, although flawed, were foundational. Like the charter governments, these frames of national government informed the constitutionalism of eighteenth-century America.

WILLIAM PENN'S PLAN OF UNION: 1697

Soon after the Committee of Trade and Plantations (the "Lords of Trade") was formed on May 15, 1696, the committee recommended that the military forces in the American colonies be consolidated under a "Captain-General," appointed by the king, who would assume the powers of government in the colonies to which his military exploits called him.[2]

On December 11, 1696, William Penn appeared before the Lords of Trade in his capacity as proprietor of East New Jersey to voice his objection to the plan. Penn "spoke also of the quota required from the neighbouring colonies for the defence of New York and said that he conceived the best way of regulating it would be, by stated Deputies from each Province, to meet in one common Assembly: the effecting of which was observed to require one Captain-General or Vice Roy to preside." Penn "promised to draw up a scheme more fully in writing."[3]

Penn submitted his plan to the Lords on February 8, 1697.[4] The plan was comprised of seven points. Penn proposed that representatives of the colonies meet once a year ("and oftener if need be") in time of war and otherwise at least once every two years in peace time. Each colony was to appoint two persons who were "well Qualified, for Sense Sobriety and Substance," as representatives, such that the congress would be composed of twenty representatives. This congress was to meet "as near as Conveniently may be, to the most Central colony," which Penn believed would "in all probability, be New York."[5]

This representative assembly would address matters of intercolonial concern and would adjudicate disputes between the colonies, such as when debtors absconded from one colony to another to avoid their "just debts" or when offenders fled the jurisdiction of a colony. Additionally, the assembly was to "prevent or cure Injuries in points of Commerce," and to "consider the ways and means to support the Union and safety" of the colonies "against the Public Enemies."[6]

The king "King's Commander" was to chair the assembly and Penn suggested that the royal governor of New York would be a suitable candidate. Penn also proposed that in time of war, the commander would have charge of all the colonies' militias "against the Common Enemy."[7]

No action on Penn's proposal was taken by the Lords of Trade. However, a half-century later, when representatives of the colonies met in general session at Albany, New York in 1754, Benjamin Franklin put forward a second plan of union which, like Penn's plan, was a blend of royal rule and colonial autonomy and which also like Penn's plan and the earlier United Colonies of New England, centered on a representative body chosen by the colonists.[8]

THE ALBANY PLAN OF UNION: 1755

The imperatives of a common defense to the threat posed by the French to British settlements in what is now western Pennsylvania and Ohio, and of the preservation of the Anglo-alliance with the Iroquois Nation, led the Lords of Trade on September 18, 1753, to request that the governor of New York call for a conference of the Maryland, Massachusetts, New Hampshire, New Jersey, New York, Pennsylvania, and Virginia colonies with a view toward forming a union for their mutual defense and assistance. In response to that request, the acting governor of New York, James Delancey, invited delegates from those colonies to convene in Albany on June 14, 1754.[9] The Lords informed Governor Delancey on July 15, 1754, that in their view, "a general union of strength and interest is become absolutely necessary."[10]

The delegates to the Albany Congress met on June 19, 1754. Although only the delegates from Massachusetts had been specifically authorized to effect a plan of union,[11] by June 24, the question was raised before the convention "whether a Union of all the Colonies is not at present absolutely necessary for the security and defense."[12] A committee was formed which included Theodore Atkinson of New Hampshire, Benjamin Franklin of Pennsylvania, Stephen Hopkins of Rhode Island, Thomas Hutchinson of Massachusetts, William Pitkin of Connecticut, William Smith of New York, and Benjamin Tasker of Maryland.[13] This committee was directed by the convention to "prepare and receive Plans and Schemes for the Union of the Colonies, and to digest them into one general plan."[14] Although the committee considered several plans offered by various delegates, the principal basis of the plan proposed by the committee was the work of Benjamin Franklin.

Franklin had long been a proponent of a united government for the colonies. As early as March 20, 1750, Franklin had written to James Parker that relations with the native peoples as well as the defense of the colonies would best be served by a council appointed by the colonies chaired by a royal governor, "to preside in the Council or in some manner to concur with and confirm their acts," as well as to "take care of the execution."[15] Franklin believed that a union of the colonies overseen by a royal governor would serve to erode or eliminate the distinction between a colonist and a British subject and so continue the evolution of the imperial relationship.[16]

Franklin came to the Albany Congress having developed an outline for the union government that reflected the influence of the United Colonies of New England, which he had styled as "short hints toward a Scheme for a General Union of the British Colonies on the Continent."

The committee submitted its proposed plan of union to the convention on June 28. After long and contentious debate, a plan of union was adopted on July 10.[17] The plan was to be submitted for approval first to the colonial legislatures and ultimately to parliament.

Under the plan, "one general government" was to be formed "including all the said colonies, within and under which government each colony may retain its present constitution." As Franklin had proposed, the government was to be administered by a "President-General," appointed by the crown, with a "Grand Council" of representatives elected proportionally by the legislatures of each of the colonies.[18]

Also as Franklin had proposed, members of the council were to serve three-year terms and after the initial three-year period, members were to be chosen from the colonies in proportion to a colony's contribution to the general treasury.[19] The council was to meet at least once a year ("and oftener if occasion require") for up to six weeks. With the consent of seven members, the president could call the council into session in the event of an emergency. The council could not be prorogued or dissolved without its consent "or the special command of the Crown."

The council was to have the power "to make laws, and lay and levy such general duties, imposts, or taxes as to them shall appear most equal and just (considering the ability and other circumstances of the inhabitants of the several colonies)."[20] However, the legislative authority of the Grand Council was restricted by the requirement that the President-General assent to all acts of the council. Also, the laws were to be "as near as may be, agreeable to the laws of England" and were to be transmitted "to the King in Council for approbation." If the laws were not approved within three years of their presentation, the laws were to remain in force. It was the "duty and office" of the President-General to see to the execution of the laws.[21]

Reflecting a balance of executive and legislative powers, the authority of the president was also subject to the assent of the council. Thus, the president was given authority, with the advice of the council, over relations with the native peoples, including the authority to declare war. Acting together, the president and the council had the authority to regulate trade with the native peoples, to purchase land from them, and to establish and regulate new settlements on those lands in the name of the Crown.[22]

The president and the council were vested with a variety of other joint powers. They were authorized to raise and equip land and naval forces and to erect fortifications for the defense of the colonies.[23] Military officers were to be appointed by the president subject to the approval of the council. Conversely, the council was to nominate all civil officials, but the approval of the president was required before they could assume their offices.[24]

Authority was given to the president and council to appoint treasurers and to disburse public funds (an annual accounting for these funds was to be provided to the colonial legislatures). In a significant departure from earlier plans of union, the president and the council were also jointly authorized to issue money.[25]

As a final matter, the plan of union made allowance for the filling of vacancies. In the event of the death of the president, the speaker of the council was to serve in his stead "till the King's pleasure be known." The colonial assemblies were to elect new representatives at their next session to replace vacancies in the council. Lastly, in the event of death or removal of any civil or military officer, the governor of the colony in which the vacancy occurred was to appoint a replacement, "till the pleasure of the President-General and the Grand Council be known."[26]

The plan of union failed to win the support and approval of the colonial legislatures.[27] In the face of this lack of acceptance, no action was taken on the plan in England.[28]

Despite this failure to gain acceptance, the Albany Plan represented a significant step forward in the evolution of the constitutional tradition in America. Notwithstanding Franklin's central role in the formation, rather than being the work of one person, as was Penn's plan, the Albany Plan was the first attempt at a unitary intercolonial government established by representatives of the colonies. The plan granted ample powers to this government,[29] while at the same time accommodating the interests and prerogatives both of the crown (through the appointment of the president-general and veto power over laws) and of the autonomous colonial governments (through proportional representation and the sub silentio reservation of judicial powers). Thus, although the Albany Plan failed to gain acceptance by either the crown or the colonial governments, the plan was, as one writer described it, "remarkably precocious,"[30] and the underlying principles informed the later work of Joseph Galloway in his Plan of Union in 1775, of Benjamin Franklin in his 1775 Articles of Confederation, and ultimately, the Articles of Confederation adopted by the Continental Congress.

JOSEPH GALLOWAY'S PLAN OF UNION: 1774

By 1774, relations between the American colonies and Britain were frayed. The colonists' opposition to the Tea Act of 1773 and the destruction of the tea cargo in Boston Harbor by Sons of Liberty "Mohawks" on December 16, 1773, led George III to remark to Lord North that the "dye had been cast" and "the colonies must either submit or triumph." Also as a consequence, Boston Harbor was closed in 1774 and individual colonists were extradited to Britain for trial.[31]

In reaction to the increasingly tense relations with Britain, Joseph Galloway[32] and a committee of correspondents in the Pennsylvania Assembly, wrote to the committee of correspondence in Massachusetts recommending that a congress of delegates from the colonies be called with a view that "something might be produced, by their united wisdom, to ascertain our rights, and establish a political union between the two countries, with the ascent of both, which would effectively secure to Americans their future rights and privileges."[33]

The First Continental Congress convened on September 5, 1774. In anticipation of the congress, Galloway formulated a plan of union, which he planned to introduce once he had taken the measure of the delegates' sentiments respecting conciliation with Britain.[34]

Galloway put his plan before the Congress on September 28 as the delegates began debate on the nonexportation proposals (the delegates had already adopted unanimously the proposal for nonimportation of British goods). Galloway urged the Congress to transmit the plan to the King and Parliament as a means of restoring union between Britain and the American colonies.[35]

The Galloway plan had been influenced by Franklin, and the plan borrowed generously from the Albany Plan of twenty years earlier. The plan eschewed independence from Britain and instead contended that the delegates "most ardently desire the establishment of a Political Union, not only among themselves, but with the Mother State, upon those principals of safety and freedom which are essential in the constitution of all free governments, and particularly that of the British Legislature."[36]

Like the Albany Plan, Galloway's plan provided for a president-general to be appointed by the king, who would hold office at the king's pleasure. The assent of the president was required for legislation to become effective and the president was responsible for seeing to the law's execution.[37]

Also like the Albany Plan, there was to be a representative assembly, called the grand council. Representatives were to be chosen by the colonial assemblies every three years and the membership of the council was to be proportionate.[38] The council was to meet at least once each year and was to have the power to select its own speaker and to determine the time and place of future meetings. The Galloway Plan mirrored the Albany Plan in these respects as well.[39]

However, the Galloway Plan represented a significant departure from the Albany Plan in the relationship of the union government to the British Parliament. Under the Galloway plan, the president and the council were to exercise legislative power to regulate the affairs of the colonies, but the president and council would be, "an inferior and distinct branch of the British legislature, united and incorporated with it, for the aforesaid general purposes." Laws enacted either by the colonial government or by the parliament in Britain were required to be "transmitted to the other for their approbation or dissent," and the validity of any law affecting the colonies required the assent of both bodies.[40]

The Galloway proposal was opposed by Samuel Adams and Patrick Henry, who may have viewed the plan as diverting support for their nonexportation initiative. Their opposition prevailed and, on September 29, 1774, the Congress postponed consideration of the plan and later (probably October 22), Galloway's plan was deleted from the minutes of the Congress.[41]

THE ARTICLES OF ASSOCIATION: 1774

Instead of pursuing union with Britain, the Continental Congress resolved to take action against the "coercive acts," or the "intolerable acts" as they were also called, which had been adopted by the parliament in March 1774 and that included the Boston Port Act, the Massachusetts Government Act, the Quartering Act, and the Administration of Justice Act. On September 7, the congress appointed a committee to prepare a statement of the rights of the colonies "and the means most proper to be pursued for obtaining a restoration of them."[42] The committee presented its draft Declaration of Rights and Grievances to the congress on September 22 and 24. The declaration proposed a "non-importation, non-consumption and non-exportation agreement or association" for the colonies.[43]

The following Friday, September 30, the congress appointed a second committee to develop a plan for unified action to interrupt commercial intercourse with Britain. The committee proffered its draft plan to the congress on October 12, and following the adoption of the Declaration of Rights and Grievances on October 14, a final draft of Articles of Association was agreed to by congress on October 18 and signed by the delegates on October 20.[44]

Under these Articles of Association, delegates from twelve of the colonies agreed not to import "goods, wares or merchandise" from Britain and not to purchase "East India tea."[45] Merchants were to direct their factors in Britain not to ship goods "on any pretence whatsoever." In like fashion, it was agreed that merchandise would not be directly or indirectly exported to Britain, "except rice to Europe." Trading in slaves was discontinued.[46] The Articles of Association also obliged the signatories to take certain actions domestically.

The articles also provided for a degree of interior governance and supervision. There was to be rudimentary price controls, under which merchants and manufacturers were to sell goods at "reasonable prices,"—i.e., "rates we have been respectively accustomed to do, for twelve months last past"—so that "no undue advantage be taken." Committees were to be chosen in the cities, towns, or counties "to observe the conduct of all persons touching this association." Merchants who violated the provisions of the articles were themselves to be boycotted. Goods imported contrary to the embargo were subject to seizure and sale by the committees, and the profits (after the owners were reimbursed for their costs) were "to be applied towards relieving and employing such poor inhabitants of the town of Boston as are immediate sufferers by the Boston port-bill."[47]

It has been noted that what was remarkable about the Articles of Association was not the economic embargo on commerce with Britain, but rather that the delegates to the congress agreed to measures that would be taken by all of the colonies in concert.[48] The failure of Galloway's plan and the success of the radical separatists in the Declaration of Rights and Grievances and the Articles of Association advanced the consensus that preservation of the colonists' rights and liberties required concerted action, decided upon by their delegates in congress. Thus, it was resolved that delegates should be elected to a second congress that would meet the following May if their grievances remained unredressed.[49]

FRANKLIN'S ARTICLES OF CONFEDERATION AND PERPETUAL UNION: 1775

Franklin returned to Philadelphia from England on May 5, 1775. The following day, the Pennsylvania Assembly selected him as a delegate to the Second Continental Congress. The congress convened on May 10, 1775, and on July

21, Franklin presented to the congress his proposed Articles of Confederation and Perpetual Union.[50]

Under Franklin's plan, the colonies would join together in a "firm League of Friendship," to provide for their common defense and the preservation of liberty and welfare. The confederation was to be known as the "United Colonies of North America."[51]

Representation in the governing body of the confederation differed from that under the plan Franklin had brought to the Albany Congress in 1754. Under Franklin's confederation plan, delegates to the national congress were to be elected annually by their colonial legislatures rather than for three-year terms, and although the concept of proportional representation was carried over from the Albany Plan, the proposed proportional representation was not to be based on a colony's contribution to the treasury (as it was under the Albany Plan), but rather was to be based on population to be determined every three years.[52]

The Franklin confederation plan included other provisions that were similar to those in the Albany Plan. As in the previous plan, each colony was to "enjoy and retain" its own laws and jurisdiction. There was also to be a national treasury. However, unlike the Albany Plan which relied on voluntary contributions by the colonies to fund the treasury, Franklin's confederation plan provided for assessments based on the number of males between the ages of sixteen and sixty years of age.[53]

Like the Albany Plan, the confederation congress was to have authority to legislate in matters affecting the colonies as a whole. However, in Franklin's Articles of Confederation, congress's power extended to matters of war and peace; sending and receiving ambassadors; entering into alliances, including reconciliation with Great Britain; resolving disputes among individual colonies; and planning new settlements. Franklin's confederation plan further provided that the congress was to adopt ordinances governing commerce, a general currency, and regulation of the armed forces. Congress would also have authority to appoint civil and military officers.[54]

Also like the Albany Plan, Franklin's confederation plan conferred on the national congress the authority to govern relations with the native peoples, and unlike the Albany Plan, the colonies were specifically prohibited from going to war with the native peoples without the consent of the congress. The plan further required that the confederation enter into an alliance with the Six Nations of the Iroquois, which would secure their boundaries from encroachment.[55]

Among the innovations of the confederation plan, Franklin proposed that a twelve-member executive council be constituted that would be authorized to act while congress was in recess. The members of the executive council were to serve staggered terms of up to four years (in contrast to the one-year term of congressmen) and a quorum of two-thirds was necessary for the council to act (again in contrast to the 50 percent requirement for the congress).[56]

The Articles of Confederation were subject to amendments approved by a majority of the colonial assemblies. Also, membership in the confederation was open, upon application, to "every Colony from Great Britain Upon the Continent of North America" (i.e., the West India Islands, Quebec, St. Johns, Nova Scotia, Bermuda, and the East and West Floridas).[57]

Lastly, the plan required approval of the articles by the colonial assemblies or by colonial conventions. Thereafter, "the Union thereby established" was to continue until

> the Terms of Reconciliation proposed in the Petition of the last Congress to the King are agreed to; till the Acts since made restraining the American Commerce and Fisheries are repealed; till Reparation is made for the Injury done to Boston by shutting up its Port, for the Burning of Charlestown; and for the experience of this unjust War; and till all the British troops are withdrawn from America.

Should those conditions be met, the plan stated that the colonies would return to "their former Connection and Friendship with Britain," otherwise the confederacy thus formed was to remain in effect.[58]

No action was taken on Franklin's proposal, although Franklin's plan has been seen as having formed the basis of the Articles of Confederation taken up by congress the following year.[59]

ARTICLES OF CONFEDERATION AND PERPETUAL UNION OF THE SECOND CONTINENTAL CONGRESS: 1777

The declaration by the colonies of their independence from England necessitated a new paradigm for an intercolonial union. Where the previous plans of union put forward by Galloway and Franklin, and by Penn before them, had been predicated on a definition of the colonial relationship with the superior British government, independence required the former colonies to find common ground for defining their relationship, and for structuring a federal government to address those issues as to which there was common cause. Just as the necessity of defending against French encroachments had called forth the Albany Plan in 1754, the imperatives of defending their newly declared independence, as well as of mediating conflicts between the former colonies over territory and commerce, led the Second Continental Congress to fashion a form of union government.[60]

However, the new states had developed independently. As colonies, they had been chartered independently, they were distinct legal entitles, and there were profound differences socially and culturally. Indeed, each of the former colonies conceived itself to be an independent, sovereign state, and for that reason, the confederation government has been described as "a federal league of states independent of each other, formed principally for mutual defense against a common enemy." [61] It was incumbent on any plan of union to recognize that autonomy.[62] Accordingly, it has been said that any other form of national government would have been unacceptable.[63]

Thus, it was on November 15, 1777, the states entered into a "firm League of Friendship with each other," the purpose of which was "their common defence, the Securing of Liberties, and their mutual and general Welfare."[64] In so doing, the states bound themselves "to assist each other against all Force offered to, or attacks made upon them, or any of them, on account of religion, sovereignty, trade, or any other pretense whatever." However, it was specifically made clear that "Each state retains its sovereignty, freedom, and independence, and every power, jurisdiction, and right, which is not by this Confederation expressly delegated to the United States, in congress assembled."[65]

Nevertheless, the Articles of Confederation established a framework for a national government to carry out the purposes of the "firm League of Friendship" among the states "for their common defense, the security of their liberties, and their mutual and general welfare."[66] To that end, the articles fixed certain principles for the relations among the states; defined the powers of the national congress; and endeavored to harmonize those powers with the prerogatives of the states.

With respect to the relations among the individual states, the articles guaranteed that the citizens of any state (except for "paupers, vagabonds and fugitives") were to be accorded "all privileges and immunities of free citizens in the several States, including "free ingress and regress to and from any other State," and "all the privileges of trade and commerce."[67] The articles acted as a treaty among the states for the extradition of fugitives who had been charged with or convicted of "treason, felony, or other high misdemeanor." Lastly, the articles established that each state would give "full faith and credit" to another state's "records, acts and judicial proceedings."[68]

The articles enumerated the authority of the national congress. In some instances, these rights and powers were in derogation of the authority of the states, whereas in other instances, the states preserved their privileges and prerogatives. The articles conferred on the congress "the sole and exclusive right and power" over: decisions concerning peace and war[69] ; conducting foreign relations[70] ; regulating trade and managing affairs with the native peoples[71] ; providing for the common defense[72] ; coining money[73] ; establishing a postal system[74] ; borrowing money and emitting bills on the credit of the United States[75] ; and appropriating funds for defraying public expenses."[76] The assent of nine states was required for the Congress to exercise these powers.[77]

Additionally, the Congress was to establish a civil government. Congress was to appoint a "committee of the states," comprised of one delegate from each state, to sit during the time Congress was in recess. Congress was also to appoint "such other committees and civil officers as may be necessary for managing the general affairs of the United States under their direction." A member of Congress was to be appointed president, subject to a term limitation of "one year in any term of three years."[78]

Congress was to appoint courts for the trial of piracy and other felonies committed on the high seas. Courts were to be established by Congress to determine appeals of captures according to rules established by Congress governing "what captures on land or water shall be legal, and in what manner prizes taken by land or naval forces in the service of the United States shall be divided or appropriated."[79]

Congress was also empowered to resolve cases and controversies between states. Upon petition of either the legislative or executive authority of a state, a dispute with another state could be brought before congress, which was to appoint commissioners to adjudicate the dispute and issue a judgment that would be "final and conclusive."[80]

States were to be represented in congress by at least two, but not more than seven delegates, but in determining questions before the congress, each state was to have one vote. Delegates were to be selected in the manner directed by the legislatures of the states for one-year terms. Delegates were subject to term limits of no more than "three years in any term of six years," and they were prohibited during their service in congress from holding any other office.[81]

Delegates to the congress were guaranteed the freedom of speech and debate. Delegates could not be impeached or questioned outside of congress. Delegates were also immune from arrest or imprisonment while going to, coming from or attending a session of Congress, except upon charges of treason, felony, or breach of the peace.[82]

As an effective national government, the confederation was deeply flawed. However, the root cause for these failures was in the essential nature of the government contemplated by the Articles—that is, a union of sovereign states rather than a federal republican government—in which the locus of governmental authority remained in the states.[83] Nevertheless, the Articles of Confederation, and the plans of union that preceded them, represent a significant development in the American constitutionalism leading to the convention of 1787.

The powers conferred on Congress by the articles formed a foundation for the federal Constitution. Accession to the articles also represented a relinquishment, however modest, of the states' autonomy and allowed the creation of a functioning national government for the first time in colonial America.[84]

CONCLUSION

At the time the newly formed states were wrestling with the creation of their governments in the wake of the flight of the crown governments and the Declaration of Independence, their delegates to the Continental Congress were actively engaged in forming a national government that could prosecute the war with Britain and that could address matters of common interest and controversy among the sovereign states. However, for at least eighty years before independence, beginning with William Penn's proposal in 1696, there had been a growing awareness of the need for some form of intercolonial government structure that could at minimum regulate the interactions of the colonies and provide for a common defense.

Although there had been an attempt at a union government of the New England colonies in 1643, the debate over an intercolonial government was propelled forward by the threat to the colonies' safety posed by the French and their allies among the native peoples as well as the imperative of preserving the alliance with the Iroquois Nation. This led to the calling of a congress of colonies in Albany, New York, in 1754 and the adoption of a plan of union, based largely on the proposal authored by Benjamin Franklin. Despite the plan's failure to gain the agreement of the colonial legislatures at the time, the principles articulated in the Albany Plan were later incorporated in the national government formed under the Articles of Confederation and later by the Constitution, including a republican government structure comprised of an executive branch and a proportionally representative legislative branch with authority to impose taxes, issue money, raise and equip armed forces, and declare war and balanced governmental structure in which the actions of the executive and legislature were subject to the approval of the other.

The breach in the relations between the colonies and the British sovereign twenty years later spawned several tentative attempts at forming a national government. In the hope of accommodating the interests of the colonies while preserving the union with the crown, Galloway put forward a proposal that incorporated central concepts of the Albany Plan, including executive and legislative branches and proportional representation in the legislature. Galloway's plan preserved supremacy of the British government by making the colonial government an inferior branch of the parliament, whose actions were subject to the approbation of the king and the privy council. By the time Galloway made his proposal, events had overtaken his sentiments and his plan was rejected.

At the same time, Franklin revived many of the principles of the Albany Plan in his proposal for a "firm League of Friendship" among the colonies that he presented to the Second Continental Congress in 1775. Among the innovations in Franklin's plan were proportional representation in congress based on population; a national treasury funded by state assessments based on population; and a mechanism for amending the Articles of Confederation. Although no action was taken by the Congress, Franklin's proposal for the first time contemplated a national government that was independent of Britain and many of its principles were incorporated into the Articles of Confederation.

These proposals envisioned a national government that would respect the authority and jurisdiction of the individual colonial assemblies while providing for united action when necessary. In those plans can be seen an evolutionary refinement of a federalist conception of a national government with enumerated powers that would address political, economic, and military issues of a national character, through a proportionally elected legislature, but which would also preserve the autonomy of the colonies over their internal governance.

Independence from Britain and the necessity of defending that independence against the British forces compelled the congress to fashion a national government under the Articles of Confederation in 1777, which has been described as "the most serious and earnest attempt that had ever been made to frame a union and a general government.[85]

Although deeply flawed, it must be recalled that contemporaneously with the framing of the national government, the newly independent states were themselves engaged in fashioning their own governance in the face of the withdrawal of the crown governments and, at the urging of the Continental Congress, the states adopted their own constitutions as sovereign governments.

The newly formed independent states were jealous of their sovereignty. Nevertheless, there was a recognition by the states "that there were certain great purposes of civil government which they could not discharge by the separate means."[86] Harmonization of state sovereignty with national purpose was the overarching challenge of confederation.[87] The Articles of Confederation gave form to the concept of union. In sum, the confederation showed that "a union of the states was both possible and necessary" and "made permanent the idea of union familiar to the people of the different states."[88]

The union under the articles was, as it was intended to be, a confederation of sovereign states to address issues of a national character.[89] The articles effectuated a national structure for that purpose and enumerated the powers of the national government to achieve that end. Thus, despite glaring flaws that subsequent experience would reveal, to a great degree, the articles were successful in achieving their purpose.[90]

NOTES

1. Thorpe pointed out, however, that "As the four provinces were practically independent of each other, slight provision was made for the federal administration of government." Francis

Newman Thorpe, *The Constitutional History of the United States 1765–1895* (Chicago: Callaghan & Co., 1901), vol. 1: 186.

2. William I. Hull, *William Penn: A Topical Biography* (London: Oxford Press, 1937), 236; Edward Corbyn Obert Beatty, *William Penn as Social Philosopher* (New York: Columbia University Press, 1939), 85. The Report of Lords of Trade and Plantations was dated August 20, 1656. Beatty, *William Penn as Social Philosopher*, 85 n.23.

3. Journal of the Lords Committee of Trade and Plantations, quoted in Hull, *William Penn*, 236.

4. Lutz, *Colonial Origins of the American Constitution*, 389.

5. Lutz, *Colonial Origins of the American Constitution*, 389.

6. Lutz, *Colonial Origins of the American Constitution*, 389–90.

7. Lutz, *Colonial Origins of the American Constitution*, 389–90.

8. Lutz, *Colonial Origins of the American Constitution*, 370. Although Penn's plan was not adopted by the Lords of Trade, his conception of a common government at the center of which was a representative congress, found resonance in later plans and in the constitutional convention of 1787. See Beatty, *William Penn as Social Philosopher*, 87; Merrill Jensen, *The Articles of Confederation: An Interpretation of the Social-Constitutional History of the American Revolution 1774–1781* (Madison: Wisconsin University Press, 1940), 107.

9. Harry M. Ward, *Unite or Die: Intercolony Relations, 1690–1763* (Port Washington, NY: Kennikat Press, 1971), 13, 143; Robert C. Newbold, *The Albany Congress and Plan of Union of 1754* (New York: Vantage, 1955), 18–23; Andrews, *The Colonial Period of American History*, vol. 4: 417; L. K. Mathews, "Benjamin Franklin's Plans for a Colonial Union 1750–1755," *American Political Science Review*, (1914), vol. 8: 397. McLaughlin suggested that for the Lords of Trade, "The pressing and immediate question appeared to be the means of securing men and money for imperial defense; but the necessity of the case demanded the establishment of a system which would not only recognize imperial unity but conserve local rights and local self-respect." Andrew C. McLaughlin, *A Constitutional History of the United States* (New York: D. Appleton-Century Co., 1935), 17.

10. Newbold, *The Albany Congress and the Plan of Union of 1754*, 35–36 (quoting a letter from the Lords of Trade to Governor Delancey dated July 5, 1754).

11. As Timothy J. Shannon noted, the reaction of the colonies to the call for the conference was decidedly mixed. Timothy J. Shannon, *Indians and Colonists at the Crossroads of Empire* (Ithaca: Cornell University Press, 2000), 107–8. Two colonies, New Jersey and Virginia, declined to participate. The four representatives of New York had not been officially commissioned as delegates and, therefore, were considered "councillors" rather than "commissioners." Although the other six participating colonies sent official delegates, their authority generally extended only to renewal of the alliance with the Iroquois Nations and to agreements for the common defense (indeed, the delegates from Connecticut and Maryland were forbidden from entering into any binding agreements). Newbold, *The Albany Congress and the Plan of Union of 1754*, 38–48. As Osgood observed, "In the very brief instructions which were given by the governors of all the colonies except Massachusetts and Connecticut, reference was made only to Indian relations and especially to the alliance with the Six Nations, which everything else was left obscure, or in the case of Maryland, positively discouraged." Herbert L. Osgood, *The American Colonies in the Eighteenth Century* (New York: Columbia University Press, 1924), 311.

12. Thomas E. Burke, "The Albany Plan of Union," in Schechter, ed., *Roots of the Republic*, 107. Shannon considered it noteworthy that the delegates were willing to entertain a general plan of union at all, "considering how few of them had specific instructions to do so." Shannon, *Indians and Colonists at the Crossroads of Empire*, 177. Osgood noted, however, that "When the commissioners had met at Albany, private discussion of this subject at once began among them and, in view of well known political weakness of the colonies, it was generally agreed that a union was absolutely necessary to their security and defence." Osgood, *The American Colonies in the Eighteenth Century*, vol. 4: 316.

13. Ward, *Unite or Die*, 13; Newbold, *The Albany Congress and the Plan of Union of 1754*, 87–88; Shannon, *Indians and Colonists at the Crossroads of Empire*, 178; Mathews, "Benjamin Franklin's Plans for Colonial Union," *American Political Science Review*, vol. 8: 399.

14. Shannon, *Indians and Colonists at the Crossroads of Empire*, 178.

15. Letter from Benjamin Franklin to James Parker dated March 20, 1750. *Papers of Benjamin Franklin*, edited by Leonard Labaree (New Haven, CT: Yale University Press, 1959), vol. 4: 117–21.

16. Shannon, *Indians and Colonists at the Crossroads of Europe*, 104; Matthews, "Benjamin Franklin's Plan for a Colonial Union, 1750–1775," *American Political Science Review*, vol. 8: 396, 406–11. Franklin acknowledged having been influenced by the constitution of the Iroquois Nation, relations with whom was a principal topic of the conference. The Iroquois constitution established a framework for the confederation of the five nations of the Iroquois: Cayuga, Oneida, Onondaga, Mohawk and Seneca. The constitution established procedures for the convening of meetings of the council and the manner in which deliberations were to be conducted. The constitution established the means by which the representatives of the nations (the Lords) were to be chosen and provided a procedure for their removal and for succession in the event of illness or death. Provision was also made for nonvoting members of the council, counselors and "Pine Tree Chiefs" (who were selected on the basis of their "great interest in the affairs of the nation" and who had shown themselves to be "wise, honest and worthy of confidence"). Provision was also made in the constitution for unified military action in time of war. Lesli J. Favor, *The Iroquois Constitution* (New York: Rosen Publishing Group, 2003), 56–61, 84–135. Two other plans may have been considered by the committee. One was a plan attributed to Thomas Hutchinson of Massachusetts (the "First New England Plan"). Under the plan, there were to be two groupings of the colonies. One group was to consist of Connecticut, Massachusetts, New Hampshire, New Jersey, New York, and Rhode Island. The second group was to be comprised of Maryland, North Carolina, Pennsylvania, South Carolina, and Virginia. It was contemplated that the two groups would join together in the event of a military emergency. The other plan (the "Second New England Plan") differed somewhat, but was also predicated on the formation of two unions of the colonies. Newbold, *The Albany Congress and the Plan of Union of 1754*, 96–103. Nevertheless, principal authorship of the plan has been attributed to Franklin. Newbold, *The Albany Congress and the Plan of Union of 1754*, 102–4; McLaughlin, *A Constitutional History of the United States*, 20. Franklin claimed credit for having been the principal influence on the committee's proposal in a letter dated December 29, 1754, to Peter Collinson. Franklin, *Papers of Benjamin Franklin*, vol. 5: 453–54; Benjamin Franklin, *The Autobiography of Benjamin Franklin* (New Haven, CT: Yale University Press, 1964), 209–10. Thomas Hutchinson also wrote that the Albany Plan "was the prosecution of Dr. F., and prepared in part before he had any consultation" with Hutchinson and that Franklin had "probably brought with him from Philadelphia." Thomas Hutchinson, *The Diary and Letters of his Excellency Thomas Hutchinson: Captain-General and Governor-in Chief of Boston* (Boston: Houghton Mifflin, 1884–1886), vol. 1: 55.

17. Newbold, *The Albany Congress and Plan of Union of 1754*, 105–15. However, there were fundamental differences among the delegates over "colonial identity." Shannon observed that "All of the commissioners swore allegiance to the same Crown, but some came from corporate colonies, some from proprietary colonies, and others from royal colonies; some sat in representative assemblies while others owed their appointments as councilors to the Crown. They thus embodied the traditional antagonists in colonial politics between centralized, prerogative power and local, popular power." These competing perspectives on the British Empire in North America were "crystallized" in the debate on union at the Albany Congress such that the opponents of the plan "defended an old imperial order in which distinct and semi-autonomous colonies governed themselves according to their particular charters and constitutional relations with the British Crown," while supporters of union, "envisioned a new imperial order in which formerly separate colonies would form a single American dominion within the British-Atlantic Empire, one governed by an inter-colonial legislature superior to colonial governments but subordinate to the British Parliament." Shannon, *Indians and Colonists at the Crossroads of Empire*, 175–76.

18. Lutz, *Colonial Origins of the American Constitution*, 371. Initial representation of the colonies in the Grand Council was to be as follows: Connecticut: 5; Maryland: 4; Massachusetts: 7; New Hampshire: 2; New Jersey: 3; New York: 4; North Carolina: 4 Pennsylvania: 6; Rhode Island: 2; South Carolina: 4; and Virginia: 7.

19. Lutz, *Colonial Origins of the American Constitution*, 372. As Franklin later explained, "though it was thought reasonable that each colony should have a share in the representative body in some degree, according to the proportion it contributed to the general treasury; yet, the proportion of wealth or power of the colonies is not to be judged by the proportion here fixed; because it was at first agreed that the greatest colony should not have more than seven members, nor the least less than two." It was contemplated that the proportion of representation "would find itself after the first election from the sums brought into the treasury." Benjamin Franklin, "Reasons and Motives for the Albany Plan of Union," in Labaree, *The Papers of Benjamin Franklin*, vol. 5: 399–47.

20. Lutz, *Colonial Origins of the American Constitution*, 374.

21. Lutz, *Colonial Origins of the American Constitution*, 372–74.

22. Lutz, *Colonial Origins of the American Constitution*, 373.

23. The colonies retained their right to defend themselves in an emergency, and the cost of that defense could be laid "before the President-General and the General [sic] Council, who may allow and order payment of the same, as far as they judge such accounts just and reasonable." Additionally, the plan provided that "the particular military as well as civil establishments of each colony remain in their present state. . . ." Lutz, *Colonial Origins of the American Constitution*, 375.

24. Lutz, *Colonial Origins of the American Constitution*, 375.

25. Lutz, *Colonial Origins of the American Constitution*, 373–74.

26. Lutz, *Colonial Origins of the American Constitution*, 372, 374–75.

27. McLaughlin attributed this failure to gain acceptance to the differences in social and industrial life of the various colonies. observed, "So varied were the colonies. McLaughin, *A Constitutional History of the United States*, 18. Andrews similarly viewed the problem as having arisen from the isolation of the colonies from each other. Andrews, *The Colonial Period of American History*, vol. 4: 414.

28. Andrews, *The Colonial Period of American History*, vol. 4: 419; Newbold, *The Albany Congress and Plan of Union of 1754*, 173; Shannon, *Indiana and Colonists at the Crossroads of Empire*, 208–12. The British government had discussed and rejected the principle of colonial union by act of Parliament before the Albany Plan was transmitted to London. Alison Gilbert Olson, "The British Government and Colonial Union, 1754," *William & Mary Quarterly*, 17 (1960): 22–34; Ward, *Unite or Die*, 17–18.

29. As McLaughlin noted, the Albany Plan "granted to the proposed central government a method and the power of raising money; it marked out a fairly definite sphere of action; and it bestowed ample authority over four subjects of supreme importance—Indian affairs, war, purchase of wild lands, and control, for a time at least, of western settlement." McLaughlin, *A Constitutional History of the United States*, 21.

30. McLaughlin, *A Constitutional History of the United States*, 21. Osgood wrote that the plan of union "was the first impression of the constitution-making instinct, which was to become so active both in Europe and America before the close of the century. Had it been put into operation, not only would a federation of the colonies have been established, but a long step would have been taken toward freeing them from the maze of ill-defined or undefined relations in which they existed under the charters and royal instructions." Osgood, *The American Colonies in the Eighteenth Century*, vol. 4: 317.

31. Samuel Eliot Morison, Henry Steele Commager, and William E. Leuchtenburg, *The Growth of the American Republic*, 6th ed. (New York: Oxford University Press, 1969), 158–60.

32. Galloway was born in 1731 into a Maryland landowning and trading family. Following his father's death, Galloway had moved to Philadelphia where he studied law. He was elected to the Pennsylvania Assembly and, in 1753, Galloway married into a socially and politically prominent Pennsylvania family. Galloway allied himself with Franklin in seeking taxation of the proprietors' estates. Galloway was elected speaker of the Pennsylvania Assembly from 1765 to 1774. Julian P. Boyd, *Anglo-American Union: Joseph Galloway's Plans to Preserve the British Empire 1774–1788* (Philadelphia: U Pennsylvania P, 1941), 17–19.

33. Benjamin H. Newcomb, *Franklin and Galloway: A Political Partnership* (New Haven, CT: Yale University Press, 1972), 237–45.

34. Newcomb, *Franklin and Galloway*, 248–49.

35. Newcomb, *Franklin and Galloway*, 253–54.

36. Philip B. Kurland, ed., *The Founders' Constitution* (Chicago: University of Chicago Press, 1987), vol. 1: 217–18.

37. Kurland, *The Founders' Constitution*, vol. 1: 212–18. The Albany and Galloway Plans were materially the same in this respect:

Albany Plan	Galloway Plan
That the said general government be administered by a President-General to be appointed and supported by the Crown . . . That the assent of the President-General be requisite to all acts of the Grand Council, and that it be his office to cause them to be carried into execution.	That the President-General should hold his office during the pleasure of the King, and his assent shall be requisite to all acts of the Grand Council, and it shall be his office and duty to cause them to be carried into execution.

38. Kurland, *The Founders' Constitution*, vol. 1:217–18. Here again, the Albany and Galloway Plans were virtually identical: Both plans provided for proportional representation. In the Albany Plan, the proportion was specified. In the Galloway Plan, the proportion was left blank.

Albany Plan	Galloway Plan
That the said general government be administered by . . . a Grand Council, to be chosen by representatives of the people of the several colonies met in their respective assemblies. That there shall be a new election of the members of the Grand Council every three years; and on the death or resignation of any member, his place should be supplied by a new choice at the next sitting of the Assembly of the colony he represented	That the said government be administered by . . . a Grand Council, to be chosen by the Representatives of the people of the several colonies, in their respective assemblies, once in every three years. That there shall be a new election of members for the Grand Council every three years; and on the death, removal, or resignation of any member, his place shall be supplied by a new choice, at the next sitting of the Assembly of the colony he represented.

39. Kurland, *The Founders' Constitution*, vol. 1: 217–18. Thus:

Albany Plan	Galloway Plan
That the Grand Council shall meet once in every year, and oftener if occasion require, at such time and place as they shall adjourn to at the last preceding meeting, or as they shall be called to meet by the President-General on any emergency . . . That the Grand Council have power to choose their speaker . . .	That the Grand Council shall meet once in every year, if they shall think it necessary, and offener, if occasions shall require, at such time and place as they shall adjourn to, at the last preceding meeting, or as they shall be caused to meet at, by the President-General, on any emergency. That the Grand Council shall have power to choose their Speaker, . . .

As Jensen observed, although the Galloway plan had much in common with Franklin's Albany Plan, the purpose of the plan differed substantially from Franklin's. Jensen wrote that "The council for which it provided represented a constitutional union between the colonies and Great Britain; it was in reality an American parliament, which was to have a veto on the acts of the

British Parliament affecting both countries, as the British Parliament was to have on similar legislation by the America parliament." Jensen, *The Articles of Confederation*, 108.

40. Kurland, *The Founders' Constitution*, vol. 1: 212–18; Fisher, *The Evolution of the Constitution of the United States*, 239.

41. Newcomb, *Franklin and Galloway*, 255–57; Boyd, *Anglo-American Union*, 37–38; Morison, Commager, and Leuchtenburg, eds., *The Growth of the American Republic*, vol. 1: 162.

42. Worthington C. Ford, ed., *Journals of the Continental Congress, 1774–1789* (Washington, DC: U.S. Government Printing Office, 1904–1937), vol. 1: 26–28.

43. Ford, *Journals of the Continental Congress*, vol. 1: 41–42.

44. Ford, *Journals of the Continental Congress*, vol. 1: 51–52, 75.

45. The Articles were signed by delegates from New Hampshire, Massachusetts Bay, Rhode Island, Connecticut, New York, New Jersey, Pennsylvania, the lower counties of New Castle (Delaware), Maryland, Virginia, North Carolina, and South Carolina.

46. Ford, *Journals of the Continental Congress*, vol. 1: 76–78.

47. Ford, *Journals of the Continental Congress*, vol. 1: 78–79.

48. Jensen, *The Articles of Confederation*, 63.

49. Jensen, *The Articles of Confederation*, 73.

50. Ford, *Journals of the Continental Congress*, vol. 2: 195; Gordon S. Wood, *The Americanization of Benjamin Franklin* (New York: Penguin Books, 2004), 154.

51. Ford, *Journals of the Continental Congress*, vol. 2: 195.

52. Ford, *Journals of the Continental Congress*, vol. 2: 196.

53. Ford, *Journals of the Continental Congress*, vol. 2: 196–97; Mathews, "Benjamin Franklin's Plans for a Colonial Union, 1750–1775," 406–11.

54. Ford, *Journals of the Continental Congress*, vol. 2: 196.

55. Ford, *Journals of the Continental Congress*, vol. 2: 197–98.

56. Ford, *Journals of the Continental Congress*, vol. 2: 197.

57. Ford, *Journals of the Continental Congress*, vol. 2: 198.

58. Ford, *Journals of the Continental Congress*, vol. 2: 198–99.

59. Edmund S. Morgan, *Benjamin Franklin* (New Haven, CT: Yale University Press, 2002), 226; Walter Isaacson, *Benjamin Franklin: An American Life* (New York: Simon & Schuster, 2003), 299–300; Thorpe, *The Constitutional History of the United States*, vol. 1: 216.

60. J. R. Pole, "Nation-Making and the American Constitutional Process," in Gary L. McDowell and Johnathan O'Neill, eds., *America and Enlightenment Constitutionalism* (New York: Palgrave Macmillan, 2006), 201.

61. George Ticknor Curtis, *History of the Origin, Formation, and Adoption of the Constitution of the United States; with Notices of Its Principal Framers* (New York: Harper, 1854), 142, 260; Jensen, *The Articles of Confederation*, 161.

62. George Ticknor Curtis described the colonial states at the time of the signing of the Articles of Confederation as "free, sovereign, and independent political communities—each possessing within itself all the powers of legislation and government, over its own citizens, which any political society can possess." Thus, Curtis described the confederation government as a "federal league of states independent of each other, formed principally for mutual defence against a common enemy. . . ." Curtis, *History of the Origin, Formation, and Adoption of the Constitution of the United States*, 142, 260. Jensen also observed, "The fundamental issue in the writing of the Articles of Confederation was the location of ultimate political authority, the problem of sovereignty." Jensen, *The Articles of Confederation*, 161.

63. Valerie A. Earle, "The Federal Structure," in Graham and Graham, eds., *Founding Principles of American Government*, 139.

64. Articles of Confederation and Perpetual Union prepared by John Dickinson were presented to the Second Continental Congress on July 12, 1776. Ford, *Journals of the Continental Congress*, vol. 5: 546. Consideration of the Articles extended for over a year. A harbinger of the debate between the Federalists and the anti-Federalists a decade later, the central issue in the Continental Congress regarding union was the independence of the states. Jensen, *The Articles of Confederation*, 116–19. Articles of Confederation were finally agreed to on November 15, 1777. Ford, *Journals of the Continental Congress*, vol. 9: 907. The Articles were

submitted to the legislatures of the states and were ratified as follows: Virginia: December 16, 1777; South Carolina: February 5, 1778; New York: February 6, 1778; Rhode Island: February 16, 1778; Georgia: February 26, 1778; Connecticut: February 27, 1778; New Hampshire: March 4, 1778; Pennsylvania: March 5, 1778; Massachusetts: March 10, 1778; North Carolina: April 24, 1778; New Jersey: November 20, 1778; Delaware: February 1, 1779; and Maryland: February 2, 1781. Merrill Jensen, ed., *The Documentary History of the Ratification of the Constitution* (Madison: Wisconsin Historical Society, 1976), 97–137. Thus, the Articles did not become effective until their ratification by Maryland on February 2, 1781. The delay in ratification was largely due to the disposition of the states' claims to the region west of the Appalachian Mountains. Jensen, *The Articles of Confederation*, 120–24; Curtis, *History of the Constitution of the United States*, 131–36.

65. Ford, *Journals of the Continental Congress*, vol. 9: 908.

66. Ford, *Journals of the Continental Congress*, vol. 9: 908.

67. Ford, *Journals of the Continental Congress*, vol. 9: 908–9.

68. Ford, *Journals of the Continental Congress*, vol. 9: 909.

69. Ford, *Journals of the Continental Congress*, vol. 9: 912–13, 915.

70. Ford, *Journals of the Continental Congress*, vol. 9: 910–11, 915.

71. Ford, *Journals of the Continental Congress*, vol. 9: 911–12, 915.

72. Ford, *Journals of the Continental Congress*, vol. 9: 912–13, 920–21; Curtis, *History of the Constitution of the United States*, 144.

73. Ford, *Journals of the Continental Congress*, vol. 9: 919.

74. Ford, *Journals of the Continental Congress*, vol. 9: 919.

75. Ford, *Journals of the Continental Congress*, vol. 9: 924.

76. Ford, *Journals of the Continental Congress*, vol. 9: 913–14, 920.

77. A majority of the states was required for other actions. Ford, *Journals of the Continental Congress*, vol. 9: 921–22.

78. Ford, *Journals of the Continental Congress*, vol. 9: 919–20.

79. Ford, *Journals of the Continental Congress*, vol. 9: 915–16.

80. Ford, *Journals of the Continental Congress*, vol. 9: 916–19.

81. Ford, *Journals of the Continental Congress*, vol. 9: 910. The provisions of Article V concerning representation and term limits clearly recall Franklin's Albany Plan. Donald S. Lutz, "The Articles of Confederation 1781, Commentary," in Schechter, ed., *Roots of the Republic*, 228.

82. Ford, *Journals of the Continental Congress*, vol. 9: 910.

83. Gordon S. Wood, "Interests and Disinterestedness in the Making of the Constitution," in Richard R. Beeman, Stephen Botein, and Edward C. Carter, eds., *Beyond Confederation: Origins of the Constitution and American National Identity* (Chapel Hill: North Carolina University Press, 1987), 72; Max M. Edling, *A Revolution in Favor of Government: Origins of the U.S. Constitution and the Making of the American State* (New York: Oxford University Press, 2003), 220.

84. McDonald, *Novus Ordo Seclorum*, 270.

85. Fisher, *The Evolution of the Constitution of the United States*, 243; Urofsky, *A March of Liberty*, 65.

86. Curtis, *History of the Constitution of the United States*, 149–50; Andrew C. McLaughlin, *The Confederation and the Constitution 1783–1789* (New York: Harper, 1907), 49–50

87. Jensen, *The Articles of Confederation*, 161–76.

88. Curtis, *History of the Constitution of the United States*, 150; Edward S. Corwin, "The Progress of Constitutional Theory Between the Declaration of Independence and the Meeting of the Philadelphia Convention," in Gordon S. Wood, ed., *The Confederation and the Constitution* (Washington, DC: UP of America, 1979), 28.

89. Wood, *The Creation of the American Republic*, 357. As Merrill Jensen pointed out, at the time of independence, "an American tended to look upon his own colony as his 'country' and upon citizens of other colonies as 'foreigners.'" Thus, Jensen observed, it had been "no slip of the pen" that John Adams referred to the Massachusetts delegation to the First Continental Congress as "our embassy" when writing to Abigail Adams in 1774. Merrill Jensen, "The

Sovereign States," in Ronald Hoffman and Peter J. Albert, eds., *Sovereign States in an Age of Uncertainty* (Charlottesville: University of Virginia Press, 1981), 227.

90. McLaughlin, *The Confederation and the Constitution, 1783–1789*, 49; Wood, *The Creation of the American Republic*, 359.

Chapter Six

The Revolutionary State Constitutions

By the spring of 1775, the American colonies were in rebellion and their crown governments were in retreat. In the face of this deterioration of the old order brought on by the seemingly inexorable movement toward revolution, the Continental Congress adopted a resolution on May 10, 1775 (which was supplemented on May 15, 1775), directing that "the exercise of every kind of authority under . . . the Crown" should be suppressed and that "all of the powers of government [should be] executed under the authority of the people of the colonies."[1]

Thereafter, in a letter dated May 16, 1775, the provisional government of Massachusetts requested that the congress provide "explicit advice respecting the taking up and exercising the powers of civil government." Massachusetts pledged to "readily submit to such general plan" as congress might "direct for the colonies, or make it our great study to establish such a form of government here, as shall not only most promote our advantage but the union and interest of all America."[2]

The Continental Congress took up the request by Massachusetts on June 2, 1775. However, instead of proposing a constitution itself or authorizing Massachusetts to formulate a constitution on its own, the congress advised Massachusetts to treat the charter of 1691 as remaining in force and to govern itself accordingly.[3]

On October 18, 1775, the provisional government of New Hampshire posed the same request to the Continental Congress that Massachusetts had. However, unlike Massachusetts, New Hampshire had no royal charter establishing a governmental structure. Instead, since 1680, each governor had ruled in accordance with a royal commission enumerating the powers of government. Thus, there was no preexisting plan of government on which New Hampshire could rely.

The Continental Congress responded to the New Hampshire request on November 3, 1775. Congress advised the New Hampshire government to "call a full and free representation of the People," and if the representatives "think it necessary, establish such form of government, as in their Judgment will best produce the happiness of the People." Congress added the caveat, however, that any government so formed should remain in effect only for the duration of the conflict with England. South Carolina received the same advice on November 4, 1775, as did Virginia on December 4, 1775.[4]

Finally, on May 10, 1776, the Continental Congress adopted a resolution

> That it be recommended to the assemblies and conventions of the United Colonies, where no government sufficient to the exigencies of their affairs had been established, to adopt such government as should, in the opinion of the representatives of the people, best conduce to the happiness and safety of their constituents and of America in general.[5]

This act of the Continental Congress has been seen as having been a "*de facto* declaration of independence."[6]

The request for advice from Massachusetts on May 16, 1775, had stated that a constitution written by the congress for the state would be accepted. Although such a course was considered by the congress, ultimately no action was taken largely because there was no consensus on what such a uniform constitution should include.[7] Instead, the individual states were left to be guided by their own lights in constructing their governments.

There followed an intensive burst of constitutionalism in the states. In 1776 alone, eight states adopted constitutions. In the months preceding the Declaration of Independence, New Hampshire enacted a constitution of government on January 5, 1776. New Hampshire was followed by South Carolina, which adopted its constitution on March 26, 1776. In both of these constitutions, it was stated explicitly that the constitution was provisional and contingent on a failure of rapprochement with Britain. Both New Hampshire and South Carolina subsequently adopted permanent constitutions of government. Also prior to independence, Virginia adopted its constitution on June 29, 1776, and New Jersey adopted its constitution on July 2, 1776. Following independence, four states adopted constitutions: Delaware (September 21, 1776); Pennsylvania (September 28, 1776); Maryland (November 8, 1776); and North Carolina (December 18, 1776). These states were joined by Georgia and New York in the early months of 1777. The newly formed state of Vermont declared its independence from both New Hampshire and New York by adopting a constitution on July 8, 1777 (Vermont would continue as essentially an independent republic until its admission to statehood by the congress on March 4, 1791). Finally, after a long and contentious process, the last of the Revolutionary constitutions was adopted by Massachusetts in 1780.

This was, Allan Nevins wrote, "The first time in the world's history that a large group of communities had begun the formation of their own governments under written constitutions."[8] Cecilia Kenyon also described this period similarly as "the first large-scale modern experiment in constitutional republicanism."[9] Thus, at the time, James Madison wrote that "it was the first instance from the creation of the world . . . that free inhabitants have been deliberating on a form of government, and selecting such of their citizens as possessed their confidence, to determine upon and give effect to it."[10]

Connecticut and Rhode Island retained their colonial charters as their constitutions until well into the nineteenth century. In May 1776, the General Assembly of Rhode Island voted simply to replace references to the king in official documents and oaths with "the Governor and Company of the English Colony of Rhode Island and Providence."[11] Likewise in October 1776, the Connecticut assembly resolved that, "The form of civil government in the State shall continue to be established by charter received from Charles the Second of England, so far as an adherence to the same shall be consistent with an absolute independence of this State to the crown of Great Britain." [12]

Both Connecticut and Rhode Island had enjoyed a significant degree of local rule, even as crown colonies, and their charters had been "essentially constitutions of self-governing republics."[13] Rhode Island had not had a royal governor but instead had been governed by its own elected officials. Connecticut too had been essentially self-governing and there was little public support to alter the frame of government.[14] Thus, it was observed that, "when now the states 'took up civil government,' their people did not break with the past; they only added to the republican foundation already laid. They brought executive and administrative functions, as they understood them, into harmony with principles which regulated the legislative and thus established forms of government according to the best political standards of the eighteenth century."[15] Hockett, too, observed with respect to the actions taken by the assemblies of Connecticut and Rhode Island, that the charters, although sanctioned by the King, had emanated from the people in the first place, and were essentially constitutions of self-governing republics. For that reason, "it was only necessary to proclaim in a formal way that they were henceforth to be constitutions of free and independent states."[16]

The writers of the Revolutionary constitutions emulated their former colonial governments in form,[17] while attempting to harmonize those governments with the Enlightenment principles they embraced. As Bailyn observed, the Revolutionary state constitution writers "were forced to think through the fundamentals of their beliefs, and establish republican policies that expressed principles they had earlier endorsed."[18] Adams too noted that this Revolutionary constitutionalism "demanded answers to questions of modern politics: how to reconcile individual freedom with the Republic's 'common good' and stable efficient government; how to have a multitude of free and equal citizens living in dispersed communities draft and agree on a set of constitutional ground rules—in the absence of a more or less enlightened monarch to give them one."[19] To accomplish their task, Bailyn wrote, these constitution writers "explored the nature of written constitutions and of constituent power; worked through the problem of separating functioning powers of government to form balances within single-order societies; and probed the nature of representation, the operative meaning of sovereignty of the people and individual rights."[20] Thus it was that Henry Steele Commager wrote, "Americans took seriously the principle of government of laws not by men and what is more they institutionalized that principle in their constitutions."[21]

In doing so, the Revolutionary constitutions gave substantive form to the moral and philosophical precepts of "fundamental law as a guide to the moral rightness and constitutionality of ordinary law and politics" shared by Englishmen of the eighteenth century. Gordon Wood explained that "Nearly everyone repeatedly invoked Magna Carta and other fundamental laws of the English Constitution. Yet all of these theoretical references to fundamental law could not have much day-to-day practical importance." In contrast, however, these constitutions "gave Revolutionary Americans a concrete handle with which to grasp this otherwise insubstantial fundamental law. Suddenly, with these written documents, the fundamental law and first principles that Englishmen referred to for generations gained a new degree of explicitness and reality."[22] As to this integration of enlightenment principles, Rakove wrote that "In its revolutionary origins, American constitutionalism displayed a remarkable confidence in the capacity of human reason to create new institutions of government organized on republican principles," and although being neither "utopians" nor "radical visionaries," the Revolutionary constitutionalists believed that "the science of politics was a body of knowledge capable of 'improvement' and that lessons drawn from experience could be applied to the task of designing institutions of constitutional government."[23]

In the majority of the royal colonies, however, there had been continuous tension between the crown governors and the legislative assemblies elected by the colonists. While the state constitution writers drew heavily from established and familiar features of colonial government, they also reacted to what they perceived as having been abuses of the royal governments.[24]

The Revolutionaries' reaction to these perceived abuses was most clearly reflected in the limitations placed on the role and powers of the governors in the newly formed states. The Revolutionary constitutions have been seen to reflect "a general distrust of the executive and, relatively, a confidence in the legislature," which was a "direct product of colonial experiences."[25]

The colonial governor was very much the vice-regal representative of the king in the colony. The colonial governor was "the central force of imperial authority within his province" and "the natural center of imperial officialdom."[26] As such, the governor "was naturally endowed with prerogatives which in Great Britain belonged solely to the king."[27]

The governor was invested with broad authority over the executive, legislative, and judicial functions of the colonial government. His role in the affairs of the colony has been described as having been

> the connecting link between the English administrators and the colonial local government. In the colony he represented the dignity and majesty of the monarch himself. He commanded the militia; he presided over the supreme colonial court; he summoned, prorogued, and dissolved the assemblies; he held power to veto; he was the source of pardons and of appointments to positions of trust and honor. Moreover, he was chief land agent; he held the power of making grants and of collecting quitrents. Thus, the colonists' sentiments toward him were complicated by the two sets of relations—political and economic.[28]

The response of the Revolutionary constitution writers was to strip away these vice-regal prerogatives.[29] Indeed, the constitutions of New Hampshire (January 1776) and Pennsylvania (September 1776) made no provision for a governor at all.[30] Other states, although retaining the office of governor, did so in a much diminished form subject to institutional checks on the governor's ability to act unilaterally.

The Revolutionary constitutions retained the privy council, which had been modeled after the House of Lords and the royal privy council that stood between the assembly and the governor.[31] The British had considered the council to be "next to the governor, the most important unit in the political framework of the province." Members of the council often performed a judicial role as well.[32] In a number of colonies, the privy council became, in effect, an upper house of the colonial legislature.[33]

From the perspective of the colonists, the elected assembly was by far the central feature of their government as being "the real organs of popular will,"[34] and eclipsing the governor as "the principal instruments of governmental power within the provinces."[35]

The supremacy of the elected legislature over the governor was a consistent feature of the Revolutionary state constitutions. In most of the new states, the governors were chosen by the legislatures.[36] Governors were thus beholden to the legislatures for their selection and their continuation in office (subject to term limitations), notwithstanding pronouncements of separation of powers to the contrary.[37] The governor's exercise of executive authority was also held in check by the prospect of legislative impeachment and consequent removal from office.[38] Thus, under the Revolutionary constitutions, the governors were reduced to "mere ciphers" as Madison pointed out."[39]

In view of this history of legislative empowerment and gubernatorial antagonism, it is not surprising that the Revolutionary constitutions afforded the governors little involvement in lawmaking.[40] Nevertheless, the Revolutionary state constitution writers also embraced the separation of powers as an organizing principle in their frames of government. Incorporation of separation of powers precepts in the Revolutionary constitutions represented a repudiation of the "mixed government" principle of British constitutionalism in favor of the theory of "balanced government."[41] Under the theory of mixed government the three principal "social estates"—monarchical, aristocratic, and democratic—were each represented in the three branches of government and thereby served to check each other.[42]

In place of mixed government, American constitution writers adopted the theory of balanced government in which "each branch was identified by its function—administrative, lawmaking and judging—not its social constituency."[43] Thus, the theory of balanced government "rested on recognition of distinct and clearly differentiated functions of government," and held that "governmental powers, not social classes, must be kept in balance in order to preserve liberty."[44]

Although the degree to which Montesquieu influenced American constitutional thinking has been a subject of scholarly debate, the American conception of balanced government at the time of the Revolution certainly owed much to Montesquieu's theory of the separation of powers, considered to be "an essential part of Montesquieu's constitutional theory."[45] It has also been said that Montesquieu's separation of powers theory "nicely complimented" the Revolutionaries' conception of political power emanating from the governed and that "In theory at least, no single branch could, separated and checked as it was by others, claim sufficient authority to become tyrannical."[46] Thus, by the time of the Revolution, "the separation of powers was being advanced as the only coherent constitutional theory upon which an alternative to colonial forms could be based."[47]

Their embrace of the separation of powers reflected the Revolutionaries' fear of concentrated power in either the executive or a unitary legislative branch.[48] Implementation of the separation of powers principle proved to be elusive, however. The absence of effective checks and balances on the powers of the legislatures left the implementation of the separation of powers principle in the state constitutions deeply flawed.[49] This lack of restraint on legislative authority was certainly due, at least in part, to the fact that it was the legislatures that framed the first constitutions of the Revolutionary period, although that had not been the case in Massachusetts and New Hampshire.[50] Nevins pointed out as well that "A fact which contributed greatly to the early supremacy of the legislatures was the general assumption during the years 1776–87 that they were the sole judges of their own constitutional powers."[51] Sturm also observed in this connection that, "In actual operation, separation of powers in the first state governments was substantially modified not only by legislative ascendancy but also by participation of each of the other two departments in the affairs of the others—a system of checks and balances."[52]

Limitations were placed on the powers of the executive and the legislature through the adoption of declarations of rights that were considered to be the inherent and inalienable rights of the state's citizens.[53] These declarations of rights included individual liberties that had been incorporated into the colonial charters and legislation, such as the right to vote in elections and to hold public office; the right to be free of arbitrary searches and seizures of persons, papers, and property; the right to trial by jury in both criminal and civil cases; the right in a criminal trial to confront one's accuser and to present evidence on one's behalf; and the right to be free from cruel and unusual punishments. The declarations of rights also secured a variety of collective civil liberties, including freedom of the press; freedom of conscience and religious worship; civil authority over military forces; maintenance of a militia for the defense of the state coupled with a prohibition of standing armies; and the prohibition of taxation by the state without the consent of the citizenry.

Although the proposal of a common constitution for the states had not been acted on by the Continental Congress, the state constitution writers were aware of developments in other states as they framed their constitutions. The influence of one state upon another is plain and, in some instances, there was wholesale importation of constitutional provisions from one state to another. Yet, it would be a mistake to view the process of constitutionalism in the states as a linear progression toward perfection. Instead, the constitutional process reflected the internal deliberations of each state to find its own balance of history and tradition with the imperatives of Revolutionary independence. This was, Vile remarked, the "remarkable achievement" of these Revolutionary constitution writers because "they not only accepted and understood the constitutional theory and experience that they were heirs to, but that they took this heritage and refashioned it, effectively and successfully, to meet a new and extraordinarily difficult situation."[54]

THE EXIGENT CONSTITUTIONS

New Hampshire: January 5, 1776

The first of the Revolutionary constitutions was enacted by the New Hampshire provisional congress on January 5, 1776. New Hampshire had recognized the need for a constitution of government well before receiving the communication from the Continental Congress, but issues such as apportionment of representation and the qualifications for voting had mired New Hampshire's congress in debate. There was also resistance in some quarters to being the first state to declare independence from Great Britain by adopting a state constitution.[55]

New Hampshire had no royal charter on which to model a government, however, and as a consequence, shortly after receiving the recommendation of the Continental Congress, a provisional congress was convened on November 14, 1775, for the purpose of adopting a constitution.[56] This provisional congress "went through the painful process of excavating, re-examining, and rebuilding the very foundations of legally constituted society."[57]

The result of this process was a frame of government enacted on January 5, 1776, that made no provision for either an executive or a judicial branch. Instead, the state's governing authority was reposed in a bicameral legislature comprised of a house of representatives, which was simply a redesignation of the provisional congress, and a twelve-member council, or upper house, that was to proportionally represent the freeholders in the five New Hampshire counties. The council was to be elected initially by the house of representatives, but thereafter both the house and the council were to be elected annually.

All legislation required the approval of both houses, as did the appointment of military officers and most state officers. Bills for the "raising and collecting of money" were required to originate in the house, but they could be amended by the council and then returned to the house for approval.[58]

New Hampshire's first constitution has been described as "a woefully makeshift piece of machinery."[59] Nevertheless, despite being intended to remain in effect only during the period of hostilities with Britain as the Continental Congress had directed, and despite the general dissatisfaction and criticism throughout the state, the provisional constitution remained in effect until a permanent constitution was adopted in 1784.[60]

South Carolina: March 26, 1776

Two months after New Hampshire acted, South Carolina became the second state to enact a constitution. A committee of the state's provisional assembly was empanelled on February 1, 1776, to draft the constitution, which was submitted to the assembly on March 4. After only two weeks of debate, the constitution was approved on March 2, 1776.[61]

Like New Hampshire, the South Carolina constitution was intended to be in effect only during "the present situation of American affairs, and until an accommodation of the unhappy differences between Great Britain and America can be obtained."[62] Unlike New Hampshire, although similarly provisional in nature, the South Carolina constitution laid out a framework of government that was much more extensive in scope.

Reflecting its Revolutionary origins, the constitution's preamble enumerated a litany of abuses against the colonies by the crown, which Lutz commented were "similar to the list to be published in the Declaration of Independence four months later."[63] South Carolina's constitution maintained the bicameral legislature that had been in place during the colonial era. The general assembly was to be elected every two years and membership was to be in proportion to the population. Provision was made for enlargement of the assembly to accommodate the growth of the population, and this has been said to be "the most notable and important change in the colonial period."[64] The second chamber was a thirteen-member legislative council whose members were to be chosen by the general assembly from among its members. Qualification for voting and for election to the assembly were left for later legislation.[65]

The most striking departure from New Hampshire's approach was the creation of an executive that was to govern alongside the legislature. There was to be a president (who was to be the commander-in-chief of the armed forces) and a vice president (who was to assume the office of the president in the event of his death or absence from the state). However, reflecting the dominance of the legislature, the president and vice president were chosen by the council and the assembly, "from among themselves, or from the people at large." If chosen from the legislature, they were required to vacate their seats.[66]

This prohibition against holding multiple offices was adopted in other state constitutions as well and has been seen as "a clear step in the direction away from the parliamentary system toward separating executive from legislative functions."[67] To Vile, this "strict prohibition upon dual membership of the legislative and executive branches," was "the most significant aspect of the doctrine forming the special character of American government."[68]

While under South Carolina's scheme, executive power was vested in the president, the constitution put in place checks on the executive's authority. The president was to govern with a seven-member privy council comprised of the vice president and three members each from the council and the assembly (who were not obliged to surrender their seats in the legislature). Military and naval officers were not eligible to serve on the privy council.[69]

In contrast to the royal governor, the president had no authority to adjourn or dissolve the legislature. Also, the president had no power to wage war, make peace, or enter into a treaty without the consent of both houses of the legislature. However, because all legislative acts required the president's assent to become law, the president was effectively given the veto power.[70]

As a further check on the president's powers, the authority to appoint the principal officers of the government was shared with the legislature. Delegates to the Continental Congress, judicial officers, and sheriffs were to be chosen jointly by the president and both legislative houses. Other officers, including the secretary of state, the attorney general, and the commissioners of the treasury were to be elected by the legislature, whereas other state officers were chosen by the governor but required the advice and consent of the privy council. It is also significant that the legislature was given the authority to remove the civil officers of the state "on address of the general assembly and the legislative counsel," which was in effect the impeachment and removal power later included in Article II, Section 4 of the federal Constitution.

Also unlike New Hampshire, the South Carolina constitution made provision for a judicial branch of the state government. Under that system, criminal trials of felonies were to be presided over by justices of the peace. There was to be an admiralty court with jurisdiction over maritime claims. Juries were to be summoned by "judges of the courts of law" and the privy council was to sit as a court of chancery.[71]

Despite being more comprehensive than that of New Hampshire, the South Carolina constitution soon came under criticism as being incomplete and undemocratic. John Harold Wolfe has suggested that the constitution would have been rejected had it been submitted to the citizenry for their approval.[72] Plans were soon underway to revise or completely rewrite the constitution and despite the demands of the war with Britain, a new and more permanent constitution was finally adopted in March 1778.[73]

THE INDEPENDENCE CONSTITUTIONS

In the meantime, the other states were furiously engaged in constitution-writing of a much more extensive kind than either New Hampshire or South Carolina. In the days immediately preceding independence, first Virginia and then New Jersey, three days later, adopted constitutions that included both comprehensive plans of government and guarantees of individual and civil rights, which modeled the later Bill of Rights in the federal Constitution.

Virginia: June 29, 1776

By the time of independence, Virginia had been a crown colony for 150 years, and as noted, there had been an elected legislature, the House of Burgesses, since 1619. On May 15, 1776, the burgesses empanelled a committee to write a constitution for the new commonwealth. The delay of almost six months from the time the Continental Congress had recommended the adoption of constitutions of government has been attributed to a reluctance primarily on the part of the aristocratic planters of the Tidewater to take action until Virginia's delegates to the Continental Congress had been authorized to vote in favor of independence.[74]

The draft of the constitution, which had been written primarily by George Mason who represented Virginia at the federal Constitutional Convention in 1787, was presented to the burgesses on May 27. Following two weeks of debate and further refinement, the constitution was adopted unanimously on June 29, 1776.[75]

Virginia's was the first constitution to include a declaration of rights that would be guaranteed to all citizens. Virginia's declaration, which was also primarily the work of George Mason, "inaugurated the practice of including separate protections for rights in state constitutions and after its adoption, only four states failed to include a declaration of rights in their constitutions."[76]

The Declaration of Fundamental Rights anticipated the Declaration of Independence by enumerating the fundamental principles on which the government was founded, that all men were "by nature equally free and independent" and that they had "certain inherent rights . . . namely, the enjoyment of life and liberty, with the means of acquiring and possessing property, and pursuing and obtaining happiness and safety."[77] Pauline Maier has suggested that both Thomas Jefferson and Mason had drawn from the English Declaration of Rights, although Mason's statement was "far more radical." Maier also noted that the Virginia drafting committee's bill of rights had been published in the *Pennsylvania Gazette* on the day that Benjamin Franklin, John Adams, and Jefferson had been appointed to draft the Declaration of Independence. In any event, Maier saw a clear relationship between Virginia's bill of rights and the Declaration of Independence.[78]

There was also a clear relationship between Virginia's bill of rights and the Bill of Rights amended to the federal Constitution a decade later. Freedom of the press and freedom in the exercise of religion were guaranteed in Virginia's bill of rights as they were in the First Amendment. As in the Second Amendment, the Virginia declaration recognized the importance of a "well regulated militia . . . trained in arms," which should be "under strict subordination to, and governed by, the civil power." Like the Fourth Amendment, the Virginia declaration prohibited general warrants for the arrest of unnamed persons "whose offense is not particularly described "and the search or premises "without evidence of a fact committed." The rights of an accused under the Fifth Amendment to the due process of law and to be free of compelled self-incrimination were provided for, as were the Sixth Amendment rights to be notified of the accusations, to confront witnesses, to mount a defense, and to a speedy trial before an impartial jury. The right to a jury trial in civil matters was guaranteed as it was in later in the Seventh Amendment. Lastly, the prohibition of excessive fines and of cruel and unusual punishments of the Eighth Amendment were similarly guaranteed in Virginia's Declaration of Fundamental Rights.[79]

The preamble to the frame of government set forth the complaints against British rule similar to the sentiments expressed in the Declaration of Independence, which is not surprising in that Jefferson is credited with having been the principal author of the preamble.[80] The preamble declared that "the government of this country, as formerly exercised by the Crown of Great Britain is totally dissolved."[81] Hockett observed that the Virginia constitution was "the first of the state constitutions based on the assumption of permanent separation from England."[82]

The Virginia constitution is also significant to the development of American constitutionalism in its establishment of the separation of powers as the organizing principle within the governmental framework. As noted, South Carolina had adopted measures in its constitution that apportioned governmental functions between the legislature and the executive, and that implemented procedures under which the power of one branch could be restricted, as by the president's veto and by the requirement of the advice and consent of the privy council for executive appointments. The Virginia constitution made the principle of separation of powers explicit.

In this regard, the Declaration of Fundamental Rights stated that "the legislative and executive powers of the State should be separate and distinct from the judiciary."[83] In accordance with this principle, the frame of government provided that "legislative, executive and judicial departments, shall be separate and distinct, so that neither exercise the powers properly belonging to the other; nor shall any person exercise the powers of more than one of them at the same time."[84] In light of those provisions, Willi Adams considered Virginia's constitution to have been "the first constitutional document since the Instrument of Government, under which Britain had been governed from 1653 to 1657, to include the principle of the separation of powers in express terms."[85]

Virginia also adopted prohibitions on holding multiple public offices and called for limitations on terms in office. The Declaration of Fundamental Rights stated that members of the executive and legislative branches "should, at fixed periods, be reduced to a private station . . . and the vacancies be supplied by frequent, certain, and regular elections."[86] To Corwin this reflected the assumption that "the rights of the individual have nothing to fear from majority rule exercised through legislative assemblies chosen for brief terms by a restricted, though on the whole democratic, electorate."[87]

Although contemporary Revolutionaries, including John Adams, considered the Virginia constitution to be "very much of the democratic kind," it has been observed that the government under the constitution did not "drastically alter the forms and institutions that had prevailed in the late colonial era."[88] The center of governing power was the legislature, which was divided into two chambers: the House of Delegates and the Senate. Two delegates were to be elected annually from each county and major city. There were to be twenty-four senators elected every four years from specially established districts. Senators were limited to serving no more than two terms.[89] Unlike other state constitutions, Virginia's constitution did not establish wealth-based qualifications for election to either chamber and thus, as Kenyon observed, "The upper house was not economically differentiated from the lower house and was accordingly not even a pale, elective imitation of the British House of Lords."[90]

Notwithstanding the constitution's explicit commitment to the principle of the separation of powers, Virginia followed the same course as South Carolina that the chief executive, the governor, was to be chosen annually by the legislature. The constitution restricted the governor to three terms after which he was to be ineligible for election for four years. An eight-member privy council known as the Council of State was to be chosen as well by the legislature, whose members were to serve staggered three-year terms. Together, the governor and council were to "exercise the executive powers of government, according to the laws of the commonwealth." With the advice and consent of the council, the governor could "embody the militia" and could grant pardons and reprieves.[91] Like South Carolina, the power to appoint state officers was apportioned between the governor and the legislature. However, the most senior state officers, including the attorney general, the secretary of the commonwealth, and the delegates to the Continental Congress were to be chosen by the house and senate.[92]

Virginia's constitution was the first to establish the judiciary as a coordinate branch of the government.[93] The constitution contemplated a statewide judicial system comprised of a supreme court, general courts, and justices of the peace. Judges were to be chosen by the legislature, but they were to be commissioned by the governor to "continue in office during good behavior," just as federal judges are today.[94]

The members of the executive and the judiciary were subject to impeachment by the house "for offending against the State, either by mal-administration, corruption, or other means by which the safety of the State may be endangered." Cases of impeachment were to be prosecuted by the attorney general and determined by the justices of the general court. If convicted, the defendant was to be removed from office, disabled from holding future office, or "subjected to such pains or penalties the laws shall direct." Impeachment cases involving justices of the general court were to be determined by the court of appeals.[95]

New Jersey: July 2, 1776

The constitution of New Jersey was enacted by the state's provisional congress on the eve of independence. There had been factions that opposed the formation of a government as being an impediment to reconciliation with Britain.[96] However, as Nevins observed, "the weight of public opinion was clearly with the radicals."[97]

Since the Concessions and Agreements of 1664 and the Agreement of Fundamentals in 1681, the colonial general assembly had exercised broad powers over the governance of the colony. Under the Concessions and Agreements as well as the Agreement of Fundamentals, the assembly was authorized to levy taxes, to enact laws for the general welfare of the colony (subject only to the requirement that those laws be "agreeable" to English law), to establish a system of courts, and to provide for the defense of the colony.

New Jersey responded to the recommendation of the Continental Congress by holding a special election for a provisional congress with authority to form a new government. A new constitution was put forward on June 21 and was enacted on July 2, 1776.[98]

Although the 1776 constitution established a legitimate government in the void left by the retreat of the British government, the basic structure of the colonial government remained in place. As Richard McCormick observed, "The framers of the state constitution were exceedingly practical men, who recognized that they must eschew any novel or theoretical institutions of government and adhere as closely as possible to the colonial model" and as a consequence, "almost the only alterations made in the government were those necessitated by the fact that there was no longer to be any connection with England." Even then, the constitution of 1776 is said to have created a "highly democratic government,"[99] that reflected the Revolutionary preference that governmental power be concentrated in an elected legislature.[100]

The New Jersey legislature was also comprised of a general assembly and a legislative council. Each was to be a representative body with three assemblymen and one councilor elected annually from each county. Although the representation of the counties could be changed "on the principles of more equal representation," the total number of representatives to the assembly could not be less than thirty-nine.

Separate wealth-based qualifications were established for election to the assembly and to the senate. Other wealth-based requirements were stipulated for the right to vote.[101] Significantly, these requirements applied to "all inhabitants" and the absence of a gender restriction was construed as granting suffrage to women.[102]

The council was to be "in all respects . . . a free and independent branch of the legislature" with the "power to prepare bills to pass into laws." With the exception of money bills, which were the sole prerogative of the assembly that the council had no authority to amend, all legislation required the assent of both chambers for a bill to become law.[103]

Following the model of South Carolina and Virginia, the governor and a privy council were to be chosen annually by the legislature. Members of the privy council were to be chosen from members of the legislative council. Thus, as Kruman noted, "the constitution both divided the functions of the old council into two institutions (a significant assertion of the separation of powers), and then reunited them in the same persons."[104]

With the privy council, the governor was to exercise "the supreme executive power" as "chancellor of the colony" and to act as commander-in-chief of the state's military forces. The real power in the new state government remained in the legislature, however. The legislature retained the power to appoint state officers and he was dependent on the legislature not only for his election to office but for his salary as well. In view of his dependence on the legislature, the governor has been seen as little more than a "figurehead."[105] McCormick attributed the governor's diminished status to "the long tradition of antagonism to the royal governors."[106]

Although the constitution contemplated a continuation of the judicial system comprised of a supreme court and courts of common pleas, the governor and privy council were the "court of last resort" with authority to grant pardons in cases of treason and felony. Kruman considered this to be an attempt by the constitution's writers to "affirm continuity with the colonial past,"[107] and led Kemmerer to remark that the governor's "chief function was a judicial one."[108]

The governor and other state officers were subject to impeachment by the assembly and removal by the council upon a finding of "misbehavior."[109] Additionally, the constitution placed restrictions on holding more than one public office concurrently, so that judges and state officers could not be elected to the legislature unless they surrendered their state office.[110]

New Jersey followed Virginia's lead by incorporating guarantees of individual and civic liberties in the constitution, although not set forth in a separate bill of rights. Chief among these rights were freedom of conscience in religious worship, the rights of the accused in criminal cases to the assistance of counsel, and to the presentation of witnesses in defense of the charges, as well as the "inestimable right of trial by jury."[111]

THE WAR CONSTITUTIONS

Delaware: September 21, 1776

Delaware distinguished itself from its predecessor states by being the first state to call a special convention to write the state's constitution, rather than treating the constitution simply as a legislative act.

There had been a representative assembly in the colony since the charter was granted by Penn in 1701. Following the withdrawal of the crown governor, the assembly formed a provisional government on June 15, 1776 by the simple expedient of directing all public officials to act "in the name of the Government and Counties of Newcastle, Kent and Sussex, upon Delaware," rather than in the name of the king.[112]

Twelve days after forming the provisional government, the assembly resolved to hold elections for delegates to attend a convention for the specific purpose of writing the constitution. Kruman noted that the members of the provisional assembly did not consider themselves to have the authority "to execute the important work" of writing the constitution and therefore had directed that delegates be elected to meet in convention "there to order and declare the future form of government for this state."[113] The calling of the constitutional convention was strenuously opposed by the loyalist citizens, and participation in the election of delegates was restricted to men who had taken an oath "to support and maintain the independence of this government."[114]

The convention met on September 2. Two committees were formed: one to draft a declaration of rights and the other to prepare the frame of government.

Penn's 1701 charter had secured the basic liberties of freedom in the practice of religion and for those accused of crimes, the right to counsel, and the right to present witnesses in defense of the charges.[115] The writers of the declaration of rights were also aided in their efforts by having available to them Pennsylvania's bill of rights, which had been published on August 21, and a copy of the unpublished draft of Maryland's declaration. The Delaware declaration was strongly influenced by the Pennsylvania and Maryland statements. As Gaspere Saldino observed in this regard, "of the declaration's twenty-three articles, eleven were lifted verbatim from the draft declaration of the Maryland constitutional convention, six were adapted from that draft, and three demonstrated the influence of Pennsylvania's declaration."[116] The draft declaration was presented to the convention and with some amendment, was promptly adopted.

Like Virginia, the Delaware declaration recognized the people as the sole source of governmental authority. The state was "founded on compact only" and the government was to be "instituted for the good of the whole." As a document born of revolution, it was declared that should the government be perverted and "public liberty manifestly endangered," the people had the right to establish a new government.[117]

As Article I of the federal Bill of Rights would later provide, the Delaware declaration recognized the right "to petition the legislature for the redress of grievances in a peaceable and orderly manner." The legislature was to be "frequently convened" and only the legislature had authority "of suspending laws or the execution of laws." Elections of representatives were to be "free and frequent" and any freeman "having sufficient evidence of permanent common interest with, and attachment to, the community" had the right to vote in elections.[118]

Other restraints on government abuses of power that would find their way into the Bill of Rights were also included in Delaware's declaration. The "liberty of the press" was to be "inviolably preserved." *Ex post facto* laws were prohibited, as was the quartering of military personnel in private homes during peacetime. The taking of private property for public use without consent was also prohibited.[119]

The importance of a "well regulated militia" was recognized. However, the maintenance of a standing army was prohibited, and it was made clear that the state's military forces were to be subject to civilian control at all times.[120]

The declaration also secured personal liberties. The freedom of worship that had been guaranteed in Penn's 1701 charter was preserved. Additionally, conscientious objection to the bearing of arms was to be respected.[121]

The rights of persons accused of crimes were also protected as they had been under Penn's charter and would be later under the federal Bill of Rights. An accused was to be free of compelled self-incrimination and was to receive a speedy trial before an impartial jury "without whose unanimous consent he ought not be found guilty." At trial, defendants were guaranteed the right to be notified of the charges, the right to be represented by counsel, the right to confront the witnesses for the prosecution, and the right to present witnesses for the defense. Lastly, like the Eight Amendment, excessive bail, excessive fines, and cruel and unusual punishments were prohibited.[122]

The declaration of rights was not incorporated into the constitution, but it was appended to the constitution as a legislative act. As a consequence, questions were raised regarding the status of the declaration.[123]

Nine days after the enactment of the declaration of rights, on September 20, the convention adopted the frame of government and then dissolved.[124] Saldino described the constitution as a "conservative document" that had been written "by men who opposed radical change." This was largely due, Saldino noted, to the fact that "their government had functioned well since 1701."[125] However, although the constitution did not represent a great departure from the colonial government, as John Monroe has pointed out, "The notable change was that the power of the legislature was enhanced and that of the governor was diminished."[126]

The unicameral legislature that had been unusual for a crown colony was replaced by a two-chamber general assembly.[127] The larger of the two houses was the assembly, which was comprised of seven representatives from each of the counties, who were elected annually. The second chamber was the council, consisting of three representatives from each county elected for staggered three-year terms. There were no wealth-based qualifications for election. With the exception of money bills, either chamber could initiate legislation that was then subject to alteration by the other.[128]

Delaware followed the example of the other Revolutionary constitutions to date by placing the executive function in the hands of a president and a four-member privy council. The president and the councilors were to be elected by the legislature to three-year terms after which they were ineligible for reelection for three years. The advice and consent of the privy council was necessary for the exercise of the executive powers including the calling up of the militia. With the advice and consent of the council, the governor could call the legislature into session, although he could not adjourn or dissolve the legislature once it was in session (as the crown governor could).

Significantly, like Virginia, the executive played no part in legislation. As an additional check on the executive, the funds for the government were appropriated by the legislature, and the president "was accountable to them for the same."[129]

As in the other constitutions, the appointment power was shared by the executive and the legislature. The general assembly was authorized to elect the delegates to the Continental Congress and the officers of the army and navy. Judicial appointments required the approval of the president and the general assembly. The president and the council were empowered to appoint state officers, including the secretary of state and the attorney general, as well as other civil officers not specified in the constitution.[130]

The limitations on the executive reflected the prevailing view of government held by the Revolutionaries. It has been noted that the authors of the Delaware constitution "were part of the revolutionary generation that sought to reform government by limiting its exercise of power. . . . Their work, like that of other emerging states, emphasized citizen's rights over government power, provided for separation of powers, and created a strong legislature coupled with a weak chief executive."[131] Nevertheless, Gordon Wood noted that "As impotent as the new Delaware president was made in 1776, he remained in the minds of the most radical Whigs a very powerful and dangerous man."[132]

The constitution interposed other checks on abuse of gubernatorial power. The holding of multiple public offices was barred and if a member of the legislature accepted a position in the executive branch, his seat would be deemed to have been vacated, requiring a new election. In like fashion, officers of the military were prohibited from election to the privy council.[133]

Members of the executive could also be removed from office for offenses against the state "either by maladministration, corruption, or other means, by which the safety of the Commonwealth may be endangered." Impeachment proceedings were to be lodged in the house and could be brought against the governor for up to eighteen months after leaving office. Trial of the impeachment was to be before the council and in the event of conviction, the official would be "either forever disabled to hold office under government or removed from office *pro tempore*, or subject to such pains and penalties as the laws shall direct."[134]

Lastly, there was to be an independent judicial branch comprised of a supreme court, an admiralty court, courts of common pleas, and orphans courts. Provision was also made for a system of justices of the peace. Although judicial appointments were to be made by the president and the general assembly, judges were not subject to reappointment but were to serve "during good behavior."[135]

In addition to establishing this frame of government, the Delaware constitution was remarkable in outlawing the importation of slaves into the state. Thus, the constitution provided that "No person hereafter imported into this State from Africa ought to be held in slavery under any presence whatever; and no negro, Indian, mulato slave ought to be brought into this State, for sale, from any place in the world."[136] Of the constitutions in this era, only Vermont was more expansive in its rejection of slavery.

Pennsylvania: September 28, 1776

The Delaware constitution was soon followed by that of Pennsylvania, and although Pennsylvania's declaration of rights had deeply influenced the Delaware constitution writers, the frame of government adopted by Pennsylvania was very much *sui generis*.

Pennsylvania's constitution has been widely regarded as the most radical of the Revolutionary period.[137] Its uniqueness among the constitutions of the time was due in large part to the strong division between those favoring independence and those who were opposed. As Paul Doutrich observed, "By early 1776 Pennsylvania's government was at the brink of revolution, as three distinct political parties emerged." There were the Tories who supported the proprietary and opposed independence. There were Radicals from the western counties who favored independence and who argued for sweeping reform of the government. Third were the Moderates who, though they opposed Penn's proprietary government, were resistant to independence, favoring a more measured approach.[138] Commenting on the divisiveness in Pennsylvania's politics, Jensen wrote that "In no other colony were the radical-political-economic lines so sharply drawn, nowhere was the ruling class so opposed to change or to concession and nowhere was the political revolution so complete in 1776."[139]

Thus, in November 1775, the Pennsylvania assembly instructed Pennsylvania's delegation to the Continental Congress to vote against independence from Britain. However, the following May, four thousand people attended a public meeting in Philadelphia to voice their approval of the recommendation of the Continental Congress that the colonies cast off the vestiges of colonial rule and form their own governments.[140]

Debate then turned, as it had in Delaware, to whether the provisional assembly was the proper body to frame the new constitution. Ultimately, in June 1776, a special constitutional convention was called. As had been the case in Delaware, only those opposed to the continuation of British rule were allowed to participate in the election of delegates to the convention. On July 15, 1776, the convention was called to order.[141]

A proposed declaration of rights was submitted to the convention on July 25, 1776, but it was not adopted until late August. The influence of Virginia's declaration of rights is clear."[142]

In language taken virtually verbatim from the Virginia constitution, the Pennsylvania declaration acknowledged the sole right of the people to govern for the common good and to alter or abolish the government "in such a manner as shall be by the community judged most conducive to the public weal." [143] Also like Virginia, the Pennsylvania declaration contained guarantees of both individual and civic rights, including prohibitions against seizures of persons and property without warrant, taking of property for public use without consent, and being compelled to take arms. Due process rights were also secured for those accused of crime. Other civil rights were secured in the body of the constitution including the right to vote and to hold public office. Standing armies were prohibited and for that reason, the constitution guaranteed the right of the people "to bear arms for the defense of themselves."[144] These rights were already established principles of constitutionalism in Pennsylvania going back to the 1682 Charter of Liberty.[145]

In some respects, the rights secured by Pennsylvania were more expansive than those of Virginia. In addition to the freedom of the press, Pennsylvania's declaration included the guaranty of "freedom of speech, and of writing and of publishing their sentiments." Along with the right to petition for the redress of grievances, the Pennsylvania constitution recognized the people's right to "assemble together," and to "consult for their common good." Pennsylvania also recognized a right to travel and "to emigrate from one state to another that will receive them."[146] Pennsylvania was the first state to establish these rights in the state's constitution.[147]

Pennsylvania's frame of government was also radically different from those of other states. Most notably, Pennsylvania made no provision for a chief executive. Instead, the executive function was to be carried out by a committee, although governing authority over the affairs of the state remained concentrated in the legislature. As Harry Tinkcom explained, the constitution "broke with the past and made Pennsylvania one of the most democratic of all the states. Fearing the power of the governor, its framers made no provision for such an office. Instead, an executive council was created with a president as presiding officer. The supreme legislative power rested in the assembly whose members were selected by an electorate no longer hampered by property qualifications."[148]

The constitution preserved the unicameral legislature that had been in place during the Penn proprietary. It has also been suggested that the constitution's framers had feared that a senate-like body would be conducive to the creation of an aristocracy.[149] This may reflect the influence of Benjamin Franklin.[150]

The House of Representatives was invested with "supreme legislative power" to "prepare bills and enact them into law," including laws "for the encouraging of virtue and the prevention of vice and immorality." The house was also authorized to exercise all the powers necessary for the legislature of a free state or commonwealth." However, as comprehensive as these policies were, the house was not given authority to alter or amend the constitution.[151]

The house exercised authority usually conferred on the executive. The house was empowered to regulate and train freemen for the defense of the state; to impeach criminals; to redress grievances; to incorporate and establish towns, cities, and counties; and to establish schools "for the convenient instruction of youth." The house had the power to appoint the officers of the state government, as well as to select the delegates to the Continental Congress. Members of the house were prohibited from holding state office, however.[152]

The legislative process was remarkable for its transparency as well. In general, sessions of the house were to be "open for admission of all persons who behave decently." Sessions could be closed to the public only when the welfare of the state so required. All bills "of a public nature" were required to be printed and distributed to the public in advance of final action, and the proceedings of the house were to be published weekly. Printing presses were to be "free to every person who undertakes to examine the proceedings of the legislature, or any part of government." These provisions were intended to ensure that the exercise of legislative power "under normal circumstances should be constantly monitored by the people," and Lutz has noted that these provisions had the effect of "restricting government to actions the population had directly approved."[153]

Those executive functions not carried out by the house were to be performed by a twelve-member Supreme Executive Council whose members were elected annually, subject to a three-year term limit. The house and the executive council jointly selected the president who was to serve for one year. It was the responsibility of this council to "take care that the laws be faithfully executed" and to that end, the council was authorized to "draw upon the treasury such sums as shall be appropriated' by the house. The council was also to correspond with other states and to "transact business as may appear to them necessary to lay before the general assembly."[154]

Executive and judicial officers were subject to removal for "mal-administration." Removal proceedings were to be initiated by the house, with trial before the president and the council.[155]

The constitution created a judiciary that included a supreme court, courts of common pleas, "courts of justice" in Philadelphia and in the counties, courts of general sessions, and orphans courts. The constitution conferred on the judiciary, "the powers usually exercised by such courts," but it was left to the house to determine any additional jurisdiction.[156] The judges were not free of control by the legislature, however. Tenure during "good behavior" was not provided for in the constitution, as was the practice in other states. Instead, judges of the "Supreme Court of Judicature" were to be commissioned by the house for seven-year terms after which they could seek reappointment. Judges were also subject to removal by the house for "misbehavior."[157]

As a further limitation on the power of the judiciary, the president and council were authorized to grant pardons and to remit fines except in cases of impeachment. Pardons could not be granted, however, "until the next session of the assembly."[158]

In yet another departure from the frames of government adopted up to that point, Pennsylvania created a fourth institution of government, the Council of Censors. Elections to the Council of Censors were to be held every seven years and two representatives were to be chosen from each city and county. The representatives were to be in office for one year.[159]

The Council of Censors was to serve two essential functions. First, the council was to oversee compliance with the constitution by the executive and legislative branches. To accomplish this, the council was to inquire into: (1) whether the executive and the legislature had "assumed to themselves, or exercised greater powers than they are entitled under the constitution;" (2) whether taxes had been "justly laid," and public monies appropriately disbursed; and (3) whether the laws had been "faithfully executed." To carry out this oversight function, the council was given broad powers to gather records and to summon witnesses.[160]

The Council of Censors was also to serve a remedial function. When warranted, the council could "pass public censures" and other impeachments. The council was to recommend the repeal of laws that in the council's view had been enacted "contrary to the principles of the Constitution." Lastly, the council was authorized to call a convention for the purpose of amending the constitution as was "necessary for the preservation of the rights and happiness of the people."[161]

Nevins described this Council of Censors as the "crowning eccentricity of the Pennsylvania Constitution."[162] Although agreeing that the council was not considered a success, Kenyon saw the council as an attempt to address the critical issues of enforcing the constitution and providing a mechanism for amendment.[163]

Indeed, the constitution itself was greeted by what Nevins described as a "perfect storm of opposition." Those who wanted a government based on a balance of power found the executive council to be "totally inadequate to keep such an unbalanced government in the straight path."[164] Bauman, who described the constitution as being "novel and distinct," attributed these flaws to the "prevailing Whig view of government" and to Pennsylvania's "inner turmoil" at the time.[165]

Opposition to the constitution delayed formation of a government until elections were held in February 1777, after the Continental Congress threatened to assume the government of the state. By March 4, both the house and the executive council were in place and a president of the council had been elected.[166] Dissatisfaction with the plan of government persisted, however, and the constitution was substantially rewritten in 1790.[167]

Maryland: November 11, 1776

Maryland's provisional legislature did not act on the recommendation of the Continental Congress until July 3, 1776, when the legislature directed that elections would be held for a convention to adopt a plan of government that would respond to the imperatives of wartime. The delegates were to be called "for the express purpose of forming a new government by the authority of the people only, and enacting and ordering all things for the preservation, safety, and general weal of the colony." The convention came together in Annapolis on August 14, 1776.

A seven-member committee was chosen on August 17 to draft the constitution, which was presented to the convention on September 10. Due to the exigencies of the war, the convention did not take up the constitution until October 4 and on November 11, the constitution and the declaration of rights were adopted.[168]

Maryland's declaration of rights has been haled as "one of the longest and most comprehensive listings of rights of any one of the states."[169] Comprised of forty-two separate provisions, the delegates reportedly debated the declaration almost every day between October 10 and November 3.[170]

The declaration of rights codified the fundamental principles on which the government was founded. Notably, specific provision was made for the legislative, executive, and judicial branches to be "separate and distinct from each other." The contemporaneous holding of more than one public office was prohibited, and provision was made for the "rotation" of public officials in the executive branch.[171] However, as contemplated by the constitution, the separation of powers was intended to prevent simultaneous office holding in the several branches of government, not a structure of offsetting powers. As David C. Skaggs observed, "Completely independent executive and judicial departments were not considered at all."[172] Nevertheless, the declaration placed restraints on the exercise of governmental power. Liberty of the press and the right to petition the legislature for the redress of grievances were guaranteed. Although the authority of the legislature over taxation was recognized, the "levying of taxes by poll" and assessments on the poor "for the support of the government" were prohibited. Instead, a more progressive, wealth-based tax system was to be employed under which taxes were to be assessed on an individual "according to his actual wealth, in real and personal property, within the state."[173]

Following Virginia's example, individual rights were also protected from government intrusion. General warrants were prohibited and due process rights were guaranteed to persons in criminal cases, including the prohibition against compelled testimony by the accused and the prohibition of "cruel and unusual pains and penalties." Also prohibited were *ex post facto* laws and the bill of attainder. Bernard Schwartz considered the prohibition against the bill of attainder to be "the most significant innovation made by the Maryland Declaration of Rights." Commenting on this, Schwartz wrote that "This was apparently the first such constitutional prohibition and was the forerunner of the Bill of Attainder Clause of Art. I, secs. 9 and 10, of the federal Constitution." To Schwartz, the Maryland provision was "the most liberal for its time."[174]

Also like Virginia, Maryland's declaration of rights placed restrictions on the state's military forces. In addition to prohibitions against maintaining a standing army and the quartering of troops in private homes without the consent of the legislature, the declaration made it clear that only military personnel would be subject to martial law. And in all events, the military forces were to be "under strict subordination and control of the civil power."[175]

Lastly, the declaration dealt with matters of religion. The declaration guaranteed religious liberty to all persons "professing the Christian religion." The effect of this provision was to remove the disability of members of the Roman Catholic Church from voting and holding office that had been imposed by the crown government, which has been deemed to have been a significant reform.[176] The legislature was empowered to "lay a general tax for the support of the Christian religion," but an individual could specify disbursemt of that revenue "for the benefit of the poor of his own denomination."[177]

Notwithstanding the liberal reforms in the declaration of rights, the Maryland constitution is considered to be the most conservative of the Revolutionary constitutions.[178] Walker Lewis wrote that "The Maryland Constitution of 1776 was one of the least revolutionary documents of that revolutionary period," and "was designed to perpetuate the existing social order."[179] Crowl too found that as a consequence of the Maryland constitution, "Maryland was to be governed for a full generation by an oligarchy of lawyers, merchants, and landed gentry."[180]

Like other revolutionary constitutions before it, the Maryland constitution located the center of political power in the legislature.[181] The composition of the House of Delegates was virtually the same as it had been under the crown government. The members of the second chamber, the senate, were elected by what was in essence an electoral college, and because its members had to have substantial wealth to qualify for election (candidates for the senate had to possess real and personal property valued at least one thousand pounds),[182] it has been said that "The senate became a refuge for wealth and an effective break upon radicalism."[183] Different wealth-based qualifications were established for election to the house (representatives had to possess real and personal property valued at five hundred pounds) and for the vote (a voter had to have a free-hold of at least fifty acres, or real or personal property valued in excess of five hundred pounds).[184] Thus, Crowl remarked that under the Maryland constitution, "Possession of property was made the *sine qua non* of civic participation."[185]

The differentiation in methods of electing the house and the senate was said by Nevins to be the "chief distinction" of the Maryland constitution from those of the other states of the era.[186] Only Massachusetts, New Hampshire (in 1784), and New York created a senate whose constituency differed significantly from the general assembly.[187]

The indirect election of senators for five-year terms of office was said to be a calculated effort to ensure the continued influence of the propertied elite in a mixed government. Commenting on Maryland's scheme, Gordon Wood wrote that

> No senate in all the states was more favorably regarded by those who clung desperately to the traditional meaning of mixed government than that of Maryland. With its small membership, its five year term of office, and its unique indirect method of election by an electoral college, it seemed to many to be the most successful republican expedient for accomplishing the end of a hereditary nobility in a balanced constitution.[188]

Despite the creation of the senate as a haven for the propertied elite, the house was invested with significant power. Only the house could originate money bills, although the house was prohibited from attaching legislation as a rider to money bills that did not relate to the raising of revenue. Otherwise, either chamber could initiate legislation for consideration by the other chamber.[189]

The house was also the "grand inquest" of the state. The house was to "examine and pass on all accounts" of the state regarding the collection and expenditure of funds, and to inquire into "all complaints, grievances and offences." Anticipating the investigatory authority of congressional committees under the federal Constitution, the house was authorized to engage auditors, order the production of "public or official papers and records," and to summon and examine witnesses under oath "concerning affairs relating to the public interest."[190]

Legislators of both chambers were guaranteed the "freedom of speech and debate" such that their proceeding "ought not be impeached in any other court or judicature."[191] This immunity for speech and debate in legislative sessions anticipated the Speech and Debate Clause of the Constitution in Article I, Section 6.

Both legislative houses could punish by imprisonment persons who were "guilty of contempt in their view," or who threatened a member or who engaged in "any obstruction to their proceedings." Anyone who interfered with members "during their sitting, or on their way to or return from" a legislative session was similarly subject to imprisonment as were persons who obstructed a witness in a legislative inquiry. Members were subject to expulsion for "great misdemeanor," although they could not be expelled a second time "for the same cause."[192]

As was typical of the Revolutionary constitutions, the powers of the governor were both limited and circumscribed. The governor was to administer the affairs of the state with the advice and consent of a five-member council. Both the governor and the council were chosen by the legislature. Although the constitution specified certain areas of authority, such as the appointment and removal of some state officers, the granting of pardons and reprieves, and the imposition of embargoes on goods, the constitution contemplated that the legislature would determine the breadth of the governor's powers.[193]

A judicial system was also established that was comprised of courts of chancery and admiralty, general courts, and justices of the peace. A three-member court of appeals was established with "final and conclusive jurisdiction." Judges were appointed by the governor and were to hold their commissions during "good behavior." Judges were subject to removal from office "only for misbehavior, on conviction in a court of law."[194]

The constitution dealt extensively with limitations on office holding and restrictions on the activities of public officers. The framers' distrust of a perpetuation of executive officers was made explicit in the declaration of rights, which stated that "A long continuance in the first executive departments of power and trust is dangerous to liberty."[195] Accordingly, the governor and other state officers (save those who occupied their offices during good behavior) were to be elected annually by the legislature as were delegates to the Continental Congress. The governor was limited to serving three consecutive terms after which the incumbent would not be eligible for reelection for four years. Delegates to congress could serve only three years in a six-year period.[196]

The constitution directly addressed conflicts of interest and corruption. The governor, the council, delegates to congress and the members of the legislature were prohibited from holding a "place of profit," on pain of removal from office, disqualification from future office, or possibly banishment from the state. Anyone found to have given "any bribe, present or reward, or any promise, or any security for the payment or delivery of any money or any other thing," in order to "obtain or procure a vote to be governor, senator, delegate to congress or assembly, member of the council, or judge, or to be appointed to any of said offices, or to any office of profit or trust," would be "forever disqualified to hold any office of trust or profit in this State," as would the person who received such a corrupt payment.[197]

A significant innovation of the Maryland constitution was the establishment of a procedure for amending the constitution. An amending bill had to be first enacted by the house and the senate. Thereafter, the bill was to be published for public study at least three months before the next election of the assembly. The amendment could then be confirmed by the house and the senate at the first session following that election. It has been noted that the requirement of an intervening election served as a popular referendum on the proposed amendment.[198] An amendment that altered the structure of the government required the concurrence of at least two-thirds of each house of the assembly, both in the first instance and in the confirmation.[199]

North Carolina: December 18, 1776

After adopting a "temporary constitution" on May 11, 1776, following the withdrawal of the crown government, elections were held in August for representatives to a state congress specifically for the purpose of writing a permanent constitution, as well as enacting other necessary legislation.[200] Unlike other Revolutionary states, North Carolina had been caught short by the departure of the royal government because, as Jensen noted, "The administration of the colony was so firmly in the hands of the royal governor that local government was almost non-existent."[201]

This new congress met on November 12, 1776. A frame of government and declaration of rights were taken up on December 11, and after three days of intense debate between the conservatives and the radicals, the constitution of government was agreed to on December 14. The declaration of rights was adopted on December 17 and incorporated into the constitution.[202]

The declaration of rights and the plan of government drew extensively from the constitutions of Maryland, Pennsylvania, and Virginia. As a consequence, there was little that was new or novel in either the constitution of government or the declaration of rights.

The center of power remained in the bicameral legislature composed of the House of Commons and the Senate. Although the declaration of rights enshrined the principle that the legislature, the executive and the judiciary were to be "forever separate and distinct from each other," as a practical matter, the executive and the judiciary were relegated to supporting roles.[203]

For example, legislation could be initiated by either house for consideration by the other. Bills were signed into law by the speakers of each house, thus effectively eliminating the governor from any substantive role in the legislative process.

The appointment power was also firmly in the hands of the legislature. The governor and the seven-member council of state were elected annually by joint action of the two houses. Delegates to the Continental Congress, state officers, and military officers were all appointed annually by the legislature. Judges were appointed by the legislature but were to serve during good behavior.[204]

The governor and other state officers could be removed by the legislature for "offending against the State," either by violating the constitution or on grounds of mal-administration or corruption. These officials could be prosecuted criminally either by legislative impeachment or by presentment of the grand jury.[205]

The restrictions on the governor have been described as the "chief fault" of the constitution resulting from "an excess of radicalism." As a result, Nevins observed, "No more hapless governor existed any where south of Pennsylvania," and led Nevins to remark that under the constitution, the governor was "simply an ornament."[206]

Different qualifications were established for election to the two houses based on ownership of real property (senators had to hold three hundred acres in fee, while representatives had to hold one hundred acres either in fee or "for the term of his own life"). In contrast to other states, North Carolina established different qualifications for voting for members of the house and of the senate.[207]

Like other states, North Carolina forbade the holding of "more than one lucrative office." Officers of the armed forces, suppliers of goods to the armed forces, and members of the judiciary were ineligible for election to the legislature. The state treasurer and others who received public monies were similarly ineligible until their accounts with the public treasury had been settled.

The constitution also put religious restrictions on holding public office. Members of the clergy were considered to be incapable of public office.

Anyone who "denied the being of God or the truth of the Protestant religion or the divine authority either of the Old or New Testaments" were prohibited from public office as were those "who shall hold religious principles incompatible with the freedom and safety of the State."[208]

In contrast to these restraints, the constitution also forbade the preference of one church denomination over another. No one was to be compelled to attend or to support a church if to do so would be "contrary to what he believes is right."[209]

Lastly, the constitution addressed various civic interests. Schools were to be established at public expense "for the convenient education of youth." Purchases of land from the native peoples were restricted to land for public use when authorized by the legislature. Imprisonment for debt was prohibited absent a "strong presumption of fraud" after delivery of all real and personal property for the benefit of creditors.[210]

Georgia: February 5, 1777

Immediately after the royal governor, Sir James Wright, absconded from the colony carrying with him the great seal, the provisional congress adopted Rules and Regulations "to curb the lawless and protect the peaceable." This enactment provided for the election of a President and Commander-in-Chief who was to serve for six months. Although the president was invested with "all executive powers of government," he was "bound to consult with and follow the advice" of a Council of State comprised of thirteen persons and the five delegates to the Continental Congress, all of whom were appointed by the provisional legislature. A rudimentary judicial branch was also appointed to serve "during the pleasure of congress."[211] The government under the Rules and Regulations was always intended to be a stopgap measure, "to serve as a frame until a more stable form could be arranged."[212]

After news was received that independence had been declared, an election for a new congress to enact a constitution, as well as other legislation, was held on August 8, 1776. Although this congress convened in October, a committee to draft the constitution was not formed until the following January. The constitution was enacted on February 5, 1777.[213]

Georgia followed New Jersey's model and integrated the guarantees of individual and civic rights in the constitution rather than adopting a separate declaration of rights. Nevertheless, the constitution secured freedom of religion (so long as the exercise of that right was not "repugnant to the people and safety of the state"); freedom of the press; the right of *habeas corpus*; protection from excessive bail and excessive fines; and the right to trial by jury. The constitution also provided that individuals could not be compelled to support teachers without their consent, "except those of their own profession."[214]

Also like the other constitutions of that time, despite the stated principle that the branches of government should be "separate and distinct," political power remained centered in the legislature, as it had been under the Rules and Regulations.[215] As Ware observed, the separation of powers, "was easier said than done and was not followed throughout the rest of the document, or in practice thereafter." This was because "The governor was too much associated in [the minds of the Framers] with royal control. The judiciary, held down by revision by the privy council, governor's whim, or transfer of jurisdiction to England, had not developed its position as it was later to do. It was to the legislature that these men entrusted the royal government of the new state."[216]

The constitution preserved the unicameral legislature. In that, Georgia joined Pennsylvania and Vermont (which adopted much of the Pennsylvania constitution verbatim) as the only revolutionary states to do so. The unicameral structure remained a source of controversy in Georgia until 1789, when Georgia eventually adopted a bicameral General Assembly.[217]

Representatives to the House of Assembly were to be elected annually, as were the delegates to the Continental Congress, who were considered to be members of the assembly as well. The constitution provided for proportional representation based on population, and Georgia was the first state to establish a graduated system permitting an increase in representation as population grew.[218]

The governor and an executive council were to be chosen by the assembly from among the elected representatives. Bills adopted by the assembly were to be sent to the executive council (but not the governor, who was not to preside over the council when it considered legislation) for the council's "perusal and advice." The council's comments and explanation of proposed amendments were to be considered by the assembly but neither the governor nor the council had the authority to veto legislation enacted by the assembly.

The assembly also exercised close oversight of the executive. The constitution provided that "every officer of the state shall be liable to be called to account by the House of Assembly."[219] In light of the restraints on his authority, the governor has been considered little more than a puppet of the assembly.[220]

The constitution expanded on the judicial system established under the Rules and Regulations. There were to be superior courts in each county and "Courts of Conscience" to decide cases in which the amount in controversy did not exceed ten pounds. Grand juries of at least eighteen members were required to bring an indictment charging violations of the criminal law. All trials were conducted by a superior court composed of a chief justice and three judges who resided in the county and who were to act as "judges of law as well as fact."[221]

As with other Revolutionary constitutions, restrictions were placed on multiple office holding. In particular, no one holding a commission in the military (other than in the militia) or who held an "office of profit" could serve in the assembly. In the event a representative accepted such an office, his seat was immediately vacated, and he was ineligible for re-election while in office. Members of the clergy were also ineligible for election to the assembly.[222]

The constitution established an elaborate procedure for amendment. All alterations of the constitution required approval by a majority of the voters in each county.[223] In practice, however, the assembly was able to substantially alter several provisions of the constitution by simply reinterpreting them.[224]

Eventually, a constitutional convention was held in November 1788 to consider amendments to the constitution. However, rather than considering amendments as the delegates were charged to do, a new constitution was put forward that was modeled after the new federal Constitution then under consideration by the states. The new Georgia constitution was adopted on May 6, 1789.[225]

New York: April 20, 1777

Even before the Continental Congress made its recommendation, New York had been embroiled in debate whether to adopt a constitution, opinion being deeply divided whether a new constitution was needed at all. Following receipt of the congress's recommendation, an election was called for a new state congress with authority to frame a constitution. Kruman viewed this election as having been a referendum on the question *vel non* of a new constitution, and if there was to be a new constitution, who would write it.[226]

Even though this congress convened on July 9, 1776, action was not taken on writing the constitution until August due to the exigencies of the war with Britain. As Nevins explained, after independence was declared, the New York congress was a "government on the run" and the congress had resolved that "the dangerous situation of the state demanded its undivided attention, and that consideration of a constitution should wait until August 1."[227]

Events soon overtook the constitution writing when the British occupied a substantial part of the state, including New York City. The war consumed the attention of the congress, and it was not until March 12, 1777, that a draft constitution was submitted for consideration by the congress. After a month of debate and revision, the constitution was enacted on April 20, 1777.[228] Even then, the constitution was approved by less than a third of the delegates to the congress.[229]

The plan of government that emerged has been described as "Unarguably . . . one of the most conservative forms of government established by any of the thirteen rebellious colonies."[230] Despite being chartered to do so, the congress did not adopt a bill of rights, and New York was one of the four states not to do so. Milton Klein has suggested that the absence of a specific bill of rights to be secured by the constitution reflected the Lockean view that "with the renunciation of British rule, New Yorkers were in a state of nature, and since under the contract theory of government all rights not surrendered to the civil magistrates were retained by the people as inalienable, no specific enumeration of such rights would be necessary."[231] A view that would be expressed by a prominent New Yorker, Alexander Hamilton, among others in respect of the necessity of a bill of rights in the federal Constitution.[232]

But in any event, the constitution contained several guarantees of individual rights. Due process, including the right to a jury trial, was to be provided before an individual could be disenfranchised or deprived of property. Attainder was abolished as to acts committed after "termination of the present war," thus preserving the punishment for those whose loyalties remained with the crown. Freedom of "religious profession and worship" was to be enjoyed but would not excuse "acts of licentiousness or justify practices inconsistent with the peace and safety of the State."[233]

Far and away, the most significant innovation of the New York constitution was the conception of the governor as chief executive with a dignity equal to that of the legislature. In this regard, Howard Lupert observed that "The power granted to the governor is a leading feature of the 1777 constitution and marks a departure from a strict conception of separation of powers that characterized other constitutions adopted in 1776 and 1777."[234]

The governor was to be elected for a three-year term by a majority of the freeholders. As Nevins noted, New York's constitution was the first revolutionary constitution to provide for popular election of the governor rather than selection by the legislature.[235] The governor was thus freed from dependence on the legislature for appointment and was made directly accountable to the voters.

In another significant departure from precedent, unlike the governments of the Carolinas, Delaware, Georgia, Maryland, Pennsylvania, and Virginia, the governor's exercise of his executive functions was not subject to a privy council. Rather, the governor was invested with the "supreme executive power" to "take care that the laws are faithfully executed to the best of his ability," including the implementation of "all such matters as may be resolved upon by the legislature." The governor was also to conduct relations with the Continental Congress and the other states to "transact all necessary business."[236]

The constitution arrayed the governor with other powers typical of the office. The governor was commander-in-chief of the state's military and naval forces. The governor could grant pardons and reprieves for persons convicted of crimes (other than murder and treason, which were the prerogative of the legislature). The governor could summon the legislature "on extraordinary occasions," and in contrast to other states that prohibited the governor from doing so, the New York constitution authorized the governor to prorogue the legislature for up to sixty days.[237]

Thus, under New York's plan of government, the governor was a much more fully realized chief executive and counter-weight to the legislature. In that, as Tarr wrote, "The New York constitution inaugurated the second wave of state-constitution making in providing a model for republican government with a substantially enhanced executive."[238]

The legislature was comprised of the Assembly and the Senate. Representation in the Assembly was to be proportional and representatives were to be chosen for one year. The Senate was also to be chosen proportionally from "four great districts." There were wealth-based qualifications for voting (among other requirements, voters had to "actually pay taxes") and for election to the senate. There were no similar qualifications for election to the assembly. Voting was by "*viva voce*," but the constitution contemplated a "fair experiment" with the secret ballot once the war with Britain was concluded.[239]

The new legislature was to enjoy the same privileges and to conduct its business in the same way as the colonial legislature had. The proceedings were to be open to the public "except when the welfare of the State shall require their debates be kept secret." Disagreements between the assembly and the senate over legislation were to be resolved by a conference committee whose members were selected by each house for that purpose.[240]

Another unusual feature of the New York constitution was the absence of restrictions on simultaneously serving in the legislature and holding office in the executive branch.[241] However, "ministers of the gospel and priests" were ineligible to hold any public office. Also, members of the judiciary (the chancellor, judges of the supreme court, and "first judges" of the county courts, who held their positions during good behavior) were prohibited from holding other public office.[242]

The constitution's procedures for appointing public officers reflected the Revolutionaries' fear of concentrating the appointment power in either the executive or the legislature. The lieutenant governor was to be elected along with the governor. Delegates to the Continental Congress and the state treasurer were to be selected by joint action of the legislature, although not from among the members of either house. Military officers were to be commissioned to serve at the pleasure of the governor.

An independent body, the Council of Appointment, was created to appoint those state officers not otherwise specified in the constitution,. The council was devised by three of the principal authors of the constitution, John Jay, Governeur Morris, and Robert R. Livingston, and reflected the reluctance of the constitution writers to confer patronage authority on the governor.[243] The council was to be composed of a senator from each of the Great

Districts and was to be presided over by the governor, who could exercise only the "casting vote" in case of a tie, but no other. Officers appointed under this procedure were to serve at the pleasure of the council.[244] Although considered to have been innovative, the council proved to be burdensome and ineffective, becoming mired in partisanship.[245]

The constitution also provided checks on the powers of the executive and the legislature. State officers were subject to removal for "mal and corrupt conduct of their offices." A bill of impeachment could be returned by a two-thirds vote of the assembly and trial was to be conducted before a court of impeachment composed of the senate and the judges of the Supreme Court. An impeached officer was suspended from duty and on conviction, was removed from office and disqualified from holding future office. Criminal prosecution could also follow impeachment and removal.[246]

As a check on the governor's power, the constitution required the governor to keep the legislature apprised of the status and activities of the government. Much like the requirement of Article II, Section 3 of the Constitution, the governor was to report on the condition of the state at every session of the legislature, and to make recommendations "as shall appear to him to concern its government, welfare and prosperity."[247]

As a check on the legislature, the constitution conferred the veto power on the Council of Revision, composed of the governor and the judges of the Supreme Court. The council was to review all enacted bills before they became law and if found to be objectionable, a bill was returned to the legislature with a written statement of the council's objections. A two-thirds vote of both the assembly and the senate was required to override the council's veto. [248] It has been suggested that this procedure was intended to limit the legislature's power while keeping the governor from having the sole authority of the veto.[249]

Vermont: July 8, 1777

At the time independence was declared from Britain, Vermont stood on very different ground from the other Revolutionary states. As a consequence, Vermont's constitution had a significance beyond that of establishing the frame of government. That is because, at the time of independence, Massachusetts, New Hampshire, and New York all laid claim to the territory. Indeed, New York's constitution had provided for the election of nine representatives and three senators from Vermont.[250]

Thus, the Vermont constitution was very much a declaration of the state's independence. Gary Aichele has noted that the fundamental challenge facing the constitution's framers "was to create a new political commonwealth where no true political community had previously existed." In essence and effect, the constitution established Vermont as an independent nation until

Vermont's admission to statehood by the federal congress in 1791. As Aichele observed, "No longer part of the British Empire and not yet part of the American union of states, Vermont found itself to be an independent—if isolated and vulnerable—republic.[251] Peter Onuf noted as well that admission of Vermont as a state under the Articles of Confederation "would probably have depended on unanimous endorsement by the thirteen states," which was unlikely in view of the claims of Massachusetts, as well as New Hampshire and New York.[252]

The settlers proclaimed themselves the independent state of New Connecticut on January 15, 1777. The name was changed the following June to Vermont. A weeklong constitutional convention was held in July and on July 8, a declaration of rights and a constitution of government were adopted by the convention.

The majority of the constitution was taken verbatim from the Pennsylvania constitution. There were, however, several substantial differences.

Chief among these differences, Vermont's declaration of rights prohibited the enslavement of women after the age of eighteen and of men after the age of twenty-one. Unlike Delaware's constitution that had prohibited the importation of slaves but left unaffected those who were already enslaved at the time the constitution was adopted, Vermont's constitution erected a bar to slavery that included those already enslaved. For that reason, Vermont is considered to be the only state to have prohibited slavery in its constitution.[253]

Vermont's plan of government included a unicameral legislature and a council of censors. Although Vermont substituted a governor and lieutenant governor in place of a president, the "supreme executive power," such as it was, was to be exercised by the governor and an executive council.[254] Unlike Pennsylvania, however, the governor and lieutenant governor were to be directly elected by the adult male citizens of the state, and because the constitution imposed no property requirement for voting, Vermont was the only state to grant the vote to all adult males.[255]

In another significant departure from Pennsylvania's plan, Vermont required all legislation to be presented to the governor and the executive council for their "perusal and proposal of amendment" before being enacted into law.[256] Also unlike Pennsylvania, Vermont's constitution made no provision for a judiciary.

Massachusetts: October 25, 1780

The last of the Revolutionary constitutions was that of the Commonwealth of Massachusetts. It was the most fulsome expression of constitutionalism in the revolutionary era and served as a guide both for the substance of the federal Constitution and for the procedure of adoption and ratification.

The gestation period had been more than three years, during which time, the government had operated under the Charter of 1691 with references to the crown stricken out.[257] The charter preserved the governor, lieutenant governor, and privy council as well as a General Court elected by the freemen who met wealth-based qualifications. The governor was authorized to appoint judges and other judicial officers with the advice and consent of the privy council. All other civil officers were appointed by the General Court, which had authority to enact "wholesome and reasonable" laws, subject to gubernatorial veto. The governor had authority to raise a militia and to impose martial law. However, the militia could not be transported out of the jurisdiction without the consent of the General Court.[258]

The process of writing and ratifying the constitution followed a tortured path. In January 1776, following the withdrawal of the royal government, the Massachusetts legislature, the General Court, issued a proclamation to the effect that a government based on the Charter of 1691 would be adequate to meet the needs of the commonwealth now freed from the authority of the crown. On May 1, 1776, the General Court reversed itself and in June, a committee was formed to draft a constitution.[259]

When, due to the press of other business, the committee had not produced a draft by September, the General Court made requests to the towns for authority to proceed with the writing of the constitution. In so doing, the General Court acknowledged that constitution writing was fundamentally different from other legislative acts. The General Court also proposed that the constitution be submitted to the towns for popular ratification.[260]

Although the majority of the responses from the towns were in favor of the General Court undertaking the task, twenty-five of the ninety-seven replies objected on the grounds that the General Court did not have the authority to enact a constitution like any other legislative act and in any event, the General Court was not a sufficiently representative body to do so.[261]

Calls were made for the convocation of a special constitutional convention. As a consequence of these calls, the recommendation was made to the General Court in January 1777 that a constitutional convention be organized. Instead, however, the General Court resolved after protracted debate that in the next general election, representatives to the General Court would be authorized to draft a constitution that would then be transmitted for consideration at special town meetings called for that purpose. At this election, the qualification for voting would be relaxed such that free males who were at least twenty-one years old could vote without regard to the usual wealth-based requirements. The results, both for and against the constitution, were to be transmitted to the General Court in order to determine whether two-thirds of those voting had approved the constitution.[262]

On June 17, 1777, a second committee was empanelled to draft the constitution. The final draft was agreed to by the General Court in February 1778 and was transmitted to the towns for their consideration in March. This was the first time that a constitution had been voted upon in an election that was open to all adult males and has been seen as an "unprecedented event in the history of modern constitutionalism."[263]

The proposed constitution was rejected by a vote of five-to-one. A variety of reasons have been ascribed to the failure of the constitution to win acceptance including the disqualification of African-Americans and native peoples from voting; establishment of property qualifications for voting that were considered to be too exclusive; and an unfair distribution of representation in the House of Representatives. Among the critiques of the proposed constitution was the Essex Result, which emanated from a convention of towns held in Ipswich on April 29, 1778.[264] Among the convention's objections were: the failure to establish a bill of rights; the failure to adequately secure the rights of conscience (i.e., the free exercise of religion and the security of persons and property); the failure to adequately provide for the independence of the branches of government; the failure to vest the executive with "proper authority"; and various inadequacies in the mode of electing representatives to the General Court and delegates to the Continental Congress. The convention enunciated eleven principles upon which the republican government of the commonwealth should be based:

1. That the supreme power is limited and cannot control the unalienable rights of mankind, nor resume the equivalent (that is, the security of person and property) which each individual receives, as a consideration for the alienable rights he parted with in entering into political society.
2. That these unalienable rights and this equivalent, are to be clearly defined and ascertained in a BILL OF RIGHTS, previous to the ratification of any constitution.
3. That the supreme power should be so formed and modeled, as to exert the greatest possible power, wisdom and goodness.
4. That the legislative, judicial, and executive powers, are to be lodged in different hands, that each branch is to be independent, and further, to be so balanced, and be able to exert such checks upon the others, as will preserve it from a dependence on, or a union with them.
5. That the government can exert the greatest power when its supreme authority is vested in the hands of one or a few.
6. That the laws will be made with the greatest wisdom, and best intentions, when men, of all the several classes in the state concur in enacting of them.
7. That a government which is so constituted, that it cannot afford a degree of political liberty nearly equal to all its members, is not founded upon principles of freedom and justice, and where any mem-

ber enjoys no degree of political liberty, the government, so far as it respects him, is a tyranny, for he is controlled by laws to which he has never consented.

8. That the legislative power of a state hath no authority to control the natural rights of any of its members, unless the good of the whole requires it.
9. That a majority of the state is the only judge when the general good does require it.
10. That where the legislative power of the state is so formed, that a law may be enacted by the minority, each member of the state does not enjoy political liberty. And
11. That in a free government, a law affecting the person and property of its members, is not valid, unless it has the consent of a majority of the members, which majority should include those, who hold a major part of the property in the state.[265]

Almost a year passed before the General Court acknowledged that the proposed constitution had failed to garner a majority vote. The advice of the towns was again solicited, and in April 1779, it was reported that a majority of the voters favored the calling of a special convention for the purpose of framing the constitution. On June 21, 1779, elections were announced for delegates to the constitutional convention to be held the following September.[266]

The convention met in Cambridge, Massachusetts, on September 1, 1779. It has been considered to be the first constitutional convention in western history and a definitive break with Britain's parliamentary system.[267] As John M. Murrin observed, "more dramatically than other Americans, the people of Massachusetts by 1780 had forced their government to establish a sharp institutional distinction between the power to enact ordinary legislation and the power to implement a constitution and define the rights of citizens." In so doing, Murrin wrote, "Massachusetts had created the definitive model of constitution-making for the United States. It formed the single most important difference that separated republican states in America from Britain's parliamentary system, in which kings, lords and commons answered to no higher authority."[268]

A committee composed of John Adams, Samuel Adams, and James Bowdoin was given the responsibility of preparing the draft. John Adams became the constitution's principal author.[269]

Debate on the draft constitution began on October 8, 1779, and continued well into 1780. The convention finally agreed to the text on March 20, 1780, after which the proposed constitution was submitted for ratification by the towns. Each article was to be considered separately.[270]

The constitutional convention reconvened on June 7, 1780, to consider the responses from the towns. These responses were not uniform, rendering it difficult to determine whether the constitution had received the necessary two-thirds approval. Nevertheless, the convention declared that the constitution had been approved, and consequently the constitution went into effect on October 25, 1780.[271]

The constitution that emerged in June 1780 is considered to be one of the most significant documents of the Revolutionary period, "arguably deserving of a place along side the Declaration of Independence, the Constitution of the United States, the Bill of Rights, and the *Federalist*, as one of the five most important documents of the revolutionary era."[272] As Gordon Wood wrote, the 1780 constitution "eventually came to stand for the reconsidered ideal of a 'perfect constitution,'" in that it "seemed to many to have recaptured some of the best elements of the British constitution that had been forgotten in the excitement of 1776."[273]

The constitution contained both a declaration of rights and a plan of government. The preamble to the constitution explicitly acknowledged that the constitution being formed was grounded on a compact between the individual and the larger society. Thus, the preamble declared that the "body politic" was a "social compact by which the whole people covenants with each citizen and each citizen with the whole people that all shall be governed by certain laws for the common good." Accordingly, in framing the constitution, it was the duty of the people "to provide for an equitable mode of making laws, as well as for impartial interpretation and a faithful execution of them; that every man may, at all times find his security in them."[274] Therefore, the government was one of limited powers. This limitation on the government's powers was effected through the interplay of individual and civic rights set forth in the declaration of rights and the rigorous separation and balancing of powers in the frame of government.[275]

DECLARATION OF RIGHTS

The declaration of rights in the Massachusetts constitution closely mirrored that of Virginia, blending guarantees of individual liberties with the duties owed by individuals to each other and to the state. Prominent among these rights were the provisions concerning freedom of religion. Recalling the state's Puritan and Pilgrim foundations, the declaration stated that "It is the right as well as the duty of all men in society . . . to worship the Supreme being, the Great Creator and Preserver of the universe." In keeping with that right and obligation, the declaration went on to state that no one should be "hurt, molested, or restrained, in his position, liberty or estate, for worshipping God in the manner and season most agreeable to the dictates of his own conscience," so long as "he doth not disturb the peace or obstruct others in their worship." Under the constitution, all Christian denominations were to enjoy the law's protection and "no subordination of any sect or denomination to another shall ever be established by law."[276]

In what has been considered to be among the most controversial of the constitution's provisions, the declaration established the right of the people "to invest their legislature with the power to authorize and require" their towns and religious societies to provide at their own expense, "the institution of public worship of God and for the support and maintenance of public Protestant teachers of piety, religion, and morality." However, an individual who was called upon to support public worship and moral teaching could insist that public funds "be uniformly applied to the support of the public teacher or teachers of his own religious sect or denomination."[277]

The declaration spoke to political rights and obligations as well. Underlying the constitution was "the sole and exclusive right" of the people to govern themselves "as a free, sovereign, and independent State." As all public officials were "the substitutes and agents" of the people and therefore, were, "at all times accountable to them," provision was made for the people "to cause their public officers to return to private life" and to replace them "by certain and regular elections and appointments." Although such elections were to be "free," it was necessary to meet the wealth-based qualifications established in the constitution, which differed for the election of senators and representatives.[278]

Obligations accompanied these political rights. Along with the individual's right to the protection of life, liberty, and property was the concomitant responsibility "to give his personal service, or an equivalent when necessary." However private property could not be taken for public use without the consent either of the individual or the legislature. If property were so taken, the owner had the right to receive "a reasonable compensation therefore."[279]

Other individual liberties later enshrined in the Bill of Rights were secured by the constitution. All persons were to be "secure from all unreasonable searches and seizures of his person, his houses, his papers, and all his possessions." Individuals could not be compelled to give testimony against themselves. In the event of conviction, magistrates were prohibited from imposing excessive bail or fines and from inflicting cruel and unusual punishments. Access to the courts was to be granted without cost "for all injustices or wrongs" which an individual "may receive in his position, property, or character." Trials were to be conducted by impartial judges who held their commissions during good behavior. Fundamental due process was also guaranteed to persons accused of crime. *Ex Post Facto* laws and attainder for treason were prohibited.[280]

The declaration secured a variety of civic rights, as well. With respect to the military, the maintenance of a standing army in time of peace was prohibited as was the quartering of soldiers in private homes.[281] The right of the people "to keep and bear arms for the common defence" was guaranteed and the imposition of martial law on the civilian population was prohibited.[282] The benefit of *habeas corpus* was also guaranteed in the constitution.[283]

Civil rights and liberties were secured as well. The liberty of the press was guaranteed by the declaration of rights as was the right of the people to peaceably assemble and to "consult upon the common good, give instructions to their representatives, and to request of the legislative body . . . redress of the wrongs done to them and grievances they suffer."[284]

Legislators were guaranteed the "freedom of deliberation, speech, and debate," for which they were to be immune from prosecution. The legislature was to meet frequently "for address of grievances, for correcting, strengthening, and confirming the laws, and for making new laws, as the common good may require." Authority was given to the legislature to suspend the execution of the laws and to lay taxes, imposts, and duties.[285]

Like that of Virginia, the constitution established the separation of powers as an organizing principle of the government. Unlike Virginia, however, the Massachusetts constitution endeavored to construct a "balanced government" of three independent and coordinate branches.[286] The government of the commonwealth was declared to be "a government of laws, and not men." Therefore, the declaration provided that "the *legislative* department shall never exercise the executive and judicial powers or either of them; the *executive* shall never exercise the legislative and judicial powers, or either of them; the *judicial* department shall never exercise the legislative and executive powers, or either of them."[287]

THE LEGISLATURE

The constitution maintained the bicameral legislature comprised of the House of Representatives and the Senate, which comprised the General Court. There were to be forty senators elected from districts designated by the General Court.[288] Representation in the house was to be proportionally based on the population of the towns. The members of the General Court were to be elected annually and there were different wealth-based qualifications for membership in each chamber, reflecting the tension between populism and aristocracy in a democratic society.[289] Wood observed that references to the "social polarity" between democracy and the aristocracy "attained an intensity that was not duplicated elsewhere in the [1780s]," and that the Essex Result had proposed a legislature that would represent the persons and the property of the state in a different house. Wood wrote that, "No other state in the period so boldly interpreted the bicameral principle in this way."[290] Kenyon similarly observed that "If property qualifications for voting and for holding office are a sure index to the degree of democracy or aristocracy established in a constitution, this constitution must be characterized as leaning toward a moderate aristocracy, particularly with respect to the requirements for office holding." Thus, she said, "the Massachusetts constitution stands out as unambiguously reflective of the conviction that a government purely popular could not possibly be a good government, and possibly could not long endure."[291]

The General Court was invested with "full power and authority" to enact "wholesome and reasonable laws, statutes and ordinances, directions and instructions . . . not repugnant or contrary to this constitution, as they shall judge to be for the good and welfare of this commonwealth," and was empowered to establish the offices of the state government. Authority was given for "the naming and settling" of "all civic officers." The legislature was also to fix "the several duties, powers, and limits of the several civil and military officers." The General Court was given the further power to establish a system of judicial courts.[292]

As with other state constitutions, the Massachusetts constitution required that money bills originate in the house. However, the constitution also provided in regard to money bills that "the senate may propose or concur with amendments, as on all other bills."[293] To fund the government, the General Court was empowered to "impose and levy proportional and reasonable assessments, rates and taxes" upon the state's residents and to levy "reasonable duties and excises upon any produce, goods, wares, merchandise, and commodities," produced, manufactured, or imported into the state.[294]

Provision was made in the constitution for the removal of state officers by the General Court. The house was to serve as "the grand inquest of this commonwealth" with jurisdiction to impeach "any officer or officers of the commonwealth, for misconduct or maladministration in their offices." The senate was to sit as a court "with full authority to hear and determine all impeachments made by the house of representatives." A conviction by the senate in cases of impeachment could not "extend further than to removal from office, and disqualification to hold or enjoy any place of honor, trust or profit under this commonwealth," but conviction would not be a bar to subsequent indictment, conviction or punishment "according to the laws of the land."[295]

The General Court was given limited judicial authority to " try and determine all cases where the rights and privileges concerned and which, by the constitution, they have authority to try and determine." Each house was authorized to punish persons who were not members, "who shall be guilty of disrespect" or "any disorderly or contemptuous behavior in its presence" or who, while the General Court was in session, threatened

> harm to the body or estate of any of its members, for anything said or done in the house, or who shall assault any of them therefore; or who shall assault or arrest any witness, or other person, ordered to attend the house, in his way in going to or returning; or who shall rescue any person arrested by order of the house.[296]

In addition to their immunity from prosecution arising from "deliberation, speech, and debate" secured in the declaration of rights, representatives and senators were immune from interference in connection with their attendance at legislative sessions. Thus, like Article I, Section 6, Clause 1 of the Federal Constitution, the Massachusetts constitution provided that "no member . . . shall be arrested, or held to bail . . . during his going unto, returning from, or his attending the general assembly.[297]

THE EXECUTIVE

Similar to the government framed in New York, a strong executive was an essential element of Adams's plan for a balanced government under the constitution. Kenyon wrote that Adams intended the governor "to stand between the two houses of the legislature, the lower representing the common people, the upper representing the natural aristocracy." Thus performing "the function ideally attributed to the monarch in the classical theory of mixed government."[298]

Under the Adams plan, the governor was to be the "supreme executive magistrate" who would be elected annually by those qualified to vote for senators and representatives.[299] There was to be a lieutenant governor having the same qualifications and being elected in the same manner as the governor.[300]

Kenyon noted that the constitution erected safeguards against an "excessively powerful governor."[301] Unlike New York's executive, the authority of the Massachusetts governor was moderated by a nine-member executive council chosen by the General Court "from among the persons returned for councilors and senators." With the lieutenant governor, this council was to advise the governor "for the ordering and directing of the affairs of the commonwealth, agreeably to the constitution and the laws of the land." The council was authorized to act in the absence of the governor and lieutenant governor.[302] Kruman pointed out that, "Once established, the council possessed considerable power," particularly with respect to appointments. Thus, "by compelling the governor to share the appointive power, convention delegates made clear their desire to curb the governor's power."[303]

The advice and consent of the council was required for the governor to prorogue the General Court (but only for up to ninety days) and to pardon persons convicted of crimes, other than by impeachment. The council's consent was required for the appointment of a variety of state officers, including judges, the attorney general, and the solicitor general. Council consent was also required for the expenditure of public funds "for the necessary defense and support of the commonwealth, and for the protection and preservation of the inhabitants thereof."[304]

The governor was otherwise vested with considerable executive and military power. The governor was the commander-in-chief of the state's land and naval forces. The governor had "full power" to train the military forces, to assemble the state's male inhabitants "in military array" and to put the military forces "in a warlike posture." The governor could impose martial law "in time of war and invasion,"[305] and he was authorized to make war on those who "attempt or enterprise the destruction, invasion, detriment or annoyance of this commonwealth."[306] The governor was to receive quarterly reports from military officers, as well as civilian officers and public boards, of all public property entrusted to their care.[307]

The most significant power conferred on the governor from the perspective of balanced government was the authority to revise legislation before being signed into law and to veto legislation of which he did not approve. It was observed that "John Adams was convinced that the executive needed the veto as a defense against the legislature's persistent attempts to arrogate all power to itself." To override a gubernatorial veto, the house originating the legislation had to approve the bill by a two-thirds vote.[308] Kruman made a similar observation.[309]

THE JUDICIARY

As noted, the declaration of rights guaranteed due process in the courts, including trial by jury presided over by an impartial judge. It was the responsibility of the General Court to erect the system of courts.[310]

Under the constitution, judges were to be appointed by the governor with the advice and consent of the council. With the exception of justices of the peace, whose terms in office were fixed at seven years, judges were to hold their commissions during good behavior. Judges could be removed by the governor, with the consent of the council, "upon address of both houses of the legislature."[311]

In addition to their judicial duties, the constitution provided that the legislature and the governor could call on the judges of the Supreme Judicial Court for their opinion "upon important questions of law, and upon solemn occasions."[312]

RESTRICTIONS ON OFFICE HOLDING

The constitution placed restrictions on holding multiple offices in the government. The governor, lieutenant governor, and the judges of the Supreme Judicial Court were prohibited from holding any other offices.[313] Similar restrictions were placed on other executive officers.[314] Appointment of a senator or representative to certain state offices operated as a resignation of his seat, as did acceptance of a place on the executive council by a judge.[315] The constitution further provided that conviction for "bribery or corruption in obtaining an election or appointment" would disqualify a person from membership in the General Court or from holding "any office of trust or importance under the government of the commonwealth."[316]

PUBLIC EDUCATION

In addition to establishing the plan of the state government, the constitution made provision for the encouragement of higher education and literature. It was declared that the president and fellows of Harvard College, which had been founded in 1636, would continue to "have, hold, use, exercise and enjoy all the powers, authorities, rights, liberties, privileges, immunities, and franchises which they now have . . . for ever," along with the gifts, devises and conveyances that had already been made to the college. The constitution also charged the General Court with the promotion of "agriculture, arts, sciences, commerce, trades, manufactures,, and a natural history of the country." The General Court was also to "countenance and inculcate the principles of humanity and general benevolence, public and private charity, industry and frugality, honesty and punctuality in their dealings; sincerity, and good humor and social affections and generous sentiments, among the people."[317]

AMENDMENT OF THE CONSTITUTION

Lastly, as had the constitutions of Maryland, Pennsylvania, South Carolina, and Vermont, the Massachusetts constitution made provision for amendment. In 1795, fifteen years after the constitution became effective, qualified voters were to meet in their towns "for the purpose of collecting their sentiments on the necessity or expediency of revising the constitution." In the event that two-thirds of the voters favored revision or amendment, the General Court was to call for an election of delegates to a convention for that purpose.[318]

THE REVISED CONSTITUTIONS

During the period between independence and the writing of the federal Constitution, three states adopted substantially revised and enhanced constitutions to replace their preliminary plans of government. South Carolina and New Hampshire replaced what had been avowedly temporary measures that had been intended simply to fill the gap left by the flight of the crown government until the "unhappy differences" with Britain were resolved.[319]

South Carolina: March 19, 1778

The frame of government under the revised South Carolina constitution remained substantially unchanged. Significantly, the constitution guaranteed a degree of freedom of worship as well as freedom of the press and due process for those accused of crime. Governing power was centered in the legislature, with restrictions placed on multiple office holding. Authority to impeach and remove the "governor and other officers of the state . . . not amenable to other jurisdiction" was conferred on the legislature. In contrast, the powers of the governor were circumscribed by a privy council and by the elimination of the veto.[320]

New Hampshire: June 2, 1784

New Hampshire's second constitution, adopted on June 2, 1784, was based largely on the 1780 Massachusetts constitution. New Hampshire's bill of rights was virtually identical in all material respects to that for of Massachusetts, except that New Hampshire's constitution expressly guaranteed the right to trial by jury in capital cases and provided the first express guaranty against double jeopardy.[321]

The frame of government adopted in the 1784 constitution was grounded on the principle of separation of powers that like Massachusetts, was explicitly enshrined in the bill of rights. The "supreme legislative power" was to be in the hands of the house and the senate, each of which could have "a negative of the other." The legislature was to be given a significant role in structuring both the executive and judicial branches and was to exercise oversight of the government as "the grand inquest of the state."[322]

The "supreme executive magistrate" of the state was the president who was to be elected annually by popular vote. The constitution blended the executive and the legislative functions in several respects. The president was to preside over the senate and was to have a vote equal to the other senators. In the event of a tie vote, the president had the "casting vote." With respect to the executive function, the president was to be advised "in the executive part of government" by a five member council elected jointly by the house and the senate from among their own members. The advice and consent of the council was required for the expenditure of public funds, "for the necessary protection and preservation of the inhabitants thereof." In that connection, all public officers were to provide an accounting every three months to the president of the goods and stores entrusted to them. As a further check on executive power, officers of the executive as well as the judiciary were subject to impeachment and removal by the legislature.[323]

Limitations were placed on holding multiple offices in the government simultaneously. The governor and the justices of the supreme court were prohibited from holding any other office "except by this constitution they are permitted to hold." Other state officers were specified in the constitution as being ineligible to occupy more than one office, as well as being ineligible to serve as governor, councilor, or member of the legislature. Additionally, persons who had been convicted of bribery or corruption in connection with either an election or an appointment were disqualified from serving in the legislature.[324]

Vermont: July 4, 1786

As noted, Vermont's 1777 constitution was as much a declaration of independence from Massachusetts, New Hampshire, and New York, and had been a source of dissatisfaction within the state virtually from inception. The almost verbatim reproduction of the Pennsylvania constitution bespoke the haste with which the weeklong constitutional convention had deliberated. However, the 1777 constitution had provided a mechanism for revision through the Council of Censors, which under the constitution was to meet on the last Wednesday of March in 1785. In accordance with that directive, the Council of Censors met in 1785 and a convention for the purpose of revising the constitution was called. On July 4, 1786, a new constitution was adopted.[325]

Rather than a wholesale revision, the constitution adopted in 1786 made limited though substantive changes to the 1777 constitution. Like the other constitutions of the time, the constitution mandated the separation of powers among the branches of government. The legislature was authorized to suspend the execution of laws, but the imposition of martial law on the civilian population was prohibited.[326] Under the new constitution, the legislature was denied the authority enjoyed by the British parliament of declaring persons guilty of treason and other felonies.[327]

The plan of government with respect to the executive remained virtually unchanged, and only minor modifications were made to the judiciary.[328] The new constitution imposed a broad prohibition against simultaneously holding multiple offices in the state government, however.[329]

NOTES

1. Ford, *Journals of the Continental Congress*, vol. 4: 342, 357–58.
2. Ford, *Journals of the Continental Congress*, vol. 2: 77; McLaughlin, *A Constitutional History of the United States*, 106–07.
3. Adams, *The First American Constitutions*, 51–52.
4. Ford, *Journals of the Continental Congress*, vol. 3: 319; Adams, *The First American Constitutions*, 56-57; McLaughlin, *A Constitutional History of the United States*, 106–7.
5. Ford, *Journals of the Continental Congress*, vol. 4: 342. McLaughlin, *Foundations of American Constitutionalism*, 92–93.
6. Adams, *The First American Constitutions*, 59.
7. Adams, *The First American Constitutions*, 53–54.
8. Allan Nevins, *The American States: During and After the Revolution, 1775–1789* (New York: Macmillan, 1924), 117.
9. Cecilia M. Kenyon, "Constitutionalism in Revolutionary America," in J. Roland Pennock and John W. Chapman, eds., *Constitutionalism*. (New York: New York University Press, 1979), 85.
10. Morison, Commager, and Leuchtenburg, eds., *The Growth of the American Republic*, vol. 1: 207.
11. Elmer Cornwell, "Constitutionalism in Rhode Island: Continuity of Colonial Design," in Connor and Hammons, eds., *The Constitutionalism of the American States*, 64.
12. The modified Connecticut charter served as the state's constitution until 1818. Adams, *The First American Constitutions*, 64–65.
13. Curtis, *History of the Origin, Formation, and Adoption of the Constitution of the United States with Notices of its Principal Framers*, vol. 1: 6.
14. Elizabeth Beaumont, "The Slow Evolution of the 'Constitution State'," in Connor and Hammons, eds.,, *The Constitutionalism of the American States*, 19.
15. Thorpe, *The Constitutional History of the United States*, vol. 1: 166–67.
16. Hockett, *The Constitutional History of the United States*, 114.
17. Thorpe, *The Constitutional History of the United States*, vol. 1: 166–67.
18. Bailyn, *The Ideological Origins of the American Revolution*, 324.
19. Willi Paul Adams, "The State Constitutions as Analogy and Precedent," in Howard, *The United States Constitution*, 4.
20. Bailyn, *Ideological Origins of the American Revolution*, 324.
21. Commager, *The Empire of Reason*, 123.
22. Gordon S. Wood, "The American Enlightenment," in McDowell and O'Neill, eds., *American and Enlightenment Constitutionalism*, 162–63.
23. Jack N. Rakove, "Ticklish Experiments: The Paradox of American Constitutionalism," in McDowell and O'Neill, eds., *America and Enlightenment Constitutionalism*, 219.
24. Rakove, "Ticklish Experiments," 219; Hockett, *The Constitutional History of the United States*, 116.
25. McLaughlin, *A Constitutional History of the United States*, 114; Nevins, *The American States*, 166; Hockett, *The Constitutional History of the United States*, 117.
26. Evarts Boutwell Greene, *The Provincial Governor in the English Colonies of North America* (New York: Longman, Green & Co., 1907), 43–45; Carl Ubbelohde, *The American Colonies and the British Empire, 1607–1763* (New York: Thos. Y. Crowell & Co., 1968), 80–81.
27. Labaree, *Royal Government in America*, 123.
28. Kellog, *The American Colonial Charter*, 66. Labaree also noted that the provincial governor "was the head of the local legislature, standing in much the same relation to the council and assembly as did the King to the Lords and Commons in Great Britain." Additionally, although the governor might be obliged to consult with the council on certain matters, the governor "was armed with the powerful weapon of an absolute veto which he was expected to employ vigorously in the defense of good government and British interests." Labaree, *Royal Government in America*, 99.

29. M. J. C. Vile, *Constitutionalism and the Separation of Powers* (Oxford: Oxford University Press, 1967), 132.
30. Thorpe, *The Federal and State Constitutions*, vol. 4: 2451; vol. 5: 3081.
31. Labaree, *Royal Government in America*, 167.
32. Labaree, *Royal Government in America*, 134.
33. Greene, *The Provincial Governor*, 74, 80–84.
34. Curtis, *History of the Constitution of the United States*, vol. 1: 7.
35. Ubbelohde, *The American Colonies and British Empire, 1607–1763*, 83.
36. Governors were selected by the legislatures under the constitutions of Virginia (June 1776); New Jersey (July 1776); Delaware (September 1776); Maryland (November 1776); North Carolina (December 1776); Georgia (February 1777); and South Carolina (March 1778). The New York constitution (April 1777) was the first to provide for a popularly elected governor. New York was followed by Vermont (July 1777); New Hampshire (June 1778); and Massachusetts (June 1780).
37. G. Alan Tarr, *Understanding State Constitutions* (Princeton: Princeton University Press, 1998), 87.
38. The constitutions of Delaware, Georgia, Maryland, Massachusetts, New Hampshire, New Jersey, New York, North Carolina, Pennsylvania, South Carolina, Vermont, and Virginia all made provision for impeachment and removal.
39. Albert L. Sturm, "The Development of American State Constitutions," *Publius* (1980), vol. 12: 61.
40. Wood, *The Creation of the American Republic*, 141.
41. Vile, *Constitutionalism and Separation of Powers*, 125–26.
42. Kermit L. Hall, *The Magic Mirror: Law in American History* (New York: Oxford University Press, 1989), 62–63; Kelly Harbison, and Belz, *The American Constitution*, vol. 1: 71.
43. Hall, *The Magic Mirror*, 63.
44. Kelly, Harbison and Belz, *The American Constitution*, vol. 1: 71.
45. Alan S. Rosenbaum, *Constitutionalism: The Philosophical Discussion* (New York: Greenwood Press, 1988), 61.
46. Hall, *The Magic Mirror*, 63.
47. Vile, *Constitutionalism and the Separation of Powers*, 122, 126.
48. Kruman, *Between Authority and Liberty*, 111.
49. David Freeman Hawke, *The Colonial Experience* (Indianapolis, Bobbs-Merrill, 1966), 645; Hockett, *The Constitutional History of the United States*, 118.
50. Hockett, *The Constitutional History of the United States*, 118.
51. Nevins, *The American States*, 168.
52. Sturm, "The Development of American State Constitutions," *Publius*, Vol. 12: 62.
53. Kruman, *Between Authority and Liberty*, 36.
54. Vile, *Constitutionalism and the Separation of Powers*, 122.
55. Jere R. Daniell, *Experiment in Republicanism: New Hampshire Politics and the American Revolution, 1741–1794* (Cambridge, MA: Harvard University Press, 1970), 107–12.
56. Adams, *The First American Constitutions*, 68.
57. Lynn Warren Turner, *The Ninth State: New Hampshire's Formative Years* (Chapel Hill: University of North Carolina Press, 1983), 13.
58. Thorpe, *The Federal and State Constitutions*, vol. 4: 2452–53.
59. Turner, *The Ninth State*, 13.
60. Daniell, *Experiment in Republicanism*, 109.
61. Adams, *The First American Constitutions*, 68–69.
62. Thorpe, *The Federal and State Constitutions*, vol. 6: 3242–43.
63. Lutz, *The Origins of American Constitutionalism*, 103.
64. Jerome J. Nadelhaft, "South Carolina: A Constitutional Revolution," in Patrick J. Conley and John P. Kaminski, eds., *The Constitution and the States* (Madison: Madison House, 1988), 159.
65. Thorpe, *The Federal and State Constitutions*, vol. 6: 3243, 3246.
66. Thorpe, *The Federal and State Constitutions*, vol. 6: 3244.

67. Adams, *The First American Constitutions,* 264–65.
68. Vile, *Constitutionalism and the Separation of Powers*, 134.
69. Thorpe, *The Federal and State Constitutions*, vol. 6: 3244.
70. Thorpe, *The Federal and State Constitutions*, vol. 6: 3244, 3247.
71. Thorpe, *The Federal and State Constitutions*, vol. 6: 3246.
72. John Harold Wolfe, *Jeffersonian Democracy in South Carolina* (Chapel Hill: University of North Carolina Press, 1940), 43.
73. Michael E. Stevens, "South Carolina: Their Liberties, Properties and Privileges," in Patrick T. Conley and John P. Kaminski, eds., *The Bill of Rights and the States* (Madison: Madison House, 1992), 412.
74. Adams, *The First American Constitutions*, 70; Jensen, *The Articles of Confederation*, 21–24.
75. Adams, *The First American Constitutions,* 70–71.
76. Tarr, *Understanding State Constitutions*, 75.
77. Thorpe, *The Federal and State Constitutions*, vol. 7: 3813.
78. Maier, *American Scripture*, 126, 134.
79. Thorpe, *The Federal and State Constitutions*, vol. 7: 3813–14.
80. David N. Mayer, *The Constitutional Thoughts of Thomas Jefferson* (Charlottesville: University of Virginia Press, 1994), 55–56; Maier, *American Scripture*, 55–56.
81. Thorpe, *The Federal and State Constitutions*, vol. 7: 3814–15.
82. Hockett, *The Constitutional History* of t*he United States*, 109.
83. Thorpe, *The Federal and State Constitutions*, vol. 7: 3813.
84. Thorpe, *The Federal* and *State Constitutions*, vol. 7: 3815.
85. Adams, *The First American Constitutions*, 265.
86. Thorpe, *The Federal and State Constitutions*, vol. 7: 3813.
87. Edward S. Corwin, *The "Higher Law" Background of American Constitutional Law* (Ithaca: Cornell University Press, 1955), 83.
88. Robert E. Brown and B. Katherine Brown, *Virginia 1705–1786: Democracy or Aristocracy?* (East Lansing: Michigan State University Press, 1964), 294; Warren M. Billings, John E. Selby, and Thad W. Tate, *Colonial Virginia: A History* (White Plains: KTO Press, 1986), 356.
89. Thorpe, *The Federal and State Constitutions*, vol. 7: 3815–16.
90. Kenyon, "Constitutionalism in Revolutionary America," in Pennock and Chapman, eds., *Constitutionalism*, 96.
91. Thorpe, *The Federal and State Constitutions*, vol. 7: 3816–17.
92. Thorpe, *The Federal and State Constitutions*, vol. 7: 3817.
93. Adams, *The First American Constitutions*, 265–66.
94. Thorpe, *The Federal and State Constitutions*, vol. 7: 3817.
95. Thorpe, *The Federal and State Constitutions*, vol. 7: 3818.
96. Adams, *The First American Constitutions*, 72.
97. Nevins, *The American States,* 127.
98. Kruman, *Between Authority and Liberty*, 20–24.
99. McCormick, *New Jersey from Colony to State*, 122.
100. Eugene R. Sheridan, "New Jersey: A Study in Paradox," in Conley and Kaminski, eds., *The Bill of Rights and the States*, 267; Melissa Scueier, "Constitutionalism in New Jersey: Constitutional Failures in a Changing Political Environment," in Connor and Hammons, eds., *The Constitutionalism of American States*, 114–15.
101. Thorpe, The Federal and State Constitutions, vol. 5: 2595.
102. Kruman, *Between Authority and Liberty*, 105–6.
103. Thorpe, *The Federal and State Constitutions*, vol. 5: 2595–96.
104. Kruman, *Between Authority and Liberty*, 127.
105. Donald L. Kemmerer, *Path to Freedom: The Struggle for Self-Government in Colonial New Jersey, 1703–1776* (Princeton: Princeton University Press, 1940), 349.
106. Richard P. McCormick, *Experiment in Independence: New Jersey in the Critical Period, 1781–1789* (New Brunswick, NJ: Rutgers University Press, 1950), 70.
107. Kruman, *Between Authority and Liberty*, 127.
108. Kemmerer, *Path to Freedom*, 349.

109. Thorpe, *The Federal and State Constitutions*, vol. 5: 2596.
110. Thorpe, *The Federal and State Constitutions*, vol. 5: 2597.
111. Thorpe, *The Federal and State Constitutions*, vol. 5: 2598.
112. Adams, *The First American Constitutions*, 72.
113. Kruman, *Between Authority and Liberty*, 38–39.
114. Adams, *The First American Constitutions*, 72.
115. Thorpe, *The Federal and State Constitutions*, vol. 1: 559.
116. Gaspere J. Saldino, "Delaware: Armed in the Cause of Freedom," in Conley and Kaminski, *The Bill of Rights and the States*, 294.
117. Kurland, *The Founders Constitution*, vol. 5: 5–6.
118. Kurland, *The Founders Constitution*, vol. 5: 6.
119. Kurland, *The Founders Constitution*, vol. 5: 6.
120. Kurland, *The Founders Constitution*, vol. 5: 6.
121. Kurland, *The Founders Constitution*, vol. 5: 5–6.
122. Kurland, *The Founders Constitution*, vol. 5: 6.
123. Saldino, "Delaware: Armed in the Cause of Freedom," in Conley and Kaminski, eds., *The Bill of Rights and the States*, 294.
124. Adams, *The First American Constitutions*, 73–74.
125. Saldino, "Delaware: Armed in the Cause of Freedom," in Conley and Kaminski, eds., *The Bill of Rights and the States*, 295.
126. Munroe, *Colonial Delaware*, 253.
127. Carol E. Hoffecker and Barbara E. Benson, "*Festina Lente*: The Development of Constitutionalism in Delaware," in Connor and Hammons, eds., *The Constitutionalism of the American States*, 168.
128. Thorpe, *The Federal and State Constitutions*, vol. 1: 562–63.
129. Thorpe, *The Federal and State Constitutions*, vol. 1: 563–64.
130. Thorpe, *The Federal and State Constitutions*, vol. 1: 564–65.
131. Hoffecker and Benson, "*Festina Lente*," 171.
132. Wood, *The Creation of the American Republic*, 149.
133. Thorpe, *The Federal and State Constitutions*, vol. 1: 563, 565–66.
134. Thorpe, *The Federal and State Constitutions*, vol. 1: 566.
135. Thorpe, *The Federal and State Constitutions*, vol. 1: 564.
136. Thorpe, *The Federal and State Constitutions*, vol. 1: 567.
137. Wood, *The Creation of the American Republic*, 438; Hawke, *The Colonial Experience*, 645; Kenyon, "Constitutionalism in Revolutionary America," in Pennock and Chapman, eds., *Constitutionalism*, 99.
138. Paul Doutrich, "Pennsylvania from Revolution to Constitution," in Conley and Kaminski, *The Constitution and the States*, 37–38.
139. Jensen, *The Articles of Confederation*, 16–17.
140. Adams, *The First American Constitutions*, 74–75.
141. Adams, *The First American Constitutions*, 76–77.
142. As Kenyon has pointed out, Pennsylvania's declaration, "like those of the majority of other states, borrowed heavily from that of Virginia." Kenyon, "Constitutionalism in Revolutionary America," in Pennock and Chapman, eds., *Constitutionalism*, 103.
143. Thorpe, *The Federal and State Constitutions*, vol. 5: 3081–83.
144. Thorpe, *The Federal and State Constitutions*, vol. 5: 3083.
145. John K. Alexander, "Pennsylvania: Pioneer in Safeguarding Personal Rights," in Conley and Kaminski, eds., *The Bill of Rights and the States*, 321.
146. Thorpe, *The Federal and State Constitutions*, vol. 5: 3084.
147. Alexander, "Pennsylvania: Pioneer in Safeguarding Personal Rights," in Conley and Kaminski, eds., *The Bill of Rights and the States*, 321.
148. Harry M. Tinkcom, *The Republicans and Federalists in Pennsylvania 1790–1801* (Harrisburg: Pennsylvania Historical and Museum Commission, 1950), 3.
149. Adams, *The First American Constitutions*, 177, 261.
150. Jeffrey P. Bauman, "Pennsylvania: Virtue, Liberty and Independence," in Connor and Hammons, eds., *The Constitutionalism of the American States*, 149.

151. Thorpe, *The Federal and State Constitutions*, vol. 5: 3085, 3091.
152. Thorpe, *The Federal and State Constitutions,* vol. 5: 3085.
153. Thorpe, *The Federal and State Constitutions*, vol. 5: 3085–86, 3090; Lutz, *The Origins of American Constitutionalism*, 15.
154. Thorpe, *The Federal and State Constitutions*, vol. 5: 3084, 3087–88.
155. Thorpe, *The Federal and State Constitutions,* vol. 5: 3088.
156. Thorpe, *The Federal and State Constitutions*, vol. 5: 3084, 3088–89.
157. Thorpe, *The Federal and State Constitutions*, vol. 5: 3088.
158. Thorpe, *The Federal and State Constitutions*, vol. 5: 3087–88.
159. Thorpe, *The Federal and State Constitutions*, vol. 5: 3091.
160. Thorpe, *The Federal and State Constitutions*, vol. 5: 3091–92.
161. Thorpe, *The Federal and State Constitutions,* vol. 5: 3092.
162. Nevins, *The American States*, 152.
163. Kenyon, "Constitutionalism in Revolutionary America," in Pennock and Chapman, eds., *Constitutionalism*, 106.
164. Nevins, *The American States*, 153.
165. Bauman, "Pennsylvania: Virtue, Liberty, and Independence," in Connor and Hammands, eds., *The Constitutionalism of the American States*, 151.
166. Nevins, *The American States*, 156.
167. Most significant among those changes were the establishment of the office of governor invested with the "supreme executive power of the commonwealth(including command of the land and naval forces, appointment authority, and authority to convene and adjourn the legislature in certain circumstances), abandonment of the Executive Council, and the elimination of the Council of Censors. The governor was subject to impeachment and removal by the General Assembly for "any misdemeanor in office." Alexander James Dallas, ed., *Laws of the Commonwealth of Pennsylvania, From the Seventh Day of December One Thousand Seven Hundred and Ninety, to the Twentieth Day of April, One Thousand Seven Hundred and Ninety Five* (Philadelphia: Hall and Sellers, 1795), vol. 3: xxii–xxxix.
168. Adams, *The First American Constitutions*, 77–78; Kruman, *Between Authority and Liberty*, 39.
169. Gregory A. Silverstein, "To Maintain Inviolate Our Liberties: Maryland and the Bill of Rights," in Conley and Kaminski, *The Bill of Rights and the States*, 386.
170. Adams, *The First American Constitutions*, 78.
171. Thorpe, *The Federal and State Constitutions*, vol. 3: 1687, 1689.
172. David Curtis Skaggs, *Roots of Maryland Democracy, 1753–1776* (Westport: Greenwood Press, 1973), 192.
173. Thorpe, *The Federal and State Constitutions*, vol. 3: 1687; Kruman, *Between Authority and Liberty*, 43–44.
174. Bernard Schwartz, *The Bill of Rights: A Documentary History* (New York: Chelsea House, 1971), vol. 1: 276.
175. Thorpe, *The Federal and State Constitutions,* vol. 13: 1688.
176. Phillip A. Crowl, *Maryland During and after the Revolution: A Political and Economic Study* (Baltimore: Johns Hopkins University Press, 1943), 33.
177. Thorpe, *The Federal and State Constitutions*, vol. 3: 1689.
178. Crowl, *Maryland During and After the Revolution*, 31–32; Thomas F. Schaller, "Pioneer and Outlier: Maryland Constitutionalism in its Third Century," in Connor and Hammons, eds., *The Constitutionalism of American States*, 99; Jensen, *The Articles of Confederation,* 21.
179. H. H. Lewis, *The Maryland Constitution of 1776* (Baltimore: Maryland State Bar Association, 1976), 1.
180. Crowl, *Maryland During and After the Revolution*, 32.
181. Kruman, *Between Authority and Liberty*, 67.
182. Thorpe, *The Federal and State Constitutions*, vol. 3: 1694.
183. Jensen, *The Articles of Confederation*, 21.
184. Thorpe, *The Federal and State Constitutions*, vol. 3: 1691–92.
185. Crowl, *Maryland During and After the Revolution*, 32.
186. Nevins, *The American States,* 158.

187. Kruman, *Between Authority and Liberty*, 139.
188. Wood, *The Creation of the American Republic*, 251.
189. Thorpe, *The Federal and State Constitutions*, vol. 3: 1692–93.
190. Thorpe, *The Federal and State Constitutions*, vol. 3: 1692.
191. Thorpe, *The Federal and State Constitutions*, vol. 3: 1687.
192. Thorpe, *The Federal and State Constitutions*, vol. 3: 1692-93.
193. Thorpe, *The Federal and State Constitutions*, vol. 3: 1693-96.
194. Thorpe, *The Federal and State Constitutions*, vol. 3: 1700.
195. Thorpe, *The Federal and State Constitutions*, vol. 3: 1689.
196. Thorpe, *The Federal and State Constitutions*, vol. 3: 1699.
197. Thorpe, *The Federal and State Constitutions*, vol. 3: 1697–700.
198. Adams, *The First American Constitutions*, 138; Kruman, *Between Authority and Liberty*, 56–57.
199. Thorpe, *The Federal and State Constitutions*, vol. 3: 1701.
200. Adams, *The First American Constitutions*, 78–79.
201. Jensen, *The Articles of Confederation*, 25.
202. Thorpe, *The Federal and State Constitutions*, vol. 5: 2794.
203. Thorpe, *The Federal and State Constitutions*, vol. 5: 2787.
204. Thorpe, *The Federal and State Constitutions*, vol. 5: 2791–93.
205. Thorpe, *The Federal and State Constitutions*, vol. 5: 2792.
206. Nevins, *The American States*, 141.
207. Thorpe, *The Federal and State Constitutions*, vol. 5: 2790.
208. Thorpe, *The Federal and State Constitutions*, vol. 5: 2792–93.
209. Thorpe, *The Federal and State Constitutions*, vol. 5: 2793.
210. Thorpe, *The Federal and State Constitutions*, vol. 5: 2793–94.
211. Walter McElreath, *A Treatise on the Constitution of Georgia* (Atlanta: Harrison Co., 1912), 59–62.
212. Ethel K. Ware, *A Constitutional History of Georgia* (New York: AMS Press, 1967), 24–25.
213. Albert Berry Saye, *A Constitutional History of Georgia* (Athens: Georgia University Press, 1948), 96–99; Ware, *A Constitutional History of Georgia*, 26–32; Kenneth Colemen, "Frontier Haven: Georgia and the Bill of Rights," in Conley and Kaminski, eds., *The Bill of Rights and the States*, 453; Adams, *The First American Constitutions*, 80–81.
214. Thorpe, *The Federal and State Constitutions*, vol. 2: 783–85.
215. Thorpe, *The Federal and State Constitutions*, vol. 2: 778; Saye, *A Constitutional History of Georgia*, 102.
216. Ware, *A Constitutional History of Georgia*, 35.
217. Adams, *The First American Constitutions*, 81.
218. Thorpe, *The Federal and State Constitutions*, vol. 2: 778–80; Adams, *The First American Constitutions*, 238.
219. Thorpe, *The Federal and State Constitutions*, vol. 2: 781–82.
220. Saye, *A Constitutional History of Georgia*, 109; Ware, *A Constitutional History of Georgia*, 39–40.
221. Thorpe, *The Federal and State Constitutions*, vol. 2: 783–84.
222. Thorpe, *The Federal and State Constitutions*, vol. 2: 780–81, 785.
223. Thorpe, *The Federal and State Constitutions*, vol. 2: 785.
224. Kruman, *Between Authority and Liberty*, 36.
225. Thorpe, *The Federal and State Constitutions*, vol. 2: 785–90; Saye, *A Constitutional History of Georgia*, 136–45; Ware, *A Constitutional History of Georgia*, 62–70.
226. Kruman, *Between Authority and Liberty*, 21.
227. Nevins, *The American States*, 158.
228. Nevins, *The American States*, 160; Adams, *The First American Constitutions*, 82–83.
229. Nevins, *The American States*, 160.
230. John P. Kaminski, "Adjusting to Circumstances: New York's Relationship with the Federal Government," in Conley and Kaminski, eds., *The Constitution and the States*, 225.

231. Milton M. Klein, "Liberty as Nature's Gift: The Colonial Origins of the Bill of Rights," in Conley and Kaminski, eds., *The Bill of Rights and the States*, 215–16.

232. Alexander Hamilton (writing as Publius), "Federalist 84," in Benjamin F. Wright, ed., *The Federalist* (New York: Barnes and Noble, 1996), 534.

233. Thorpe, *The Federal and State Constitutions*, vol. 5: 2632, 2636–37.

234. Howard L. Lupert, "The New York Constitution: Emerging Principles in American Constitutional Thought," in Conley and Kaminski, eds., *The Constitution and the States*, 131–32.

235. Nevins, *The American States*, 161.

236. Thorpe, *The Federal and State Constitutions*, vol. 5: 2633.

237. Thorpe, *The Federal and State Constitutions*, vol. 5: 2632–33.

238. Tarr, *Understanding State Constitutions*, 87.

239. Thorpe, *The Federal and State Constitutions*, vol. 5: 2630–31.

240. Thorpe, *The Federal and State Constitutions*, vol. 5: 2631–32.

241. Kruman, *Between Authority and Liberty*, 122.

242. Thorpe, *The Federal and State Constitutions*, vol. 5: 2634, 2637.

243. Kruman, *Between Authority and Liberty*, 125.

244. Thorpe, *The Federal and State Constitutions*, vol. 5: 2633–34.

245. Nevins, *The American States*, 162–63.

246. Thorpe, *The Federal and State Constitutions*, vol. 5: 2635.

247. Thorpe, *The Federal and State Constitutions*, vol. 5: 2633.

248. Thorpe, *The Federal and State Constitutions*, vol. 5: 2628–29.

249. Nevins, *The American States*, 163; Kruman, *Between Authority and Liberty*, 125.

250. Thorpe, *The Federal and State Constitutions*, vol. 5: 2630–31; Adams, *The First American Constitutions*, 90–91.

251. Gary J. Aichele, "Making the Vermont Constitution," in Michael Sherman, ed., *A More Perfect Union: Vermont Becomes a State, 1777–1816* (Montpelier: Vermont Historical Society, 1991), 17, 19; William C. Hill, *The Vermont State Constitution: A Reference Guide* (Westport: Greenwood Press, 1992), 3–7.

252. Peter S. Onuf, "Vermont and the Union," in Sherman, ed., *A More Perfect Union*, 155.

253. Thorpe, *The Federal and State Constitutions*, vol. 6: 3739–40; Adams, *The First American Constitutions*, 4. Although not as extensive as in other states, the ownership of enslaved Africans and Native Peoples had been pervasive in New England from the earliest colonial period. As Wendy Warren observed, "did the New England colonists disapprove of slavery? The answer is a resounding no." Warren pointed out that slavery was seen as having a theological basis and even the 1691 Massachusetts Body of Liberties allowed slavery. Thus, Warren wrote, "By the opening of the eighteenth century slavery was embedded in the New England colonies as an accepted and financial part of society." Indeed, it was not until 1783 that slavery was declared to be contrary to the Massachusetts constitution and Connecticut and Rhode Island moved toward "general emancipation." Wendy Warren, *New England Bound: Slavery and Colonization in Early America* (New York: Liverwright Publishing Corp., 2016), 31–35, 349–50.

254. Thorpe, *The Federal and State Constitutions*, vol. 6: 3742.

255. Thorpe, *The Federal and State Constitutions*, vol. 6: 3744; Adams, *The First American Constitutions*, 194.

256. Thorpe, *The Federal and State Constitutions*, vol. 6: 3744.

257. Adams, *The First American Constitutions*, 84; Kruman, *Between Authority and Liberty*, 24.

258. Thorpe, *The Federal and State Constitutions*, vol. 3: 1877–86.

259. Adams, *The First American Constitutions*, 83–84.

260. Kruman, *Between Authority and Liberty*, 30.

261. Adams, *The First American Constitutions*, 84–85; Louis Adams Frothingham, *A Brief History of the Constitution and the Government of Massachusetts* (Cambridge, MA: Harvard University Press, 1916), 21–22; Kruman, *Between Authority and Liberty*, 31

262. Adams, *The First American Constitutions*, 86–87.

263. Adams, *The First American Constitutions*, 3, 87–88.

264. Adams, *The First American Constitutions*, 87–88; Ronald M. Peters, *The Massachusetts Constitution of 1780: A Social Compact* (Amherst: Massachusetts University Press, 1978), 18–19; Kenyon, "Constitutionalism in Revolutionary America," 109.
265. Charles S. Hyneman and Donald S. Lutz, eds., *American Political Writing During the Founding Era 1760–1805* (Indianapolis: Liberty Press, 1983), vol. 1: 481–522.
266. Adams, *The First American Constitutions*, 88–89; Frothingham, *A Brief History of the Constitution and Government of Massachusetts*, 25; Kenyon, "Constitutionalism in Revolutionary America," in Pennock and Chapman, eds., *Constitutionalism*, 106–7 (emphasis original).
267. Adams, *The First American Constitutions*, 89; Peters, *The Massachusetts Constitution of 1780*, 20–21.
268. John M. Murrin, "From Liberties to Rights: The Supreme Struggle in Colonial Massachusetts," in Conley and Kaminski, eds., *The Bill of Rights in the States*, 63–65.
269. Kenyon, "Constitutionalism in Revolutionary America," in Pennock and Chapman, eds., *Constitutionalism*, 109; Frothingham, *A Brief History of the Constitution and Government of Massachusetts*, 25–26.
270. Adams, *The First American Constitutions*, 90.
271. Adams, *The First American Constitutions*, 89–90; Frothingham, *A Brief History of the Constitution and Government of Massachusetts*, 27. With respect to whether the constitution had received the required two-thirds vote, Kenyon wrote that "It seems quite impossible to arrive at an exact conclusion as to whether the ratification was strictly in accordance with the requirement that two-thirds of the voters approve the constitution. The basic reason is that the returns from the towns did not follow a uniform pattern." Kenyon, "Constitutionalism in Revolutionary America," in Pennock and Chapman, eds., *Constitutionalism*, 113.
272. Peters, *The Massachusetts Constitution of 1780*, 13; Lutz, *The Origins of American Constitutionalism*, 98.
273. Wood, *Creation of the American Republic 1776–1787*, 434.
274. Thorpe, *The Federal and State Constitutions*, vol. 3: 1889. In this regard, Peters commented that "In establishing their new government, the people of Massachusetts attempted to limit the power of government procedurally, in order to protect individuals from arbitrary actions by the government. In so doing, they also provided a measure of protection for individuals against a tyrannical majority."
275. Peters, *The Massachusetts Constitution of 1780*, 189.
276. Thorpe, *The Federal and State Constitutions*, vol. 3: 1889–90.
277. Thorpe, *The Federal and State Constitutions*, vol. 3: 1890; Kenyon, "Constitutionalism in Revolutionary America," 111–12.
278. Thorpe, *The Federal and State Constitutions*, vol. 3: 1890–91, 1895–96, 1898.
279. Thorpe, *The Federal and State Constitutions*, vol. 3: 1891.
280. Thorpe, *The Federal and State Constitutions*, vol. 3: 1892.
281. Thorpe, *The Federal and State Constitutions*, vol. 3: 1891–93. Even in time of war, soldiers were not to be quartered in private homes unless directed by a magistrate in accordance with rules prescribed by the legislature.
282. Thorpe, *The Federal and State Constitutions*, vol. 3: 1892–93.
283. Thorpe, *The Federal and State Constitutions*, vol. 3: 1910.
284. Thorpe, *The Federal and State Constitutions*, vol. 3: 1892.
285. Thorpe, *The Federal and State Constitutions*, vol. 3: 1892.
286. Adams, *The First American Constitutions*, 267; Kenyon, "Constitutionalism in Revolutionary America," in Pennock and Chapman, eds., *Constitutionalism*, 110.
287. Thorpe, *The Federal and State Constitutions*, vol. 3: 1893 (emphasis added).
288. Thorpe, *The Federal and State Constitutions*, vol. 3: 1893–95. Representation in the senate was to be in proportion to the taxes paid by each district, subject to a maximum representation of six senators from one district.
289. Thorpe, *The Federal and State Constitutions*, vol. 3: 1897–98.
290. Wood, *The Creation of the American Republic 1776–1787*, 576.
291. Kenyon, "Constitutionalism in Revolutionary America," in Pennock and Chapman, eds., *Constitutionalism*, 110–11.

292. Thorpe, *The Federal and State Constitutions*, vol. 3: 1894.

293. Thorpe, *The Federal and State Constitutions*, vol. 3: 1899. Wood pointed out, however, that by 1785, the senate had established parity with the house in regard to money bills. Wood, *The Creation of the American Republic 1776–1787*, 243.

294. Thorpe, *The Federal and State Constitutions*, vol. 3: 1894.

295. Thorpe, *The Federal and State Constitutions*, vol. 3: 1897–99.

296. Thorpe, *The Federal and State Constitutions*, vol. 3: 1899.

297. Thorpe, *The Federal and State Constitutions*, vol. 3: 1899.

298. Kenyon, "Constitutionalism in Revolutionary America," in Pennock and Chapman, eds., *Constitutionalism*, 111.

299. Thorpe, *The Federal and State Constitutions*, vol. 3: 1899–1900. To be eligible to serve as governor, a man had to be an inhabitant of the commonwealth for the preceding seven years and to possess a freehold valued at least one thousand pounds. He also had to have declared himself "to be of the Christian Religion." In the event no one garnered a majority of votes, the constitution established a procedure for election by the house and the senate. Thorpe, *The Federal and State Constitutions*, vol. 3: 1900.

300. Thorpe, *The Federal and State Constitutions*, vol. 3: 1903–4.

301. Kenyon, "Constitutionalism in Revolutionary America," in Pennock and Chapman, eds., *Constitutionalism*, 111.

302. Thorpe, *The Federal and State Constitutions*, vol. 3: 1904–5.

303. Kruman, *Between Liberty and Authority*, 128.

304. Thorpe, *The Federal and State Constitutions*, vol. 3: 1900–2.

305. Thorpe, *The Federal and State Constitutions*, vol. 3: 1901. However, as Frothingham noted, "Martial law can be applied to civilians in Massachusetts only by vote of the legislature, and this restriction is found in the constitutions of only two other States, namely New Hampshire and South Carolina." Frothingham, *A Brief History of the Constitution and Government of Massachusetts*, 31–32.

306. Thorpe, *The Federal and State Constitutions*, vol. 3: 1901.

307. Thorpe, *The Federal and State Constitutions*, 1903.

308. Thorpe, *The Federal and State Constitutions*, vol. 3: 1893–94. Adams, *The First American Constitutions*, 271.

309. Kruman, *Between Liberty and Authority*, 125.

310. Thorpe, *The Federal and State Constitutions*, vol. 3: 1894.

311. Thorpe, *The Federal and State Constitutions*, vol. 3: 1905–6.

312. Thorpe, *The Federal and State Constitutions*, vol. 3: 1905.

313. Thorpe, *The Federal and State Constitutions*, vol. 3: 1909.

314. Thorpe, *The Federal and State Constitutions*, vol. 3: 1909–10.

315. Senators and representatives were prohibited from simultaneously holding the offices of "judge of the supreme judicial court, secretary, attorney general, solicitor general, treasurer- or-receiver general, judge of probate, commissary general, president, professor or instructor of Harvard College, sheriff, clerk of the house of representatives, registrar of probate, registrar of deeds, clerk of the supreme judicial court, clerk of the inferior court of common pleas, or officer of customs, including . . . naval officers." Thorpe, *The Federal and State Constitutions*, vol. 3: 1909–10.

316. Thorpe, *The Federal and State Constitutions*, vol. 3: 1910.

317. Thorpe, *The Federal and State Constitutions*, vol. 3: 1906–8.

318. Thorpe, *The Federal and State Constitutions*, vol. 3: 1911.

319. Thorpe, *The Federal and State Constitutions*, vol. 4: 2452; 6: 3243.

320. Thorpe, *The Federal and State Constitutions*, vol. 6: 3248–55; Michael E. Stevens, "South Carolina: Their Liberties and Privileges," in Conley and Kaminski, eds., *The Bill of Rights and the States*, 412; Wood, *The Creation of the American Republic*, 141 n.27.

321. Thorpe, *The Federal and State Constitutions*, vol. 4: 2453–57; Frank G. Mevers, "New Hampshire Accepts the Bill of Rights," in Conley and Kaminski, eds., *The Bill of Rights and the States*, 166–71; Thomas Schuman, "New Hampshire and the Constitutional Movement," in Connor and Hammonds, eds., *The Constitutionalism of the American States*, 57–58.

322. Thorpe, *The Federal and State Constitutions*, vol. 4: 2458–62.

323. Thorpe, *The Federal and State Constitutions*, vol. 4: 2463–66.
324. Thorpe, *The Federal and State Constitutions*, vol. 4: 2469–70.
325. Celise Schneider, "The Green Mountain Boys Constitute Vermont," in Connor and Hammons, eds., *The Constitutionalism of the American States*, 89–91; Hill, *The Vermont Constitution*, 8–9; Thorpe, *The Federal and State Constitutions*, vol. 6: 3749 note a.
326. Thorpe, *The Federal and State Constitutions*, vol. 6: 3752.
327. Thorpe, *The Federal and State Constitutions*, vol. 6: 3757.
328. Thorpe, *The Federal and State Constitutions*, vol. 6: 3754–56.
329. Thorpe, *The Federal and State Constitutions*, vol. 6: 3758.

Chapter Seven

The American Constitutional Tradition in the Revolutionary Era

The colonial charters of the sixteenth and seventeenth centuries set the course for the way Americans would conceive of a constitution of government. The charters established the legitimacy of the governing authority; enumerated the powers that could be exercised according to that authority; and provided an institutional structure for implementation of those powers. Of equal importance, the royal charters assured the colonial settlers that they would possess and enjoy all liberties, franchises, immunities, and privileges of free and natural subjects of England.

By virtue of these authoritative writings establishing the form of government and securing fundamental rights against encroachment by those governments, it has been said that the American constitutionalists became accustomed to "a written document defining the context of their politics," reference to which was "the focus of their link" with the vast corpus of rights and authorities that in Britain was comprised of the common law and parliamentary enactments. Accordingly, although the federal Constitution was rooted firmly in British constitutional principles, there is nevertheless a "continuity to be found . . . from the earliest colonial documents of foundation to the written constitutions of the [1770s] and [1780s]," and therefore, it was observed, "we should look to our shores as well when seeking a constitutional tradition for America."[1] The revolutionary constitutions of the 1770s, culminating with the Massachusetts constitution of 1780, drew on the earlier seminal documents to give form to the fundamental tenets of American constitutionalism and as a consequence, their influence on the federal constitution cannot be ignored or under estimated.[2]

The Revolutionary era was a time of intensive constitutionalism, perhaps even more so than during the drafting of the federal Constitution a decade later. It was a time when political realists, infused with revolutionary idealism and confronted with the void left by the collapse of the established order under the crown governments and the imperatives of war, were propelled by events to fashion a new political order in the newly independent states.[3] To Bernard Bailyn, this Revolutionary constitutionalism was nothing less than a reconception of both the fundamentals of government and of the relationship of society to government.[4]

To accomplish their task, the framers of the state constitutions drew on the experiences of their colonial governments over the preceding two hundred years. From these experiences, the Framers fashioned plans of government as well as statements of fundamental law and guarantees of individual rights and civic liberties that would be inviolable by the state governments.

The Revolutionary constitutions also carried on the charter tradition of establishing governments with enumerated powers. Unlike the charters, however, the powers enumerated in the constitutions were delegated by the people and not by the crown. The delegation of these limited, enumerated powers was founded on republican principles of elected representation and the separation of legislative, executive, and judicial functions. Informed by their experiences under the crown governments, the newly independent states adopted plans of government based on elected representation. All of the state constitutions provided for an elected legislature, which in the majority of states was comprised of two chambers. Qualifications for election often differed,[5] as did the constituencies that each represented.[6]

To a greater or lesser extent, the frames of governments under the Revolutionary constitutions sought to distribute powers within the governments by separating the executive and judicial functions from those of the legislature and over time, by augmenting the role of the executive and by providing greater independence to the judiciary. Although the locus of power remained primarily in the legislature, restraints in the form of bicameralism,[7] executive veto of legislation,[8] and the sharing of the appointment power,[9] furthered the implementation of mixed government.

Each of the Revolutionary constitutions incorporated principles of the separation of powers. The majority of the constitutions explicitly referenced the separation of powers as an organizing principle.[10] Implementation varied widely. For example, with the exception of Massachusetts, New York, and Vermont, the governor was chosen by the legislature.[11] Virginia was the first state to establish the judiciary as an independent branch of the government, and Virginia's example was followed in Georgia, Maryland, Massachusetts, New Hampshire (in 1784), New York, North Carolina, Pennsylvania, and Vermont. In other states (Delaware, New Jersey, and South Carolina), either the executive or the legislature performed at least some judicial functions. The independence of the judiciary was preserved in a majority of the states by providing that judicial offices were to be held "during good behavior."[12]

In addition to the separation of governmental functions, the Revolutionary constitutions included mechanisms for limiting powers particularly of the executive and legislature. A common feature was a prohibition against holding more than one governmental office simultaneously.[13] Limitations were also imposed on the length of time in which some offices could be held.[14] The authority of the governor to act unilaterally was restricted by the requirement of the advice and consent of a privy council that was usually appointed by the legislature.[15] Civil officers, including the governor, were subject to impeachment and removal from office by the legislature in several states for malfeasance or misfeasance in office.[16]

Of even greater significance, however, the constitutionalism of the Revolutionary era gave rise to the recognition of constitutional law as having greater dignity and weight than other legislative enactments. Indeed, elevation of constitutional law to a paramount position has been considered "*the* great innovation and achievement of eighteenth century American constitutionalism."[17]

Although the Revolutionary constitutions differed substantially in their structure, they all embraced the principal that the governments they created derived their legitimacy from the consent of the governed (even though those empowered to express their consent were limited by gender, race, and wealth). The manner in which constituent power of the governed was exercised in the formulation and adoption of the Revolutionary constitutions evolved over time and reflected the evolution in the conception of what a constitution was.

Thus, in their earliest essays in constitution making in the heat of rebellion, the Revolutionary states of New Hampshire, South Carolina, and Virginia enacted constitutions of government in the same manner in which they enacted other legislation. However, in May 1776, a committee of the New York provisional congress called for an election to be held for representatives to a new congress that would be authorized to frame the civil government for the state. Thereafter, first in Pennsylvania and then in Delaware, special conventions were called for the express purpose of adopting constitutions.[18] In Maryland, a provincial congress was elected for the stated purpose of adopting a constitution as well as enacting other necessary legislation. A similar approach was taken in Georgia, New York, and North Carolina.

In July 1776, elections were held in Delaware, Maryland, and Pennsylvania. In August elections were held in Georgia and North Carolina. Elections were held the following May in New York (whose proceedings had been delayed by the war). In these states, although the congresses conducted other legislative business and despite their constitutions being enacted in the same manner as other legislation, the calling of the special elections evidenced a recognition that the creation of a constitution was not simply an ordinary legislative act and that the representatives engaged in constitution writing should be specifically deputized by the electorate for that purpose.

In 1777, the citizens of Vermont (which had just declared its independence from Massachusetts, New Hampshire, and New York) broke with the accepted practice of legislative enactment of a constitution, and in June, a convention was convened solely for the purpose of adopting a constitution.

Later, like Delaware, Maryland, Pennsylvania, and Vermont, Massachusetts decoupled the process of constitution writing from ordinary legislation by convening a "true constitutional convention" of delegates that had been elected exclusively for the purpose of framing a constitution.[19] The necessity of calling a special constitutional convention had been the subject of communications from various town meetings, which had objected to the writing of the constitution by the General Court. The Pittsfield town meeting advised the General Court on May 29, 1776, that "the formation of a fundamental Constitution is absolutely necessary to give Liberty & being to it," and it was "then & not 'till then" that the foundation for legislation would be laid.[20]

The sentiments of Pittsfield were echoed in the communication from Concord to the General Court on October 22, 1776. At the town meeting the day before, it had been resolved that the General Court, either as a whole or in committee, was "by no means a body proper to form & establish a constitution or form of government," for several reasons. First, the constitution was to be "a system of principles established to secure the subjects in the possession & enjoyment of their rights and privileges, against any encroachments of the governing part." Second, it was noted that because "the same body that forms a constitution has as a consequence a power to alter it," a constitution enacted by the legislature "is no security at all to the subjects against any encroachment of the governing part on any or on all of their rights and privileges." It was therefore "highly necessary & expedient that a convention, or a congress be immediately chosen, to form & establish a constitution, by the inhabitants of the respective towns in the state."[21]

Although an attempt was made to authorize the General Court to adopt a constitution that would then be submitted to the voters for approval, a variety of objections were made to the proposed constitution and the constitution was rejected. Finally, on June 21, 1779, elections were announced for a constitutional convention, and on September 1, the convention came together in Cambridge. The draft that emerged from the convention was submitted to the towns for ratification. It was only after the ratification process had run its course that the convention declared the constitution to have been ratified by the necessary two-thirds vote.[22]

By following this course, Massachusetts not only established the precedent for the 1787 convention and the ratification of the constitution by the states, the Massachusetts approach gave concrete recognition of constitution writing as being fundamentally different from ordinary legislation and to constitutional law as being those immutable principles on which the government would be founded and individual rights secured.

Thus, the constitution was established as a body of fundamental law for the governance of a state that was wholly distinct from the body of the state's legislative enactments, and adopted through a process of ratification of delegated authority by the voting citizens of the state. As Peterson observed, "No model theory or model of a constitutional convention existed in 1776. It came about gradually through trial and error. As finally realized, the new institution involved three main elements: first, the popular election of delegates to a convention specifically authorized to frame a constitution; second, the convention's deliberate choice of a frame of government reduced to written form; and third, the consent (or dissent) of the people to the proposed constitution through a process of ratification. . . . The institution rested on a distinction unknown to English theory and practice, between the constitution-making authority and the law-making authority."[23]

The Revolutionary era was also a time when American statesmen sought to fashion centralized governmental structures for a national government and for their states that would respect the authority of peripheral governments (that were themselves centers of political authority in their own spheres). Both the Revolutionary state constitutions and the Articles of Confederation and Perpetual Union in 1777 attempted to provide for collective security and to create a structure of governance over matters of mutual interest and concern while leaving to the states (or local governments in the case of state constitutions) authority over internal matters that were unique to them.

The earliest of these efforts was the 1643 confederation of the Connecticut, Massachusetts Bay, New Haven, and Plymouth settlements to form the United Colonies of New England. The agreement to form this union were set forth in a written document specifying the powers and limiting the authority of the union government. The governing body of the union was comprised of commissioners representing each of the member colonies (two commissioners from each). Their agreement specifically enjoined the union government from "intermeddling" in the internal affairs of the colonies, which were "preserved entirely to themselves." In this, the confederation of New England colonies was little more than an overture to federalism.

Nevertheless, interest in forming an intercolonial government continued despite the failure of the New England union. In 1697, William Penn, the proprietor of the East New Jersey and Pennsylvania colonies, submitted his plan to the Lords of Trade and Plantations for a government that would comprehend all of the American colonies. Like the New England union, there was to be a deliberative body comprised of two representatives from each of the colonies. However, unlike the New England body, there was to be a presiding officer appointed by the king. Penn incorporated into his plan the same jurisdiction over matters of mutual interest, as had been the basis of the

New England confederation with the significant addition of authority to regulate commerce among the various colonies. Although no action was taken on Penn's proposal, there continued to be initiatives put forward for uniting some or all of the colonies under a central governmental authority.[24]

In 1754, at the instance of the Board of Trade, representatives of the Maryland, Massachusetts, New Jersey, New York, Pennsylvania, and Virginia colonies met in Albany, New York, for the purpose of reaching agreement on how the alliance with the Iroquois Nation could be preserved in the face of aggression by the French and their allies among the native peoples. The conference soon turned to consideration of forming a confederation of the colonies. The written plan of union approved by the Albany conference called for the formation of a "general government" of the colonies administered by a "President-General" appointed by the crown and a legislative "Grand Council" comprised of representatives elected by the legislatures of the colonies in proportion to the colony's contribution to the common treasury.

Under the Albany Plan, the legislature was given broad authority to enact laws of general application and to raise revenue through the laying of taxes, duties and imposts. However, the acts of the legislature were subject to the agreement (and thus, the veto) of the president (and ultimately the crown). The president was charged with seeing that the laws were carried out. The president's authority was also subject to the consent of the legislature.

Despite failing to garner the approval of the colonial legislatures, the Albany Plan of Union, authored primarily by Benjamin Franklin, represented a significant conceptual advance toward a federal government grounded on republican principles of proportional representation coupled with real executive authority. It was also significant in the respect that the Albany delegates set out the plan in a unitary document that defined how the government was to be constituted, the authorities granted to the branches of government, and the limitations imposed on the exercise of those authorities.

The salient features of the Albany Plan were recalled in the proposals for union of the colonies by Joseph Galloway and Franklin two decades later as the colonies were propelled toward insurrection. While prompted by diametrically opposed motives (Galloway sought to avoid a rupture of relations with Britain whereas Franklin advocated independence), both plans contemplated a representative central government that was by varying degrees independent of Britain. Under Franklin's plan, representation of the colonies was to be proportional based on population (and not predicated on contribution to the public fisc as in his Albany Plan) that was subject to review every three years. Franklin's plan would require ratification by a majority of the colonial legislatures and allowed for amendments.

Franklin's plan was not acted upon by the Continental Congress, but the influence of Franklin's plan can be seen in the Articles of Confederation and

Perpetual Union that were adopted by the Continental Congress and served as the constitution of government until ratification of the federal Constitution in 1789. The Articles of Confederation were written under the exigencies of war at a time when the newly independent states, which were in the process of writing their own constitutions, were jealous of their sovereignty and fearful of the abuses of centralized governmental power that they attributed to the metropole. Under those circumstances, the Continental Congress produced a written plan of government which, although deeply flawed, sought to harmonize the individual interests of the sovereign states with the necessity of mounting a common defense, conducting relations with foreign governments, and facilitating domestic trade. This balance of sovereign interests informed the conception of federalism underlying the Constitution of 1787.

In retrospect, we can only reflect with envy on the constitutionalism of the Revolutionary era expressed by John Adams when in 1776 he wrote to a contemporary that "You and I, my dear friend, have been sent into life at a time when the greatest law givers of antiquity would have wished to live. How few of the human race have ever enjoyed an opportunity for making an election of government . . . for themselves and for their children."[25]

Firmly grounded on first principles derived from the colonial experience, the constitutions of the Revolutionary era "stand as a fulcrum of American constitutional history,"[26] and their framers as the originators of the modern constitution.[27] The "American invention,"[28] the Constitution of 1787, that articulated the powers of a republican federal government and the fundamental rights of citizens in relation to that government, had its beginnings in the charters granted by the crown for the exploration and settlement of America. On the basis of those charters, the colonial settlers fashioned their social structures and asserted their rights against the king and parliament when they believed their liberties to be in jeopardy. From their experience under the charters, a constitutional tradition emerged that was uniquely American, which found its most lasting expression in the US Constitution.

NOTES

1. Lutz, *Colonial Origins of the American Constitution*, xxxi.

2. Willi Adams described the influence of the state constitutions on the drafting of the 1787 Constitution as having been "profound," noting that "they were the constitutions that Americans knew best." Adams, "The State Constitutions as Analogy and Precedent," in Howard, ed., *The United States Constitution*, 3. This was also the view of Winton U. Solberg, *The Constitutional Convention and the Formation of the Union* (Urbana: University of Illinois Press, 1990), lxxxv.

3. Thus, Willi Adams observed that "After the decision for independence was made, there was no alternative to the establishment of republican state constitutions. Their drafting demanded answers to core questions of modern politics: how to reconcile individual freedom with the republic's 'common good'; and stable and efficient government; how to have a multitude of free and equal citizens living in dispersed communities draft and agree on a set of constitutional

ground rules—in the absence of a more or less enlightened monarch to 'give' them one." Adams, "The State Constitutions as Analogy and Precedent," in Howard, ed., *The United States Constitution*, 4.

4. Bailyn wrote, "To conceive of legislative assemblies as mirrors of society and their voices as mechanically exact expressions of the people; to assume, and act upon the assumption, that human rights exist above law and stand as a measure of the law's validity; to understand constitutions to be ideal designs of government, and fixed, limiting definitions of it permissible sphere of action; and to consider the possibility that absolute sovereignty in government need not be the monopoly of a single all-engrossing agency but (*imperium in imperio*) the shared possession of several agencies each limited by the boundary of others but all-powerful within its own—to think in these ways as Americans were doing before independence, was to conceive the fundamentals of government and of society's relation with government." Bailyn, *The Ideological Origins of the American Revolution*, 230.

5. Different qualifications for election to the two chambers were specified in the constitutions of Massachusetts, Maryland, New Hampshire, New York, North Carolina, South Carolina, and Virginia.

6. In Massachusetts, Maryland, New Hampshire, New York, North Carolina, South Carolina, and Virginia, members of the state senates represented different geographic divisions of the state than those represented by members of the lower houses.

7. Bicameral legislatures were established under the provisional constitutions of New Hampshire and South Carolina and under the more permanent constitutions of Delaware, Maryland, Massachusetts, New Jersey, New York, North Carolina, and Virginia.

8. Gubernatorial veto was provided for in the constitutions of Massachusetts, New York, and South Carolina. The veto in the first South Carolina constitution was not carried over in the second constitution. In New York and New Hampshire, the veto could be overridden by the legislature. In Georgia and Vermont, legislation was required to be submitted to the governor and the council for their "perusal and advice," after which they could propose amendments. Additionally, in Vermont, if the governor and the council were not satisfied with the legislature's response to their proposed amendments, they could suspend passage of the legislation until the next legislative session.

9. The appointment power was shared by the executive and the legislature in Delaware, Massachusetts, New York, South Carolina, Vermont, and Virginia.

10. Explicit reference to the principle of separation of powers was made in the constitutions of Georgia, Maryland, Massachusetts, North Carolina, Vermont, and Virginia.

11. Provision was made later for the direct election of the governor in the New Hampshire constitution of 1784.

12. Judicial tenure during good behavior was secured in the constitutions of Delaware, Maryland, Massachusetts, New Hampshire, New York, North Carolina, South Carolina, and Virginia. Fixed terms for judicial offices were established in New Jersey and Pennsylvania.

13. The holding of multiple offices was prohibited in Delaware, Georgia, Maryland, Massachusetts, New Hampshire, New York, North Carolina, Pennsylvania, and South Carolina.

14. Such limitations were established in the constitutions of Delaware, Georgia, Maryland, North Carolina, Pennsylvania, South Carolina, Vermont, and Virginia.

15. The advice and consent of the privy council was required in Delaware, Georgia, Maryland, Massachusetts, New Hampshire, North Carolina, South Carolina, and Virginia.

16. The impeachment power was conferred on the legislatures in Delaware, Massachusetts, New Hampshire, New York, North Carolina, Pennsylvania, South Carolina, Vermont, and Virginia.

17. Gerald Stourzh, "Constitution: Changing Meanings of the Term from the Early Seventeenth to the Eighteenth Century," in Ball and Pocock, eds., *Conceptual Change and the Constitution*, 47 (emphasis original)

18. Willi Adams described the actions of Pennsylvania and Delaware as "a great step forward in the practical development of modern constitutionalism." Adams, *The First American Constitutions*, 73.

19. Adams, *The First American Constitutions*, 89.

20. The Pittsfield town meeting stated that "we have been persuaded that the people are the foundation of power. That since the dissolution of the power of Great Britain over these colonies they have fallen in a state of nature. That the first step to be taken by a people in such a state for the enjoyment and restoration of civil government amongst them, is the formation of a fundamental constitution as the basis & ground work of legislation. That the approbation of the majority of the people of this fundamental constitution is absolutely necessary to give life & being to it. That then & not 'till then is the foundation laid for legislation." Pittsfield Petition to the House of Representatives, May 29, 1776, in J. R. Pole, ed., *The Revolution in America 1754–1788: Documents on the Internal Development of America in the Revolutionary Era* (Palo Alto, CA: Stanford University Press, 1970), 419.

21. Pole, *The Revolution in America*, 430.

22. Despite some legerdemain on the part of the reconvened convention in tabulating the towns' responses, the constitution was declared to have been ratified by at least two-thirds of the voters.

23. Peterson, "The Idea of a Written Constitution in the Thought of the Founders," in Howard, ed., *The United States Constitution*, 45.

24. Fisher, *The Evolution of the Constitution of the United States*, 227–31.

25. Charles Francis Adams, ed., *Works of John Adams* (Boston: Little & Brown, 1850–1856), vol. 4: 200.

26. Lutz, *The Origins of American Constitutionalism*, 97.

27. Hall, *The Magic Mirror*, 60–61.

28. Merrill D. Peterson, "The Idea of a Written Constitution in Thought of the Founders," in Howard, ed., *The United States Constitution*, 43.

Bibliography

Adams, Charles Francis, ed. *The Works of John Adams*. Boston: Little & Brown, 1850–56.
Adams, James Truslow. *The Founding of New England.* New York: Atlantic Monthly Press, 1921.
Adams, Samuel. *The Rights of the Colonists: The Report of the Committee of Correspondence to the Boston Town Committee*, Old South Leaflets No. 173. Boston, Directors of Old South Works, 1906.
Adams, Willi Paul. *The First American Constitutions: Republican Ideology and the Making of the State Constitutions in the Revolutionary Era.* Lanham, MD: Rowman & Littlefield, 2001.
Amar, Akhil Reed. *America's Constitution: A Biography*. New York: Random House, 2005.
American Political Science Association and the American Historical Association, eds. *The Constitution: Our Enduring Legacy*. Washington, DC: Congressional Quarterly, 1986.
Andrews, Charles M. *Colonial Self-Government 1652–1689.* New York: Harper Brothers, 1907.
———. *Our Earliest Colonial Settlements*. Ithaca: Cornell University Press, 1933.
———. *The Colonial Period of American History.* New Haven: Yale University Press, 1934.
Andrews, Kenneth R. *Trade, Plunder and Settlement: Maritime Enterprise and the Genesis of the British Empire, 1480–1630*. London: Cambridge University Press, 1984.
Andrews, Kenneth R., Canny, Nicholas P. and Haires, P. H. eds., *The Westward Enterprise: English Activities in Ireland, the Atlantic and America.* Liverpool: Liverpool University Press, 1978.
Bailyn, Bernard. *The Ideological Origins of the American Revolution*. Cambridge, MA: Harvard University Press, 1992.
———. *The New England Merchants in the Seventeenth Century.* Cambridge, MA: Harvard University Press, 1979.
Ball, Terence, and J. G. A. Pocock, eds. *Conceptual Change and the Constitution*. Lawrence: University of Kansas Press, 1988.
Barnes, Viola F. *The Dominion of New England: A Study in British Colonial Policy.* New Haven: Yale University Press, 1923.
Beatty, Edward Corbyn Obert. *William Penn As Social Philosopher*. New York: Columbia University Press, 1939.
Beeman, Richard R., Stephen Botein, and Edward Carter, eds. *Beyond Confederation: Origins of the Constitution and American National Identity.* Chapel Hill: University of North Carolina Press, 1987.
Beer, George Louis. "The Early Colonial Movement I." *Political Science Quarterly* Volume 23 (1908).

Bilder, Mary Sarah. *The Transatlantic Constitution: Colonial Legal Culture and the Empire.* Cambridge: Harvard University Press, 2004.

Billings, Warren M., John E. Selby, and Thad W. Tate. *Colonial Virginia: A History.* White Plains: KTO Press, 1986.

Bliss, Robert M. *Revolution and Empire: English Politics and the American Colonies in the Seventeenth Century.* Manchester: Manchester University Press, 1990.

Bolingbroke, Viscount Henry. *Political Writings.* Edited by David Armitage. Cambridge: Cambridge University Press, 1999.

Bowne, William Hand. *Maryland, The History of a Palatinate.* Boston: Houghton Mifflin, 1904.

Boyd, Julian P. *Anglo-American Union: Joseph Galloway's Plans to Preserve the British Empire 1774–1788.* Philadelphia: University of Pennsylvania Press, 1941.

Brigden, Susan. *New Worlds, Lost Worlds: The Rule of the Tudors 1485–1603.* New York: Penguin Press, 2000.

Brown, Robert E., and Katherine Brown. *Virginia 1705–1786: Democracy or Aristocracy?* East Lansing: Michigan State University Press, 1964.

Burke, Edmund. *An Account of the European Settlements in America.* London: J. Dodsley, 1770.

Canny, Nicholas, ed. *The Oxford History of the British Empire: The Origins of Empire.* Oxford: Oxford University Press, 1998.

Commager, Henry Steele. *The Empire of Reason: How Europe Imagined and America Realized the Enlightenment.* Garden City, NY: Anchor Press, 1977.

Commissioners of Statutory Revision. *The Colonial Laws of New York from Year 1664 to the Revolution.* Albany: James B. Lyon, 1894.

Conley, Patrick J., and John P. Kaminski, eds. *The Bill of Rights and the States.* Madison: Madison House Publishers, 1992.

———. *The Constitution and the States.* Madison: Madison House Publishers, 1988.

Connor, George E., and Christopher W. Hammons eds., *The Constitutionalism of the American States.* Columbia: Missouri University Press, 2008.

Corwin, Edward S. *The "Higher Law" Background of American Constitutional Law.* Ithaca: Cornell University Press, 1955.

Craven, Wesley Frank. *New Jersey and the English Colonization of North America.* Princeton: Princeton University Press, 1964.

Crowl, Philip A. *Maryland During and After the Revolution: A Political and Economic Study.* Baltimore: Johns Hopkins University Press, 1943.

Curtis, George Ticknor. *History of the Origin, Formation, and Adoption of the Constitution of the United States, with Notices of Its Principal Framers.* New York: Harper, 1854.

Dallas, Alexander James, ed. *Laws of the Commonwealth of Pennsylvania, from the Seventh Day of December, One Thousand Seven Hundred and Ninety, to the Twentieth Day of April, One Thousand Seven Hundred and Ninety Five.* Philadelphia: Hall and Sellers, 1795.

Daniell, Jere R. *Colonial New Hampshire: A History.* Millwood: KTO Press, 1981.

———. *Experiment in Republicanism: New Hampshire Politics and the American Revolution* Cambridge: Harvard University Press, 1970.

Davenport, Frances G., ed. *European Treaties Bearing on the History of the United States and Its Dependencies of 1648.* Washington, DC: Carnegie Institution of Washington, 1917.

Dunaway, Wayland Fuller. *A History of Pennsylvania.* New York: Prentice-Hall, 1935.

Edling, Max M. *A Revolution in Favor of Government: Origins of the U.S. Constitution and the Making of the American State.* New York: Oxford University Press, 2003.

Favor, Lesli J. *The Iroquois Constitution.* New York: Rosen Publishing Group, 2003.

Fisher, Sydney George. *The Evolution of the Constitution of the United States.* Philadelphia: Lippincott, 1897.

———. *The Quaker Colonies.* New York: United Publishers Association, 1919.

Ford, Worthington C., ed. *Journals of the Continental Congress, 1774–1789.* Washington, DC: US Government Printing Office, 1904–1837.

Foster, Stephen, ed. *The Oxford History of the British Empire: British North America in the Seventeenth and Eighteenth Centuries.* Oxford: Oxford University Press, 2013.

Franklin, Benjamin. *The Autobiography of Benjamin Franklin*. New Haven: Yale University Press, 1964.

———. *The Papers of Benjamin Franklin*. Edited by Leonard Woods Labaree. New Haven: Yale University Press, 1959.

Frothingham, Louis Adams. *A Brief History of the Constitution and the Government of Massachusetts*. Cambridge, MA: Harvard University Press, 1916.

Gambrell, Theodore C. *History of Early Maryland*. New York: Thomas Wittaker, 1893.

Graham, George J., and Scarlett G. Graham, eds. *Founding Principles of American Government: Two Hundred Years of Democracy on Trial*. Bloomington: Indiana University Press, 1977.

Greaves, H. R. G. *The British Constitution*. London: Allen & Union, 1965.

Greene, Evarts Boutell. *Political America 1690–1740*. New York: Harpers, 1905.

———. *The Provincial Governor in the English Colonies of North America*. New York: Longman, Green & Co., 1907.

Greene, Jack P. *Great Britain and the American Colonies 1606–1763*. Columbia: South Carolina University Press, 1970.

———. *Negotiated Authorities: Essays in Colonial Political and Constitutional History*. Charlottesville: University of Virginia Press, 1994.

———. *Peripheries and the Center: Constitutional Development in the Extended Polities of the British Empire and the United States 1607–1788*. Athens: Georgia University Press, 1986.

Haffenden, Philip S. "The Crown and the Colonial Charters, 1675–1688, Part I." *William and Mary Quarterly* Volume 15 (1958).

Haies, M. Edward. *Sir Humphrey Gilbert's Voyage to Newfoundland: A Report of the Voyage and Success Thereof, Attempted in the Year of Our Lord 1583 by Sir Humphrey Gilbert, Knight*. Boston: Directors of Old Southwork, 1902.

Hall, Kermit L. *The Magic Mirror: Law in American History*. New York: Oxford University Press, 1989.

Hatch, Charles E. *The First Seventeen Years, Virginia 1607–1624*. Charlottesville: University of Virginia Press, 1957.

Haven, Samuel F. *History of Grants under the Great Council for New England*. Boston: John Wilson, 1869.

Hawke, David Freeman. *The Colonial Experience*. Indianapolis: Bobbs-Merrill, 1966.

Hazeltine, H. D. "The Influence of Magna Carta on American Constitutional Development." *Columbia Law Review* Volume 17 (1917).

Hill, William C. *The Vermont State Constitution: A Reference Guide*. Westport: Greenwood Press, 1992.

Hockett, Homer Carey. *The Constitutional History of the United States 1776–1826, The Blessings of Liberty*. New York: Macmillan, 1939.

Hoffman, Ronald, and Peter J. Albert, eds. *Sovereign States in an Age of Uncertainty*. Charlottesville: University of Virginia Press, 1981.

Howard, A. E. Dick, ed. *The United States Constitution: Roots, Rights, and Responsibilities*. Washington, DC: Smithsonian Institution Scholarly Press, 1992.

Hull, William T. *William Penn: A Topical Biography*. London: Oxford University Press, 1937.

Hulsebosch, Daniel J. *Constituting Empire*. Chapel Hill: University of North Carolina Press, 2005.

Hutchinson, Thomas. *The Diary and Letters of His Excellency Thomas Hutchinson: Captain-General and Governor-in-chief of Boston*. Boston: Houghton Mifflin, 1884–86.

Hyneman, Charles S., and Donald S. Lutz, eds. *American Political Writing During the Founding Era 1760–1805*. Indianapolis: Liberty Press, 1983.

Isaacson, Walter *Benjamin Franklin: An American Life*. New York: Simon & Schuster, 2003.

Jensen, Merrill, *The Articles of Confederation: An Interpretation of the Social-Constitutional History of the American Revolution 1774–1781*. Madison: Wisconsin University Press, 1940.

———., ed. *The Documentary History of the Ratification of the Constitution*. Madison: Wisconsin Historical Society, 1976.

Jones, J. R., ed. *The Restored Monarchy, 1660–1688*. London: Macmillan Press, 1979.
Kammen, Michael. *Colonial New York*. New York: Scribner, 1975.
Kavenagh, W. Keith. *Foundations of Colonial America: A Documentary History*. New York: Chelsea House, 1973.
Kellog, Louise Phelps. *The American Colonial Charter: A Study of English Administration in Relation Thereto, Chiefly After 1688*. New York: DaCapo Press, 1971.
Kelly, Alfred H., Winfred A. Harbison, and Herman Belz. *The American Constitution: Its Origins and Development*. 7th ed. New York: W.W. Norton & Co., 1991.
Kemmerer, Donald L. *Path to Freedom: The Struggle for Self-Government in Colonial New Jersey, 1703–1776*. Princeton: Princeton University Press, 1940.
Kruman, Marc W. *Between Authority and Liberty: State Constitution-Making in Revolutionary America*. Chapel Hill: University of North Carolina Press, 1997.
Kurland, Philip B., ed. *The Founders' Constitution*. Chicago: University of Chicago Press, 1987.
Labaree, Leonard Woods. *Royal Government in America: A Study of the British Colonial System Before 1783*. New Haven: Yale University Press, 1930.
Lacey, Robert. *Sir Walter Raleigh*. New York: Athenaeum, 1974.
Land, Aubrey C. *Colonial Maryland: A History*. Millwood: KTO Press, 1981.
Lefler, Hugh T., and William S. Powell. *Colonial North Carolina—A History*. New York: Scribner, 1973.
Lewis, H. H. *The Maryland Constitution of 1776*. Baltimore: Maryland State Bar Association, 1976.
Love, William DeLos. *The Colonial History of Hartford*. Hartford: Self-published, 1914.
Lustig, Mary Lo. *The Imperial Executive in America: Sir Edmund Andros 1637–1714*. Madison, NJ: Farleigh Dickenson University Press, 2002.
Lutz, Donald S. *Colonial Origins of the American Constitution: A Documentary History*. Indianapolis: Liberty Fund, 1998.
———. *The Origins of the American Constitution*. Baton Rouge: Louisiana State University Press, 1988.
Macmillan, Ken. *The Atlantic Imperial Constitution: Center and Periphery in the English Atlantic World*. New York: Palgrave Macmillan, 2011.
Maier, Pauline. *American Scripture: Making the Declaration of Independence*. New York: Knopf, 1997.
Marshall, P. J., and Alaine Low, eds. *The Oxford History of the British Empire: Volume 2: The Eighteenth Century*. Oxford: Oxford University Press, 1998.
Martin, James K., ed. *Interpreting Colonial America*. 2nd ed. New York: Harper and Row, 1973.
Mathews, L. K. "Benjamin Franklin's Plans for a Colonial Union 1750–1755." *American Political Science Review* Volume 8 (1914).
Mayer, David N. *The Constitutional Thought of Thomas Jefferson*. Charlottesville: University of Virginia Press, 1994.
McCormick, Richard P. *Experiment in Independence: New Jersey in the Critical Period, 1781–1789*. New Brunswick, NJ: Rutgers University Press, 1950.
———. *New Jersey from Colony to State*. Princeton: Princeton University Press, 1964.
McDonald, Forrest. *Novus Ordo Seclorum: The Intellectual Origins of the Constitution*. Lawrence: University of Kansas Press, 1985.
McDowell, Gary L., and Jonathan O'Neill, eds. *America and Enlightenment Constitutionalism*. New York: Palgrave Macmillan, 2006.
McElreath, Walter. *A Treatise on the Constitution of Georgia*. Atlanta: Harrison & Co., 1912.
McFarlane, Anthony. *The British in the Americas 1480–1815*. New York: Longman Group Limited, 1992.
McIlwain, Charles Howard. *Constitutionalism: Ancient and Modern*. Ithaca: Cornell University Press, 1940.
McLaughlin, Andrew C. *A Constitutional History of the United State*. New York: D. Appleton-Century Co., 1935.
———. *The Confederation and the Constitution 1783–1789*. New York: Harper, 1907.

———. *Foundations of American Constitutionalism.* Greenwich: Fawcett Publications, 1961.

Meinig, D. W. *The Shaping of America: A Geographical Perspective of 500 Years of History.* New Haven: Yale University Press, 1986.

Mereness, Newton D. *Maryland As a Proprietary.* New York: The Macmillan Company, 1901.

Middleton, Richard, and Ann Lombard. *Colonial America: A History to 1763.* 4th ed. Chichester: Wiley-Blackwell, 2011.

Morgan, Edmund S. *Benjamin Franklin.* New Haven: Yale University Press, 2002.

Morison, Samuel Eliot, Henry Steele Commager, and William E. Leuchtenburg. *The Growth of the American Republic.* 6th ed. New York: Oxford University Press, 1969.

Munroe, John A. *Colonial Delaware: A History.* (Millwood: KTO Press, 1978).

Nevins, Allan. *The American States: During and After the Revolution, 1775–1789.* New York: Macmillan, 1924.

Newbold, Robert C. *The Albany Congress and Plan of Union of 1754.* New York: Vantage, 1955.

Newcomb, Benjamin H. *Franklin and Galloway: A Political Partnership.* New Haven: Yale University Press, 1972.

Olson, Alison Gilbert. "The British Government and Colonial Union, 1754." *William and Mary Quarterly* (1960).

Osgood, Herbert L. *The American Colonies in the Seventeenth Century.* New York: Macmillan, 1904.

———. *The American Colonies in the Eighteenth Century.* New York: Columbia University Press, 1924.

———. "The Corporation as a Form of Colonial Government, Part I." *Political Science Quarterly*, Volume 11 (1896).

———. "The Corporation as a Form of Colonial Government II." *Political Science Quarterly*, Volume 11 (1896).

Pennock, J. Roland, and John W. Chapman, eds. *Constitutionalism.* New York: New York University Press, 1979.

Pestana, Carla G. *The English Atlantic in the Age of Revolution 1640–1661.* Cambridge: Harvard University Press, 2004.

Peters, Ronald M. *The Massachusetts Constitution of 1780: A Social Compact.* Amherst: University of Massachusetts Press, 1978.

Pole, J. R., ed. *The Revolution in America 1754-1788: Documents on the Internal Development of America in the Revolutionary Era.* Palo Alto: Stanford University Press, 1970.

Polk, William R. *The Birth of America: From Before Columbus to the Revolution.* New York: Harper Collins, 2006.

Pomfret, John E. *Colonial New Jersey—A History.* New York: Scribner, 1973.

———. *Founding the American Colonies.* New York: Harper & Row, 1970.

———. *The Province of East New Jersey 1609–1702.* Princeton, Princeton University Press, 1962.

Prescott, Arthur Taylor. *Drafting the Constitution.* Baton Rouge: Louisiana State University Press, 1941.

Quinn, David Beers. *England and the Discovery of America: 1481–1620.* New York: Knopf, 1974.

Rakove, Jack N. *Original Meanings: Politics and Ideas in the Making of the Constitution.* New York: Knopf, 1997.

———. *Revolutionaries: A New History of the Invention of America.* Boston: Houghton Mifflin Harcourt, 2010.

Reid, John Phillip. *Constitutional History of the American Revolution: The Authority of Rights.* Madison: Wisconsin University Press, 1986.

Rodick, Burleigh Cushing. *American Constitutional Custom: A Forgotten Factor in the Founding.* New York: Philosophical Library, 1953.

Root, Winfred T. "The Lords of Trade and Plantations." *American Historical Review,* volume 23 (October 1917).

Rosenbaum, Alan S. *Constitutionalism: The Philosophical Discussion.* New York: Greenwood Press, 1988.

Sarson, Steven. *British America 1500–1800*. New York: Oxford University Press, 2005.

Saye, Albert Berry. *A Constitutional History of Georgia*. Athens: University of Georgia Press, 1948.

Schechter, Stephen L., ed. *Roots of the Republic: American Founding Documents Interpreted*. Madison: Madison House Publishers, 1990.

Schwartz, Bernard. *The Bill of Rights: A Documentary History*. New York: Chelsea House, 1971.

Shannon, Timothy J. *Indians and Colonists at the Crossroads of Empire*. Ithaca: Cornell University Press, 2000.

Sherman, Michael, ed. *A More Perfect Union: Vermont Becomes a State 1777–1816*. Montpelier: Vermont Historical Society, 1991.

Skaggs, David Curtis. *Roots of Maryland Democracy 1753–1776*. Westport: Greenwood Press, 1973.

Sirmans, M. Eugene. *Colonial South Carolina: A Political History*. Chapel Hill: University of North Carolina Press, 1966.

Smith, James Morton, *Seventeenth Century America: Essays in Colonial History*. Chapel Hill: University of North Carolina Press, 1959.

Solberg, Winton U. *The Constitutional Convention and the Formation of the Union*. Urbana: University of Illinois Press, 1990.

Steele, I. K. "The Board of Trade, The Quakers and the Resumption of Colonial Charters, 1699–1702." *William and Mary Quarterly* Volume 23 (1966).

Story, Joseph. *Commentaries on the Constitution of the United States*. Boston: Hilliard Gray, 1833.

Sturm, Albert L. "The Development of American State Constitutions." *Publius* Volume 12 (1980).

Swisher, Carl Brent. *American Constitutional Development*. Boston: Houghton, 1943.

Tarr, G. Alan. *Understanding State Constitutions*. Princeton: Princeton University Press, 1998.

Thorpe, Frances Newton. *The Constitutional History of the United States*. Chicago: Callaghan & Co., 1901.

———. *The Federal and State Constitutions, Colonial Charters and Other Organic Laws of the States, Territories, and Colonies Now or Heretofore Forming the United States of America*. Washington, DC: U.S. Government Printing Office, 1909.

Tinkcom, Harry M. *The Republicans and the Federalists in Pennsylvania 1790–1801*. Harrisburg: Pennsylvania Historical and Museum Commission, 1950.

Tomlinson, Howard, ed. *Before Civil War: Essays on Early Stuart Politics and Government*. London: Macmillan, 1984.

Trevelyn, Raleigh. *Sir Walter Raleigh*. New York: Henry Holt & Co, 2002.

Turner, Lynn Warren. *The Ninth State: New Hampshire's Formative Years*. Chapel Hill: University of North Carolina Press, 1983.

Ubbelohde, Carl. *The American Colonies and the British Empire, 1607–1763*. New York: Thos. Y. Crowell & Co., 1968.

Urofsky, Melvin I. *A March of Liberty: A Constitutional History of the United States*. New York: Knopf, 1985.

van Deventer, David E. *The Emergence of Provincial New Hampshire 1623–1741*. Baltimore: Johns Hopkins University Press, 1976.

Ver Steeg, Clarence L. *The Formative Years 1607–1763*. New York: Hill & Wang, 1968.

Vile, M. J. C. *Constitutionalism and the Separation of Powers*. Oxford: Oxford University Press, 1967.

Ward, Harry M. *Unite or Die: Intercolony Relations 1690–1763*. Port Washington: Kennikar Press, 1971.

Ware, Ethel K. *A Constitutional History of Georgia*. New York: Ams Press Inc., 1967.

Warren, Wendy. *New England Bound: Slavery and Colonization in Early America*. New York: Liverwright Publishing Corp., 2016.

Weir, Robert M. *Colonial South Carolina—A History*. Millwood: KTO Press, 1983.

Wertenbaker, Thomas J. *Virginia under the Stuarts, 1607–1688*. New York: Russell and Russell, 1959.

Whittington, Keith E. *Constitutional Construction.* Cambridge, MA: Harvard University Press, 1991.

Wolfe, John Harold. *Jeffersonian Democracy in South Carolina.* Chapel Hill: University of North Carolina Press, 1840.

Wood, Gordon S. *The Americanization of Benjamin Franklin.* New York: Penguin Books, 2004.

———. *The Creation of the American Republic: 1776–1787.* Chapel Hill: University of North Carolina Press, 1998.

———. *The Idea of America: Reflections on the Birth of the United States.* New York: Penguin Press, 2011.

———., ed. *The Confederation and the Constitution.* Washington, DC: UP of America, 1979.

Wright, Benjamin F., ed. *The Federalist.* New York: Barnes & Noble, 1996.

Index

About the Author

H. Lowell Brown is an attorney and historian. He has taught at the law schools of the American University and the University of Maine. He is the author of a constitutional history of impeachment, *The Meaning of High Crimes and Misdemeanors in Presidential Impeachment*, as well as books on issues of white collar crime, including *Bribery in International Commerce*, *White Collar Crime: RICO*, and *U.S. Money Laundering Law*.

Made in the USA
Coppell, TX
04 November 2026

11289009R00138